The Long Road Home

The Long Road Home

One woman's true story of reclaiming her life along the infamous Camino de Santiago

Alesa Teague

The Long Road Home

One woman's true story of reclaiming her life along the infamous Camino de Santiago

Copyright © 2013 by Alesa Teague. All rights reserved.

ISBN: 978-0-9914609-2-2 (Nook Edition)
ISBN: 978-0-9914609-3-9 (iBook Edition)
ISBN: 978-0-9914609-0-8 (Paperback Edition)
ISBN: 978-0-9914609-1-5 (Kindle Edition)

Library of Congress Control Number: Information Available Upon Request.

No part of this publication may be reproduced, stored in a retrieval system or transmitted in any way by any means, electronic, mechanical, photocopy, recording or otherwise without the prior permission of the author, except as provided by USA copyright law.

Published by Rogue Publishing
1160 Atlantis Ave.
Lafayette, Colorado 80026 USA

Editor: Janet Schwind
Cover design: Penny Hill
Interior design: Suzanne Parada

ACKNOWLEDGEMENTS

I need to thank you, Momma, for allowing me to be authentic during this process and for your blessing on this book. I tried to write around the truth and could not. I know some of this will be hard to read and I want you to know I'll always love you. We've come a long way and I value the relationship we have today.

Aunt Jan and Uncle Steve, I can't thank you both enough for being a steady influence on me. You were both there, offering a soft place to land when I needed you. You have been super supportive during this writing process and of my need to do it. I am forever grateful.

Lynne M. and Debbie, thanks for listening and being there when I needed shoulders, also for understanding when I withdrew to my cave during the writing process.

Kati J., we needed those coffee talks where we were supposed to be working and didn't get much done! Thanks for allowing me to write in your presence when I needed to get away from my self-imposed exile and for adding levity, wisdom and humor to our daily happenings. I love you, Sweetie!

Leah M., thank you for moving to Colorado and being my roommate for a year. You are an inspiration to me. Stay true to yourself! You are going to do something amazing in life and I can't wait to see what it will be! Love!

To Dave J., thank you for always being there. You are a true friend, my bro-friend. I cherish our friendship! Love you always. XO

Kyrie and Woody, I thank you for your support, friendship, and management of my business when I went through ACS, all the crazy shit. You are so much more to me than you might think. You're family.

Carolyn C., you are a wonderful woman and inspiring and helpful and, well...a good and lovely person. Thank you for you.

To my twin sister, Dana: You rock, Sis! Thank you for all of your support in watching Parker while I went on the Camino. I appreciate the help you gave while in a big transition of your own. Proud of you always! (See? It's in writing!)

A note to the whole city of Lafayette, Colorado: This community saved me. Continue to support and reach out to each other. I never knew the value of community until I moved to this sweet town. Our townspeople rock!

Finally, but **not** last, I am honored to know you and count you as a close friend, Laura Powers! Your powers of clairvoyance changed my life. You helped me through some harsh times. You showed me the value of letting go and letting my hair down. Thank you for pushing me to lighten up and have fun in life. You are precious and your powers truly are amazing.

CHAPTER ONE

I DIED RATHER SPECTACULARLY MY first night in Spain. In retrospect, it had been coming for a long time, possibly my whole life. After two full days of travel, I stepped off the bus in Pamplona feeling alone and scared, yet oddly accustomed to these lifelong feelings. I was tired. Tired in my soul. Travel fatigue added a lethargic heaviness to my limbs that I hardly noticed since my mind was so heavily entrenched in the past, both recent and distant. Images and voices from my life haunted me along the way to Spain.

Feeling lonely and alone, my travels to Spain had been accompanied by snippets of long-suppressed memories. In the DIA terminal, my high school boyfriend's voice chanted in my head, "You can't do anything right," followed with a mocking punch to the arm that I'd dared not react to for fear that another, angrier hit would follow. As I curled into the wall on my international flight, my mother's tyrannical phrases ran ruthlessly through my mind while I tried to nap next to an annoyingly optimistic young woman. As she chattered on, heedless of my disinterest, my mother's oft repeated rants rang in my memory, "I hate you kids! Hurry and grow up so I can be free...How dare you become prettier than me!"

This last one, she'd spat into my face as she scrubbed my makeup off with the rotten sponge snagged from the dish drain.

Her beautiful brown eyes shriveled into angry, hard raisins in her rage. Her bright red lips twisted in a snarl, spots of lipstick dotting her two front teeth. I'd almost laughed at her then, but instead had bitten a hole in my cheek in order to avoid more of her wrath. I'd calmly walked out the front door, my back straight, though my face smelled like soured milk. She'd ripped my new dangling earrings out of my ears. My right lobe stung and later I found it crusted with blood. I hadn't cried until I was out of sight of the house. Now in my adulthood, her voice pleaded, "I need you, LeLee. Don't leave me. I'm so depressed."

As I navigated the airport in Madrid, the weight of my red back pack was my only comfort. I listened to the buzz of languages I didn't comprehend, as images of my ex-husband's chat window with his mistress haunted me through the brightly lit corridors and escalators. "I just want to be with you now. I can't stand her anymore." Interspersed throughout my personal descent into the past, images of my daughter's large, pleading eyes would pop into my mind, making me gasp as if I was punched. With her beautiful hazel eyes full of tears, she'd clung to me, begged me not to leave Daddy.

I tried to sleep on the bus but a memory of my last trip to the hospital jolted me wide awake. My anesthesiologist had been trying to flirt with me while he fiddled with the medication that would knock me out for my third cancer surgery. His blue eyes dissolved into liquid twin lakes as my sister Renee loudly filled him in on the details of my divorce. My last semi-apathetic thought, "Hey, fuck you, Sis....you're my twin...protect me for once..." Another moment I'd chosen not to defend myself, as I'd let myself slip away into the unconscious world I was learning to embrace. I welcomed the black void, an experimentation with death.

Almost asleep, I jerked up to a sitting position, unsure if I'd missed my stop. My heart pounded in fear. I took a deep breath to calm the rapid beating. Vibrant green, rolling hills rushed past my window as I tried to shake myself out of the depressed state I'd been in for a very long time. I leaned forward and tapped a young woman on the shoulder in front of me and asked in poor Spanish if she was going to Pamplona. She nodded and pointed to her *mochilla* (Spanish for backpack). It was a soft green color and she already had her scallop shell secured to the back. This was the symbol for pilgrims who walked the Camino de Santiago. Instantly comforted, I gripped my red backpack to my chest, fingering the empty loop where I would tie my shell.

Two years ago, while recovering from the last surgery at Renee's house, I idly watched television. Feeling extremely sorry for myself, I hunched deeply into her leather recliner as I lazily held the remote and flipped through channels before landing on PBS. I wondered what my own personal tipping point was, when my internal compass would forever tip south rather than north and I would finally lose my mind. I almost looked forward to the day. I watched Rick Steves as he traipsed through some part of Europe. He sipped red wine fussily with his pinky finger held aloft. His airy travel tips floated around me with the levity of someone untouched by the trappings of real life and all its muckiness. Feeling peeved at his seeming lack of personal problems, I envied his ability to travel the globe and fill us all in on the wonders of the world. The show changed to images of people walking the Camino de Santiago, an ancient pilgrimage across northern Spain.

I knew nothing of this trek, yet I tuned in and sat forward. Medieval cathedrals and castles along the way filled the screen. With a chill of recognition shivering down my body, I knew I was going to walk this Camino. It felt familiar to me. I felt scared for a moment. Had thoughts of tipping into Crazyland sent me over the edge? I dropped the remote and stared at the new yet familiar images. Though I was not an outdoor junkie, had never felt the need to hike the Appalachian, nor felt the need to camp for weeks on end, I felt the urge to join those pilgrims with their backpacks and trek that 500 mile journey. With certainty in my soul and heart, I just knew I had to walk it.

This was the end of 2011. It was the end of my seventeen-year relationship with my husband. The end of everything I had relied on, taken for granted. My body had even tried to kill me in the midst of the divorce and my cheerful, professional persona that I wore to the coffee shop, like a cloak of invisibility, was starting to fray at the seams. My customers were noticing the wear and tear. I was gone for long stretches of time to recover from surgery and people were inquiring about these lapses. A regular customer of mine had one day walked into the kitchen, wrapped me in her arms and pleaded with me to let my feelings out. I'd stood ramrod straight as waves of unshed emotions shuddered throughout my body, making me sweat with the need to open up to someone. Rather than give in and make an emotional scene, I stepped back and, to her disappointment, insisted I was fine.

Only I wasn't. A panic attack at the local grocery store struck while I stood stupidly over the apple bins trying to remember which kind I liked. My brain had stopped functioning for a moment as I took in the Pink Ladies and Juicy Reds. I noticed spots of color swirling at the edges of my vision and felt as if my head had detached like a balloon before I caught myself with my hands on the bin in front of me and bent my knees. I'd knelt there for a minute until the buzzing in my ears receded.

I sensed, rather than saw, a man approach me from behind. Before he could touch me, I shot to my feet and walked as fast as my unsteady legs could carry me out of that store. He'd asked me something that I ignored. My face flamed with embarrassment as I climbed into my car. I leaned my forehead on the wheel until my breathing was under control. It felt like breathing underwater for a few minutes. When the feelings passed, I drove to Renee's home where I lived until my divorce was finalized. Still a bit shaken, I fell into the guest bed and took a 3-hour nap. I awoke to five text messages from my employees asking me if I'd forgotten the chocolate sauce and demanding quarters and dimes ASAP. Overwhelmed with their simple demands, I downed more Vicodin than I should have, turned my phone off, and slept again until noon the next day. I woke up groggy and already resenting the long list of chores I had to complete to keep the business running. For the thousandth time since the separation, I wished I could sell the store so I could be rid of every vestige of anything that remained of "us."

Until I saw Rick Steves on PBS, I had no interest in anything at all beyond functioning enough for Parker. I knew she was scared. Scared of me dying and of the divorce, Daddy's new girlfriend and what that might mean. It was a horrible time to leave and yet I felt I had no choice if I was going to survive all of the blows I'd been dealt. With iron resolve, I sold the store and made arrangements for Parker to stay with friends and family during the portion of time I was responsible for according to our parenting agreement. Here I was at the starting point of my journey, the bus station in Pamplona. I stood a bit uncertainly with my red Deuter strapped to my back. After much confusion, I found the heart of the city where the Camino trail took off and knew there would be places to stay along that path. I was looking for an *albergue*, which is a very affordable way to travel. These are places that charged from five to ten euros for a bed in a bunk room with possibly many other pilgrims snoring away near my head. At that moment, I could have slept on a concrete slab in the middle of a concourse somewhere. My muscles nearly shook with the need to lay down.

Unfortunately, it was late at night so all of the albergues displayed *"completo"* signs, meaning they were full, no beds available. I wove around the city before I was directed to another albergue on the outskirts of town, near the river. With a sinking heart, I saw the completo sign taped to the wooden door. This was a German albergue, though, and knowing a little about Germans, I knew most of them spoke English. I went inside hoping to speak with someone about my options.

I came face to face with Francesco, the *hospitalero* (a volunteer who runs the pilgrim albergues or hostels). Francesco was a short, thin old man with white hair and a stern look in his blue eyes. He took one look at my backpack and shook his head, pointing at the door. "Completo!" he reiterated. There were other pilgrims milling around in the lounge area and they all repeated, "Completo, completo!" I don't know why they thought they all had to throw in their two cents. It was obvious. I looked at Francesco, "Donde está el baño?"

I must have looked ready to cry because his face suddenly softened and he pulled a chair out for me. I let my pack fall to the ground as he said, "I'll call someone. Stay there." I sat in exhaustion as he, rather loudly, much to his wife's dismay, placed a few calls for me as she tried to shush him. I gathered that people were sleeping and she wanted him to shut up. He cast a look at me as if to say, "She's harmless," and finally got a hold of a man at a *pension* about a mile away...the direction

I had come from. He spoke to the hospitalero but watched me with large, blue eyes behind wire-rimmed glasses and nodded excitedly while holding up a finger for me to be silent.

He hung up loudly and with much gesturing toward 'town', he drew on several pieces of paper and haltingly told me what to say when I found the doorbell of this pension. He patted me on the back but as I hoisted my pack to my shoulders preparing to put it on, he noticed something about it. "Ah!" he exclaimed. "You need a shell!" With that he chose a pilgrim's big, white scallop shell from a shelf and handed it to me. "Put this on your pack. You want a stamp for your Camino passport?"

"I don't have that either, I've only just arrived," I breathed tiredly.

With a slap to his head, he waggled his finger at me in a funny manner. "One moment. We start you the right way." He took a folded Camino passport and had me fill out my name and country of origin. He checked my real passport to make sure I was really me. With that he stamped my little booklet and before handing it to me, stuck his finger in the air and waggled it again, chastising me: "You no bike, you no horse, you NO bus. You WALK!" I nodded vigorously, immediately wondering where I might find a good horse at this late hour. He gave me the booklet and wished me "Buen Camino!" as his farewell. I would have hugged him but he didn't seem the sort, and so I awkwardly took a half step forward and then another half step back as I wrestled with NOT hugging him. To cover my awkwardness, I thrust my hand out instead, which he gently shook with an odd look glimmering in his eyes.

With a tired sigh, I forced myself back into the black night. Tremors of fatigue shook me. Stars shone brightly overhead as the river behind the albergue gurgled over its rocky bed.

I climbed up the hill back toward the area I had combed for accommodations earlier. Gorgeous men lingered in the bar entrances and watched as I walked past. I felt dingy after two days of travel and couldn't imagine what drew their eyes to me. My feet dragged me to the right address. With an aggravated sigh, I realized I must have passed that very doorway a dozen times earlier. I hit the bell. A disgruntled male voice called out, "Hola!"

I'd forgotten what Francesco told me to say. I stared at the intercom and stammered in very broken Spanish. "Uh...pardona...Francesco telefono you? Peregrina uno hospitalereo?" I wanted to slap myself. I rolled my eyes and promised myself to attempt to learn more Español pronto. After a moment of which I am sure he was rolling HIS eyes behind closed doors, he replied with a stream of Spanish that I obviously had no hope of interpreting, followed by a buzz.

I pushed on the door as it grated open to admit me into a rounded stone hallway. There were no decorations on the entry walls. Stairs that wound up and around to the right lay four steps ahead. Apparently, I was on display. I heard shuffling and sniffling above my head. Looking up, I met the gazes of several sleepy children and a woman behind them. All peered straight down at me as if expecting the very worst sort of intruder. I understood. It was late. But...really? Had these kids never seen a pilgrim before? Feeling as if I was in a strange dream, I waited for the owner or manager to come forward out of the gloomy staircase.

He finally heaved forward into the dim entry. I fought to stay in place rather than step back in revulsion. He was a slimy pig of a man and his thinning black hair was greasy as snot but fanned up neatly above his ears, creating little waves curling up on either side. His tight collared polo, a throwback to 1976, was tucked smoothly over his protruding belly and disappeared into gray pants pulled up over the midpoint of his belly. I nearly snickered out loud as I imagined him to be the incarnation of Humpty Dumpty.

Humpty looked me over, nodded, and gestured for me to follow him. His family popped one by one out of view as we climbed up and around the circular entry going past the second floor. On the third floor, he exited the winding stairs, veered right and led me down a dark, narrow hallway to the farthest room. It was so silent, I wondered with a bright flare of panic if there were others staying there. I remembered Francesco. Surely he wouldn't have called this man if he was a total pig.

This being my first introduction to European hostels, I'd fully expected to share one bathroom with countless others. Theirs was tiled in a floor-to-ceiling fish-belly gray color—in fact, tile covered everything except the commode. A mop and bucket sat next to the toilet. The owner gestured to me, then the shower, and back to the mop. Aha, I had to mop up after my bath.

He showed me to my narrow room with its single twin bed, which provided just enough space for the small dresser and nightstand and a tight path to move my body around it all. The bare wooden floors were dull but swept. The room was clean enough. I felt ready to faint and knew it would feel heavenly to lie down. I didn't care what the sheets were like; I had no intention of crawling into them. I thanked the man, he nodded and left.

Unhooking the straps from my chest, I let my pack slip down my back onto the bed. The time on my iPhone said 10:30 p.m.! I decided to shower now before sleep claimed me. Ignoring my growling stomach, I quietly slipped down the hall to the single bathroom where I took care of business. After my luke-warm shower, I slipped on the wet tiles and caught the edges of the sink to keep from falling when I noticed my reflection in the mirror. Dark half-moons shadowed my hazel eyes. I didn't see the beauty people remarked on frequently as I took in my sharp cheekbones and wet strands of brown hair that straggled around my face. Sadness seeped up from the depths before I squashed it back down. My ex's face surfaced for a moment before I shoved thoughts of him away. I had given him nearly twenty years, I vowed to not give him a moment more.

Tiptoeing back to my room, I nearly threw a temper tantrum when I figured out I still needed to eat something and comb my hair. These tasks felt monumental just then. Deciding to tackle all of it at once, I sat shakily in the middle of my precious sleeping bag trying to comb my wet hair with my right hand while devouring bites of a chocolate-flavored protein bar held in my left. Without warning, I ran out of steam halfway through both jobs. With wet tangles on the left side of my head, I dropped the comb and uneaten portion of the bar to the floor and whimpered around the uneaten chunk I couldn't seem to chew. Even that required a certain level of strength I no longer possessed. I spit the chunk of food onto the floor and promised myself I would pick it up in the morning as I crawled into my sleeping bag. With my bedroom lights on, I fell instantly into the dream…

I was home in Colorado, driving west on South Boulder Road toward the heart of Old Town Louisville. The finger-shaped sign pointing the way to Old Town waved at me, signaling where to turn off onto Main Street. As I began the turn, my orange cased iPhone fell into my lap, vibrating. My daughter's name blazed across the screen, and in a moment of fear I grabbed at the phone before it could fall to the floor. A screeching train blast made me look up, my phone forgotten. Heart thundering in my chest, I knew what was happening… She'd called to tell me something and I hadn't been able to answer. Would she be okay after I died? Oh no! This couldn't happen. I had to see her again, hold her.

A huge, round yellow light sped toward my driver's side door. Too late, I realized I'd paused on the train tracks. My daughter's name flashed through my mind as the yellow light grew bigger, becoming dazzlingly mesmerizing, colored sparkles swirling inside it. The train hit my car with a loud and violent crash, then a horrendous crunch as my door crumpled triangularly toward my face. I waited for the pain, my right hand still groping for my phone. It was too late. Shards of glass flew into my hair and sprinkled the air around me. In an instant, the broken frame of my car door wrapped around me, and still the train kept coming. I thought it should hurt but I felt nothing, only shock as my vehicle and all physical ties to the earthly realm were whisked away.

I now stood in place as the train cars passed through me. The blare of the train's horn continued to blast in my head as windows and seats sped past me. Indecipherable faces of passengers in their seats flashed briefly. They were unaware of me. My car hadn't slowed the train at all. They didn't know they'd killed me!

My body began to dissolve into floating colored particles. I drifted up toward the ceiling of the last car, pulled toward the sky. I tried desperately to hold on to something. My daughter had called. "Shit! Shit! I have to call her back!" Then the wall of the end of the train came at me and, absurdly, I noticed it was tiled in an ugly fish-belly gray color. I passed through the ceiling with a shudder and drifted upward. "I'm dead!" I yelled insanely at the sky, for who could hear me?

I awoke with a violent jerk that thumped the bed hard on the floor. A cold sweat covered me, the words "I'm dead" reverberating in my skull. Fine hairs on my body stood up. I lay there in shock for a moment, feeling my heart tremble in fear. As I gripped my sleeping bag to my chest I nearly sobbed with relief. I had died? I had died! "Whoever said you can't die in your dreams is extremely stupid!' I said out loud, rather vehemently. I managed a shaky sigh before looking around. I barely remembered this room so I was glad I had fallen asleep with the light on. Vague memories of beautifully gorgeous men lounging in doorways, Francesco, and the ugly man came flooding back. I shivered again.

I still shook and I realized it wasn't just fear; I was very cold. Damn, I needed that wool blanket I'd thrown onto the dresser. I didn't want to get out of my sleeping bag so I crawled, feeling like a caterpillar, to the end of my bed and reached forward to drag the blanket off the top of the dresser as the cold night air threatened to slip underneath my covering. Reluctant to step onto the floor for some reason, I reached as far left as I could to strike off the light switch. Lying back, I dragged the blanket over my sleeping bag, still shivering on into the night, worrying that I was getting sick, but finally sleep found me again.

Light streamed through the window and found the crevices of my eyes without my permission. Somehow morning had come, overtaking a fitful sleep. Reluctantly awake, I finally sat up and noticed the sun was higher than I had wanted. I had promised myself to start each day of my Camino early so I could be ahead of the crowd. I laughed at myself. I had never been a morning person. I disentangled my body from the sleeping bag since it had managed to wrap and twist around me in my restless sleep.

My first thought was *I need coffee* but I wasn't sure where I was going and hoped to find someplace on the Camino. I was happy to leave this strange pension, so I quickly walked down the hall loaded with my pack and wearing my freshly purchased REI gear. The hallway was so narrow that the unused straps dangling from my pack brushed the walls with the sway of my hips. Down the winding stairs I went, and out the round entry. I struggled with the door for a split second before remembering to swing it toward me, rather than out, a sign of my general confusion. My goal was to head for the trail signs I'd seen the night before. After several wrong turns down cobblestone alleys that were all as charming as the last, I finally found the modern, flat silver disks set into the walking stones that were meant to guide us and keep us from losing our way through the cities.

My foot struck one of these disks, embedded in the pedestrian cobblestones in front of a quiet bar. I paused to look around, keeping my foot on the disk as if it would disappear on me. People passed me going left and right and down the alley behind me. As I stood there, I had the notion that I could stay here and just say I'd done it...who would know? I didn't really feel like walking anyway! My backpack already pinched and it felt heavier than ever. I knew it weighed less than 22 lbs. Last night's dream came barreling back into my mind. Maybe I shouldn't do this! I'd been looking forward to this for so long and now I felt lost and confused.

Furiously, I gathered my willpower again. I had to just start! The symbol I rested my foot on was a flat silver disk with the pilgrim symbol of the scallop shell and a bicyclist stamped into it. These disks were spaced about twenty feet apart on this section of the trail. I looked up and saw them spaced along the walkway in one direction, but a glance behind showed them stretching that way, too. One way led to France and the other toward my destination, Santiago. But which was the right way to go? I didn't see any other pilgrims to ask for help. I'd woken up so late!

Floundering with indecision, I hadn't noticed the man who came up behind me. A bit jarringly, I felt my backpack being grabbed. Instinctively I gripped my shoulder straps with both hands as if to keep my pack from being stolen and thought about kicking the robber. As the person bodily turned me to the right, I tried to wrench out of his grip but he was strong and pulled me back as I tried to step forward. I found myself facing in the opposite direction.

An arm, thick with black hair, shot past my face and a pudgy index finger pointed the opposite direction from which I'd almost launched my first steps into the pilgrimage. "Camino, peregrina," he said simply. He firmly held me in place until I was settled enough not to topple over. I stared down the length of his arm. Above his fingernail, on the sign post, I saw the yellow arrow pointing the same way.

He released me. I was so grateful for the direction and for being released from his grip with all of my belongings that I fairly skipped away from him. I managed to yell a proper "Gracias!" without too much American accent. I hopped away from him and followed the shiny silver disks for a dozen paces. Then, I stopped again to breathe. Standing to the side to let others pass around me, I took a long, deep inhale. Then I laughed at myself when I noticed a couple of backpacks with their obvious large, white shells on the backs of pilgrims walking the same direction, weaving through the late morning crowd. I was a bit worried then about my observational and navigational skills. Why hadn't

I noticed them? I muttered to myself. "Okay, let's just chalk this up to jet lag, scary dreams, and maybe beginner-pilgrim jitters. Get a grip now."

Setting off through the city, I looked forward to being out in the country, but first I needed coffee! To the left and right I noticed the nods and acknowledgements from passersby. People in business attire paused in their bustling walks to greet me with a smile and "Buen Camino." Something akin to wistful desire lit up a pair of eyes here and there. A couple of times, I felt hands patting my shoulder as if to encourage me. The weight of this pilgrimage began to take hold. This was a significant journey. Parents walking their children to school paused as their kids looked up at me in passing and whispered or yelled, "Buen Camino!"

The children passing me made me miss my daughter's precious face. Tears welled in my eyes and I longed to go running home to her. We both knew that I needed to do this. I had tried to talk her into coming on this journey with me. Wise beyond her twelve years, she said "Momma, you need to go. Just hurry up and do it so you can stop talking about it. Besides, you know I hate hiking anyway!"

"Okay baby. We'll have our own vacation when I come back. I promise." She knew I needed to heal. She didn't know why I needed THIS trip, but she knew something was going to change. We both hoped things would be better when I came back.

Throughout the divorce, I hadn't been the Best Mommy Ever, but when I was in the thick of all the drama I hadn't thought so much about consequences as I had about simply getting through each hurdle. I had thought our mother-daughter bond was enough. I didn't see how I was affecting my relationship with her. I snapped more often than I like to admit. I couldn't voice my hurt and frustrations, my fears...so I took them out verbally on her. The thought still makes me cry. I would never knowingly harm my child, but the knowledge that I was yelling at her more than I remembered made me take stock of my behavior. I was truly ashamed. We'd always been close and snuggled often, but there was an underlying current of distrust and I didn't know if that was just in my own mind or hers.

It was very real. She thought my cancer would come back. She'd written in her diary that she wanted to die before I did so she could be with me. We promptly signed up for family therapy. Our therapist was shocked I hadn't told Parker more about my disease. Honestly, I couldn't really acknowledge it to myself. As a result, my child wanted to die BEFORE I did. I had thought to not talk to her about my illness as we were already working through divorce, an affair that rocked my whole family—and now cancer. I was reeling for solid ground and the only rock I had was her. I leaned too heavily. Full of remorse now, I walked right in front of a car as I made a bee-line for the coffee shop I'd spied. At the last second I hopped backward to avoid the vehicle and vowed to pay more attention so I could avoid an untimely death here in Spain.

I managed to order café con leche from the charming woman behind the counter and was pleased at the small latte she produced for me. She reminded me of baristas I'd had at my coffee shop, complete with their tattoos and Bohemian hairstyles. She was a nice woman and I wished I knew more of her language. I settled into a comfy chair, my backpack resting against the wall beside me. A customer noticed my shell and offered a sweet "Buen Camino!"

"Muchas gracias, señora!" I replied, and she looked pleased enough at my Spanish and turned back to her book.

I contemplated my decision to make this trek while I sipped my latte and ate the delicious croissant. With the combination of insecurities that plagued me and the unfamiliarity of being in a foreign country, I felt as though I were running away. The familiar pangs of anxiety and uncertainty reminded me of the times I'd run away from home as a teenager. I remembered also the time I'd left my college boyfriend under cover of darkness to move back home with my mom.

It was the summer of '92. I had had a "wakeup moment" one morning when I realized I was in a nightmarish relationship with my high school boyfriend. I had started dating him when I was sixteen and had turned blind eyes to how he treated me. Both of us were now twenty. I was overcome with a wild desire to finally leave him! Suddenly infused with common sense that I'd previously totally lacked, I packed my valuables (a teapot from my aunt, a few knickknacks, and my clothes) and snuck out like a thief in the night. Of course the teapot was full of his tip money he'd been saving for a new computer.

While Shane worked the late shift, waiting tables, I packed my clothes hastily. I had been certain that would be the night he'd come home early and catch me. I thought about taking his cat, the sweetest fur ball on the planet, but quickly decided against it. Taking his cat would give him more motivation to find me. The teapot held a dismal $232. I didn't have enough money to start over in Colorado. I could probably make it back on that amount if I was careful and slept in my car. I just had to go!

Shane had been violent before, but this last year the frequency of pushing and hitting had increased. He'd even bitten me once in a childish temper tantrum over an ice cream dispute. His small teeth had left indents in my skin until morning when they faded to little purple dots in a half moon. He'd become meaner.

I suspected it was because we had moved nearer to his mean-tempered father whose influence Shane sought as his father had not raised him and he was only now beginning to know him in-depth.

I took as much time as I dared to shake out the couch cushions and dig around for more cash. I found $2.11 in the couch and $56 in singles shoved into a dirty, black waiter's apron. The roll of singles smelled like hamburger grease. Once I'd loaded up my clothes and a few meager possessions I was sure he wouldn't miss, I climbed into my little Chevette and took off without contacting any of my friends. Last time, that was how he'd found me. Someone had told him where to find me as I'd made the mistake of sleeping for a few hours at a friend's house. I hadn't been able to walk without limping for three days as he liked to hit me only where people wouldn't see it, never my face. He'd laughingly told his father that I'd fallen off my mountain bike. His father's small, beady eyes had turned to me then and I saw the cruelty light up his eyes as he laughed, too. He knew what had really happened.

I didn't say goodbye to anyone the second time. I drove for two hours while it was still dark. Just as the sun started coming up, I found a pay phone to call my mom. I hadn't talked to her in a year. Shane hadn't allowed a phone in the apartment. He was afraid I'd call my family and they'd talk me into leaving him. I shook my head at my gullibility. I dialed Mom's number, my fingers trembling. I hoped she would pick up the phone because she had no way of knowing I was about to arrive on her doorstep in a few days. I promised myself I would stop in Wyoming to see my grandparents, too. I had felt hopeful and the breeze through the booth lifted the ends of my hair. I could see the treetops outside swaying in the breeze and I wanted to hear the sound of it through the branches.

I heard her pick up and fumble the phone a little, her sleepy, scratchy throat said "mmmhello?" It was pretty typical that my mom would be asleep at 11 on a Saturday morning, so I knew this was extremely early for her or rather like the middle of the night. I hadn't expected the sound of her voice to choke me up.

I watched the phone and glass walls of the booth become wavy and sway with the movement of tears. I couldn't speak. "Hello?...anyone there?"

I was frozen with the ache in my chest. I hadn't missed her until that moment. My heart thudded heavily. All I could do was sob. I gripped the black receiver as I fought to gain control of myself.

"Alesa? Honey, is that you?! Oh my God!"

I cried harder at that. I thought she would be upset with me. She sounded so caring and worried! I hadn't expected that. I felt rocked to the core.

"Momma...." I sobbed really hard and couldn't say anything for a second while she flipped out on the other end.

"Oh my God! Are you okay? What's happening? Where ARE you? Should I call the police? Are you okay!?" She assaulted my ears with her intensity. I fought to swallow my tears enough to stammer.

"I'm-m-m f-f-f-iiine!" I managed to sob. "C-c-coming h-h-ho-ome... In my car. C-com-ming home in my car." I felt so relieved to hear her voice my knees had gone shaky. I looked up at the trees wavering in front of me. I wished I could sit in their calm branches and feel the cool of the breeze flow up and over me. I would stay there, maybe live there! A wild thing. No home. Free to go wherever I needed to be. My mind snapped back to my mom's voice now crying and sobbing as well. I couldn't stand here listening to her crying sounds. I felt sick as I listened.

Cars and semis blew by on the highway and I felt more lost than ever. "Momma, can I s-s-stay with you for a while?" My voice rose on a whine and I hated it. I stamped my foot in frustration. I'd wanted to sound more sure of myself.

"Sure, honey! Sure. Just come home. We'll figure it out! Oh, honey, I've wanted…"

I had to cut her off. "Be there in a f-f-few days," I managed. I focused on calming down. My forehead now leaned on the glass wall of the booth and I took a breath in, breath out, breath in….

"I love you, honey!"

This last comment caused the dam inside my heart to burst open and I couldn't respond. I imagined her waiting for my answering response as I tried to softly hang the receiver up so it wouldn't bang in her ear. That image made me cry so hard that no sound could be made. I thought I might die from the squeezing crush of it all. I still gripped the phone with my right hand as if she knew I was holding on. It was a link from me to her. I also needed it for balance. My left hand had curled into a fist over my heart, pressing hard. I doubled over in pain as a soundless wail rose out of my throat. I stayed like that for a couple of minutes, fighting the sobs and my body's need to breathe.

I had struggled for what seemed like a long time to regain control of myself. Leaning cautiously against the glass on the inside of the phone stall, I waited for the tears to stop. A few moments later, my legs began returning to normal so I walked to my car. I was desperate to find some soap, water and paper towels to wash my hands and face.

I dreaded the thought of seeing Mom for the first time. There was so much she didn't know. There was a lot I wouldn't tell her.

We'd had a troublesome relationship for years and I had barely managed to graduate high school. After a particularly nasty fight with Mom, I had secretly moved away with my boyfriend. I'd been absolutely positive I would never need her, nor look back.

Here it was almost a year and half later. I wanted to hug her and apologize for running off and not calling her. She must have been scared and hurt. I experienced new insight after nearly having a baby of my own. Nearly, because I hadn't been allowed to keep it. An argument over keeping the child had resulted in Shane accidently tossing me down the back staircase of our apartment complex. I'd lain there at the bottom wondering why no one bothered to come out of their homes and check on the noise I'd just created as I screamed and fell.

I lay there on my back softly crying and looking up at him. His face had registered shock as he came down to see if I was alright. I had been bruised and lucky. Lucky to not break any bones, but the little one inside me had not been fine. I went to the clinic the next morning. They checked to make sure my "trip down the stairs" hadn't caused internal bleeding. I sat numbly watching the suspicion on the aide's face as she asked questions about my relationship with Shane. Her blue eyes softened when she looked at me. I knew she could see through my quiet lies.

I had thought about that day and could not wait to leave Montana behind. I opened my hatchback to find the bar of soap, water and towels buried under the hamper of clothes I'd hastily thrown in the car, and I cleaned my face and hands. After rearranging everything for easier access, I grabbed a soda and chugged the whole can as I leaned on the tail of the open hatch. I belched as loudly as I could to drown out a semi passing me. Traffic whizzed by on the highway. The wind from their passing caused my skirt to lift and dust to settle on my shoes. I didn't mind. I turned my face up to the rising sun and felt the rays dry my face. The stubborn tears slowed to a trickle.

I'd gotten the hell out of Montana and moved back with Mom to start our reconciliation.

I shook myself out of my reminiscing fog. Here I sat in this Spanish cafe feeling like the lost teenage waif of nearly twenty years ago and feeling those same insecurities. The greatest adventure of my life was here and waiting for me to participate! There were five-hundred miles to cover and as it was, I was short on time to finish it all, would probably need to catch a bus at some point to jump ahead. Without further delay, I stood and readied myself to go. I set my dishes in the tub and smiled at the tattooed barista. She waved at me and smiled back. Feeling a bit encouraged, I set off to find a market to purchase snacks for the road.

Outside of the city, I paused to take in the stunning beauty that surrounded me. The trail wound ahead through a rolling landscape alight with jewel-bright colors in every direction. I caught my breath. The spring rain made every blade of grass shimmer with vibrant health and dewy color. Fields of grass wove up and over the hills in a shimmering velveteen cloak. Green hues sparkled as far as I could see, changing from emerald to tourmaline as sun beams danced between fluffy, white clouds suspended in a cerulean sky. Blue, distant mountains ringed me on all sides. Amidst the green, velvety swaths bright yellow-gold fields added their own patchwork draped over the hills like the softest of silk. To my right, rain clouds warred with puffy white ones in a sparring match for dominion. Here and there patches of red poppies burst gaily upright on their long stalks.

I took a deep breath as a peaceful feeling settled into my bones. Once outside the city and the crushing weight of its oppressive business districts, I started to cruise along at a steady pace, probably 3.5 miles an hour. Several miles passed before I saw the medieval palace ruins of Guendulain. These were the first medieval ruins I had ever seen. I was tempted to investigate the mysterious looking remnants of times past, but I felt the pull of being behind the others, having started so late that day, so I continued on.

The sky began to darken in a threatening manner so I pulled out my poncho in case it rained heavily. Thus far the light drizzling hadn't bothered me enough to put on rain gear. Throwing the poncho over me and my backpack, I wrestled with the neck hole for a few seconds before figuring it out. My head popped through just as a loud clap of thunder boomed and rain started. I tucked my hands inside the poncho to keep them dry and warm as I ascended a rather muddy, steep hill. Passing the steady drone of wind turbines on my left, I climbed the Hill of Forgiveness, or Alto del Perdon. At the landmark summit stood metal silhouettes of pilgrims on horseback and on foot in relief against the background of green valleys below.

I paused at the top of the hill to catch my breath as the wind pushed my hood back and wickedly whipped my hair. I looked back from where I'd come from and slowly spun to take in a 360-degree view. I was flanked by the peak of Higa to the south and the Sierra de Leyre behind it and the Arga Valley to the west.

Another crack of thunder, followed by a flash of lightning caused me to abandon the views and scurry down the other side of the steep hill. Halfway down my legs shook with muscle fatigue though I still had approximately ten kilometers to go. My guidebook suggested stopping in Puenta La Reina, but I doubted I would make it that far. I spied a tree that would be perfect to shelter from the rain while I ate a snack. It was there under the eaves when I ran into my first pilgrim!

A man sat smoking a cigarette under the tree with his legs stretched out. His dark blue poncho was gathered underneath his butt on the ground to keep him dry and he rested against his orange pack which leaned against the tree. He looked quite comfortable and his blue eyes smiled at me.

"Hola! Buen Camino!" I called as I walked toward him.

"Buen Camino!" he continued smiling. I asked him if he spoke English, he shook his head and said, "American?"

I nodded. He slid over to make room for me on the ground as I sat down next to him. He was about sixty years old with salt and pepper hair. His name was Gabriel, from France. We couldn't converse, so we watched the lightning show in silence. Every few minutes we looked at each other and smiled. It was then that the first lesson of the Camino occurred to me. We didn't have to speak out loud for we were all companions on a journey—a journey for our own personal reasons and yet a common goal, though I still had no idea what that really meant.

The rain seemed steady and so I decided to get going as soon as I'd finished eating. I packed the rest of my crackers with the tuna and wrapped my garbage in a plastic bag to bring with me. The trail was still visible but slightly muddy now and my shoes made sucking sounds with each step. Gabriel had waved goodbye to me.

CHAPTER TWO

I MADE IT TWENTY KILOMETERS (about twelve miles) that first day to a medieval village called Obanos, which is also the capital of the Navarre province. Quaint brick and mason buildings sat around the main square, complete with a cathedral. I was too tired to really investigate the rich Jesuit history of Obanos, complete with intrigue, murder and suspense that I'd briefly read about. Instead of venturing farther into town, I bee-lined to the first albergue I came across. There were a handful of pilgrims milling around outside. That was more people than I'd seen most of the day. I smiled shyly at them, but quickly learned that no one spoke English. I was feeling lonelier and lonelier as the day wore on.

Tiredly, I realized it was nearly 7 p.m.! I worried that I wouldn't find a bed. I grasped the St. Michael pendant around my neck in a weak gesture of prayer and hoped the Saint would help me out as I sought out the hospitalero. Once inside the entry, I noticed the beautiful floor mosaic made out of tiles shaped like fossils. The fossils formed a flower in the center of the entry. A desk to my left showed where the owner would stamp my passport. I let my pack slide to the floor with a dull thud and rolled my aching shoulders once the weight was gone. With the cadence of unfamiliar languages surrounding me, I waited. Finally, a short old man came out and peered at me with one eyebrow raised in question. *He must be tired of attempting to interpret these languages*, I thought.

Afraid to ask I said, "Completo?" He leaned forward and proceeded to ask me a volley of questions in Spanish but soon saw the look of confusion on my face. He pointed his finger at my chest. "Uno?"

"Si!" I responded. His eyes crinkled at the corners and he nodded, holding his hand out for my pilgrim passport. He stamped it with the same flower pattern as the inlaid pattern on the floor and handed it back. Gesturing for me to follow him, he smiled and picked up my pack. He led me down a short hallway and opened the door to a large room that housed bunk beds and quickly deposited my pack on a lower bunk. Every other bed had a pack on it. I estimated thirty total beds or so.

I was the last one! Feeling fortunate, I followed him as he showed me the women's bathroom. A shower stall to one side with a door separated the sink and toilet areas. When he'd sufficiently showed me around, he gestured to a chart showing my breakfast choices. I eyed it a little dubiously and found no other option. I was a bit worried about my gut. I'd had McDonalds in the airport in Florida during my layover and hadn't eliminated anything since then. Occasionally I suffered from gluten intolerance and severe constipation was the result. I didn't know what to do but asked my host if there was a *farmacia* (pharmacy) in town. He nodded and threw more Spanish sentences at me. To which I just nodded. I would find it. I gave him the money for *desayuno* (breakfast) and, with my lodging, paid thirteen euros.

Once I stopped moving, uncontrollable shivering set in due to the lack of heat and my sweat-soaked body. A hot shower seemed my best recourse and hope. I also intended to wash a few pieces of dirty laundry. The water though was barely warm enough to take my chills away so I hurriedly scrubbed my body and settled on washing only underwear before being blasted with freezing water. Afterward, I still shook from cold as I pulled on a pair of yoga pants and a long-sleeved, warm purple wool shirt and a jacket. Grabbing my purse and important documents, I left the chilly bunk room to find the closest restaurant, hoping for some good company after such a long day lost in personal reflections. As I searched for a restaurant, I became aware of the intensity of my hunger pains. Luckily I had only to walk a couple of blocks before I turned into the nearest restaurant and was promptly seated at a nice table near the back of the room, surrounded by couples happily filling their stomachs already. In that moment, I became nearly nauseous with hunger as I watched people eat.

An older man with white, wispy hair held a bottle of red wine aloft as he approached me. I merely nodded my agreement as he smiled, filled my glass, and set a menu in front of me. No one around me seemed to be speaking English, so I tried my best to decipher the menu. After a confusing conversation with my elderly waiter in which he insisted I order "spaghettis" along with my chicken and potatoes, I gave up and nodded at whatever he wanted me to have. He obviously thought I needed two entrees. It was the next evening when I realized this was the standard pilgrim fare, and my body did require more fuel than usual.

My attention focused on the middle-aged couple across from me. Their glasses of red wine sat untouched as my own was drained and refilled. They laughed softly at the little things they said and stole soft, brushing kisses. I watched her hands stroke his shoulders lovingly as he leaned into her and whispered in her ear. I really hoped they weren't staying in the same room as me.

My earplugs were good, but not that good. Her eyes sparkled as she peered into his.

Tears blurred my eyes momentarily as my ex-husband Derek's face flashed in my mind. We'd discussed taking trips like this one. Each time a lump rose to my throat, I swallowed it down with another gulp of wine. In an attempt to keep my emotions in check, my nails dug half-moons into the creases of my left hand, while my right kept a death grip on the stem of my glass. The dining room buzzed with muted conversations all around me. My table was the only one with a single occupant. I sighed wistfully as my first entree was set in front of me and wished I had someone to clink glasses with. Thankfully, my hunger gave me something else to focus on and I blissfully filled my stomach, not caring whether the food was tasty or not.

Under the moonlight, I staggered back to my bed and drunkenly worried about my grandmother. Would she understand my need to leave? I spent much of my life trying to be someone she could be proud of. She possessed a strength of character my mother did not. Growing up, we didn't see her much, but occasionally she breezed into our house with her glamorous 1950's movie star looks and her svelte figure swaddled in rich fabrics. She spoke loudly and filled our dull house with exuberant life. Though she was a stable influence, she worked too much during my early years while my siblings and I suffered under the narcissistic world our mother created—a world that involved Mom dragging us to parties, keeping us up all of hours of the night. A world where as soon as one of us kids stepped out of line, she threw a screaming fit and told us she never wanted kids. Grandma would not listen to us if we tried to communicate, but would tell us we needed to be more understanding and helpful to our mother.

I scoffed at this memory as I stubbed my toe on a rock and cursed violently for a moment. Help my mother? Jesus, I thought, if only they had known what she was allowing to happen to me while she was home, passed out from pot and letting her depraved friends stay over. I'd bargained with the creep who tormented me: my silence if he'd leave my sister alone. Though she and I were twins, I felt we were very different people. She had a tenderness that couldn't cope with tough things. She was like my mother, who often dissolved in emotional fits at the most insignificant things. It was sickening to watch either of them have a tantrum. So, I valiantly sacrificed myself in order to protect Renee, though she had no clue I was doing it.

Picturing my mother now in one of her hysterical fits of volatile emotion, the realization hit me—this was the reason I could not stand to cry. It reminded me of my mother. It made me feel weak. Was that what this trip was about? Was I here to cry? I hoped not, as I shuddered at the thought of all that snot and moisture leaking from my face and tried to shake the memories off.

For a moment, I stood outside the darkened Obanos Albergue wishing I had a cigarette. So many Europeans smoked that it was tempting to ask for one. I know what you are thinking—*But you survived cancer. That's not very smart.* Believe me, I know. For me, it's a seduction rather than an addiction. I can go years without one, but then something will trigger the need and they call to me until I give in and buy a pack. Now, sadly, without a cigarette, I stumbled as quietly as I could to my bed. I'd stuffed my toothbrush and paste under my pillow so I wouldn't have to dig in the dark for them. No sooner had my head touched my pillow before dreams swirled in.

I stood on my own front stoop. I wore a little black cocktail dress with my hair piled high on my head in a fancy style. Derek opened my front door. There were people mingling and talking inside. He smiled and held out his hand. I didn't take it as he continued to stare sadly at me. "Come in," he said. I had the strange sense that I almost knew some of the people in my house, but I couldn't clearly see their faces. I followed Derek to the kitchen. He served me a glass of wine and asked if I wanted spaghettis. I laughed and said, "No, but I'd love a cigarette." His eyebrow quirked in disapproval. His hand grabbed my arm just as his short, blonde girlfriend came toward him. He hurriedly asked me, "Can we work this out?" Shimmering tears stood in his eyes. I shook my head.

Weak sunlight filtered through my hazy mind and cracked open my eyes. Pilgrims bustled around to find their belongings, pack up and leave in a hurry. Both my earplugs had popped out during the night; too lazy to retrieve them, I lay there listening to the frenzied whispers of women urging their men to move and the deep-voiced, biting responses. Most seemed to be trying to be quiet, but occasionally someone bumped into my bed or dropped something, so their whispers were pointless. I lay there just taking it all in and tried to find the calm center of my mind before I'd have to get up and join the frenzied fray.

I remembered the dream vividly now. I recognized the dark, menacing shadow of Derek's mistress in one corner of my dining room. Her presence had seemed familiar but I didn't want to see her in my dream. She'd been a close, young friend to me. My heart lurched as I lay there and I turned my head to the side as tears threatened. I couldn't think of her and the love I'd had for her. I'd begun to think of her as a little sister. She was half his age. In her ploy for my trust, she had used her beauty and youth to steal away my husband. As a result, she'd irrevocably damaged my friendship with him, and herself. Thankfully, the need to pee was too urgent to dwell on these thoughts for long. I was suddenly squirming like mad to find a way out of my suddenly restrictive sleeping bag in enough time to make it to the restroom.

As I shuffled back to my bed, set on packing and joining the mad rush for the trails, a dark-haired, handsome Italian man caught my eye as I passed. He smiled charmingly as if we already knew each other. My lips quirked up at him in response. "Oh, you charming man!" I responded out loud, knowing he would most likely not understand me. I was wrong. His eyebrows quirked up in surprise as he quickly stepped forward and grasped my hand in his. He bent his carved lips over my hand and looked up at me as he lowered them to the back of my hand. I laughed and blushed. I had never been able to handle flirtations very well. He took pity on me and released me so I could run to my bunk and ignore him as I packed up and dressed in a corner out of his line of sight.

I was the last to exit the room. Hoping the handsome Italian had already eaten breakfast, I carried my belongings out to the hall and set my pack against the wall with the others, lined up like mini soldiers at attention along one wall. I hesitated at the threshold of the dining room, peering in to see if there was a spot available. The innkeeper circled the room with a coffee pot held aloft. He noticed me and waved me to an empty spot. The Italian man was on the other side of the room with his friends. It was then I noticed he wore blue and white cycling gear that matched the group he sat with. I felt a bit of relief. I wouldn't have to avoid him; he would cycle right by. When had I become so terrified of a little male attention, I wondered? I pondered this while sipping my coffee and nibbling croissants slathered with jelly and butter. I remembered how easy it had been to fall in love with Derek.

Nearing my twenty-second birthday, I'd been dating Scott for a few months, and was truthfully already bored with his neediness and babyish ways. I felt his lack of life experience made him immature, though he was a few years older than I. He still lived at home, ate his mommy's groceries, and did not drive. Which meant I had to pick him up for everything. This, fortunately, kept me from seeing him too often.

One day Scott called to say we were taking a friend of his out for his twenty-first birthday. Knowing what a bore his friends usually were, I told him I didn't want to go, but he argued and told me I would really like his friend Derek. I felt bitchy but agreed to go so Scott could have a driver. He didn't like it when I said that, and I listened with evil merriment to the silence I'd created on the other end of the line. Knowing he had no other way to "take his friend out," Scott thanked me and hung up.

Later that evening, a handsome young man exited the house just as we pulled up in the driveway. Derek was different from Scott's usual friends in that he walked with confidence. He was not some dopey slumped-over bangs in his eyes Dungeons and Dragons playing zombie-like creature that smelled of Cheetos like the rest of Scott's friends. I noticed his large, laughing eyes — an odd mixture of gray, hazel and dark blue — as he climbed into my back seat and introduced himself. His hair was sun bleached and curled around his ears and forehead. He was hilarious. He smelled like sunshine and just a hint of male cologne. I couldn't stop staring. We soon found excuses to send Scott off to the bar. We needed another drink. More water. A straw. Napkins. Each time, Scott stupidly went and we were able to steal another look at each other. We hid our attraction in the quirks of our grins, in the soft, joking shoves, which were tiny excuses to touch and feel.

Guilt washed over me each time I looked at Derek and felt excitement pulse through me. I tried to think of some redeeming qualities that Scott may have but couldn't focus for long on our relationship. My deep moral compass would never allow me to physically cheat on my boyfriend, but I sure wanted to! Derek made me laugh like no one else ever had. I drove the drunken boys home and after that night, I tried to put Derek out of my mind and refused to ask my boyfriend about him. I could not ignore the way he had made me feel that night, though. Wistful moments watching dust motes swirl in front of my eyes as I daydreamed about his smiling face happened more often than I wanted to allow.

Fate answered my silent cravings a few weeks later when Scott called to tell me that Derek had lost a roommate and needed one ASAP. I waited breathlessly for him to tell me he was moving out of his parents' house and in with the guys. He shocked me by asking if *I* would want to move in since I'd been complaining about living with my mother. He offered to help me get a better job at UPS, where he and Derek both worked. The pay would be better and close to home. A couple of heartbeats later, he cleared his throat. "Well? What do you think?" he asked a bit impatiently.

After it was obvious he was not joking, I responded with a nonchalant, "Yeah, sure. Uh, give me his number. I guess I'll call him."

"I thought you'd be more excited," he said peevishly.

You have no idea, I thought. I wanted to bang my head on the counter at his naivety.

It took me a couple of days to work up the nerve to call

Derek. We both laughed nervously at the idea of living in the same house. Our attraction sizzled unspoken over the phone line. Within three months, we were spending most of our free time together. I neglected Scott's calls as Derek and I visited museums and went to movies. I didn't call him back for days until my mom called and informed me that Scott was panicking, thinking I'd been kidnapped or worse. I reluctantly called him then and told him we would talk that afternoon. He begged me to come over to his house. Derek and I had been sitting in the sunshine on the front stoop, admiring each other as much as the autumn leaves clinging to the maple trees in their red and gold glory.

Scott's lanky frame opened his front door. Smells of his mother's awful beef stew hit my nose. Dark circles rimmed his deep-set hazel eyes. His parents' voices could be heard near the back of the house. He invited me inside with sad, puppy dog eyes. I retreated a step and told him we'd talk outside. I didn't need the triple guilt of breaking up with him in front of his parents, so I walked to my car and leaned against it. My car keys dangled from my hand in readiness to leave.

He tried to hug me but I shrugged him off. "Where have you been?" he whined. "I have been trying to find you, thought something bad happened."

Feeling stalked, I became angry. I stood up taller and looked him in the eye. "I don't belong to you, you know. I'm not your child."

"Wha...? What are you talking about? You're my girlfriend and I CARE."

I decided then and there to rip the band-aid off and not prolong the inevitable.

"I'm sorry. I just don't want to be with you anymore," I said.

"Why?" Scott asked and then blurted out, "I was going to ask you to marry me!"

I sighed and looked down at the keys dangling from my hand. I wished I could slink away now. "Listen, I'm truly sorry. You will find someone who wants to marry you, too. It's not that you've done anything wrong, it's that ...I don't love you." My heart hammered with the truth of my words. I didn't want to hurt him but there was no other way now.

His face crumpled as he cried. His hands lifted to cover his face as he bent over slightly. I felt the usual impatience with his tears as I did when anyone else I knew cried. I tried not to show my distaste for his emotional outburst as I waited a few minutes more. Then he asked, "Does this have anything to do with Derek?"

I shook my head, "NO! No, it doesn't," I lied with guilt crawling over my heart. I wasn't even sure if Derek liked me the same way. We'd never even kissed, though I felt it would happen soon. The important thing, in my mind, was that it hadn't happened yet.

Scott took a step toward me as if he wanted to cling to me and I stepped back, opened my car and told him I had to leave. His sad, hunched form shrunk in my rear view as I drove away.

Feeling only relief, I drove back to Derek's house singing badly off key, very loudly. My heart lifted when I saw that Derek still sat on the front stoop though more than two hours had gone by. (My young, eager heart thought he must have waited the whole time! He had smiled and nodded. Yes, he had! Years later, I found out the truth that he'd gone inside, made lunch, taken a nap, then come back out.)

I sat next to him in the late afternoon sunshine. We didn't speak. The sun warmed my eyelids as I tipped my head back to warm my face in the late afternoon sunshine. His hand reached for mine. I studied the shape of his fingers and decided I liked those, too. I held his hand softly in my own for just a minute, then turned to him and demanded, "Would you kiss me already?!" His multi-colored eyes widened in shock but he leaned in with that slight smile and did as I requested. He'd tasted like sunshine and maybe something like pasta salad.

I'd been incredibly in love with him in those early years and, coupled with the fiery passion we had for each other, we both believed we would be together for the long haul.

CHAPTER THREE

"Buen Camino!" I looked up from the bottom of my coffee cup into a middle-aged woman's face. I hadn't heard her approach me. She put a hand on my shoulder gently; I didn't cringe but smiled up at her. She asked me if I was okay, though her English was poor. She sat down for a moment at the end of my bench. I nodded.

"Just lost in the past for a minute," I said. She looked confused as she tried to decipher my meaning. I shook my head. "I'm okay." I smiled to show her.

They were from Finland and very sweet, though we could hardly understand each other. She must have sensed my sadness for she asked if I wanted to walk with them that morning. I shook my head, I needed to be alone, I believed. Trying to soften the rejection, I patted her shoulder and told her I was fine. She smiled a bit sadly and stood to leave. I sighed and wondered if I would always be the last to leave. I just didn't feel that urgency to go, go, go!

Beyond the glass windows in the entry, gray skies threatened as I prepared to set out for the day. My pack felt heavy on my shoulders, the weight unevenly distributed. Now I had to take it off and dig for my poncho, for rain seemed imminent. With my back turned, someone clicked toward me in bicycle shoes. I turned to see the Italian man. His friends waited beyond the windows, peering in at him as they all stood with their bicycles tucked between their legs, ready to ride away.

"Buen Camino, peregrina!" His long-lashed brown eyes flicked toward his waiting friends. "We go to Los Arcos today. And you?" he inquired.

My heart sank ever so slightly. He would be covering more than twice my distance on his bicycle. While he covered fifty kilometers, I would maybe do twenty, and so I would most likely not see him again. So much for him being my Camino romance, I sighed to myself, then shrugged.

"I have no bike, so hopefully Estella! Have to see," I gestured to the clouds.

"Ah! Well, I show you how we say goodbye to beautiful women!" he said. Before I knew what was happening, he grabbed my face with his warm hands and kissed both of my cheeks! I envisioned returning this gesture but it felt too awkward so I stuck out my hand. He laughed but kindly returned the gesture, while murmuring something about Americans. His male friends came rushing in and there were more rounds of hugging. Though I didn't know them, I was included in the well-wishing and good cheer. As suddenly as it began, everyone dispersed. I followed them out and began my walk for the day.

"Need more coffee!" the handsome cyclist laughed as he peddled after his friends. I realized later I didn't ask his name.

My pace seemed to be steady, though not fast, as I passed people I thought were long gone. Though the skies were gray and seemed as if they'd stay that way for a while, the glorious landscape took my breath away. I had to stop several times near medieval ruins or fields of poppies to breathe in the beauty. I was amazed at the quantity of air I breathed in.

My lungs were acclimated to climbing mountains in Colorado

where the air was thin. I sometimes felt I was having workout-induced asthma in Colorado from the lack of air at the highest elevations. Here in northern Spain the air filled the back of my throat and lungs quickly. I found myself taking half sips of air rather than full breaths subconsciously. When I took full breaths and walked at a moderate clip, I felt a little drunk. The headiness of the air was exhilarating!

The monotonous rhythm of my steps lulled me into thoughts of home. I missed my sweet daughter so much that my insides hurt and I wanted to hold her to stop the ache in my heart. She'd refused my offers of bringing her with me. Of course, we would have waited until summer, rather than late May, and it would have completely changed the journey. I'd had to ask her, though, and I would have brought her. She declined time and again, stating that she hated to hike, hated to carry a pack and finally in an exasperated tone had said, "Momma! Just go and do this. Hurry up, too. You've been talking about this trip for so long. Just hurry up and come back!" She'd grabbed my face in her hands and told me she would be okay, but most importantly, she wanted me to be okay, too. I'd left her in Derek's care, though Renee was helping out while he worked. Knowing she was being cared for in the best possible way still didn't assuage the guilt I felt.

The last two years had tested the bonds of our mother/daughter relationship. There were times I felt she was taking better care of me than I of her. She gave me strong hugs, discouraged me from dating the wrong men, or the right ones.... seemed to know I wasn't ready yet. She feared my cancer would come back, and in the back of my mind, I did too. I tried really hard not to say mean things about her father, but when she asked me if I would take him back, I couldn't help showing some anger and venting a bit before catching myself before revealing too much. There'd been the surreal moment in the grocery store as we stood by the bananas when she'd told me she'd seen her father kissing and holding the girl we both knew and could not name for it brought such pain for both of us. I had held her on the floor of the newly waxed wooden floors in the middle of the grocery store as she had collapsed, white-faced in my arms, as she begged me not to hate her daddy. I hadn't known that she'd known and was amazed that she had kept her secret, trying to protect me. We both cried that day, her for her father's betrayal and me for her lost innocence.

Her pain angered me. I strove to shield her from life's pains and struggles. I had tried my best to have a normal adult life, with a normal marriage, normal careers, and a normal child. We'd never actually planned to have children, so when I became pregnant, we accepted it with a healthy dose of fear but resolved to be the best parents we could be. Yet, the news that I carried a daughter rather than the son I'd prayed so hard for had nearly undone me. I couldn't bear the thought of my own daughter suffering as I had. In denial, we'd painted the nursery blue with cartoon astronauts. When my very handsome, very young doctor announced it was a girl, I told him to look again! I chose her name, Parker, from the list of boys' names I'd compiled. There was no list of girls' names.

Never really believing in any higher power before she was born, I suddenly found myself praying hard for her to be strong and confident, not a shadow of a girl like me. She gave me a gift when she was born, too. I hadn't known what it really meant to love someone. I'd been afraid that I couldn't be a good mother, afraid that I would treat her as I'd been treated growing up. Would I hate and resent my own child? Within moments of meeting my daughter face to face, I knew it wasn't possible. I would die to protect her.

Remembering those early days made me chuckle. Parker needed no protector. As if the heavens heard me, she had been endowed with a strong sense of self-protection and could vindicate herself with utter conviction. One day, when Parker was four, we'd taken her to play at the city park. We watched as a girl twice her height approached her. We thought she wanted to play with our little Parker. With her sun-bleached hair pulled into side pigtails, she was the very picture of adorable. However, the big girl had taken a rather threatening stance and my little angel squared off to face her directly. The larger girl said something with a mean glare. I had no time to react as Parker suddenly punched the mean girl with a straight right arm directly into her soft lower belly. Beside me, Derek grunted in sympathy as the big girl doubled over. Parker turned and flew toward us, her large eyes opened wide and legs pumping hard. She came at me like a rocket. I scooped her up, barely able to keep from falling over. She pointed at the girl and said, "She said she was going to beat me up. I told her, 'No, you won't.' I hit her first!" I admired her quick processes and self-preservation skills. My relief at her strength of character caused delirious laughter to rise up as I tried to very seriously tell her she did the right thing between snickers of laughter. We took our little bruiser out for celebratory ice cream.

Over the years, Derek and I were called in to the principal's office on a few occasions to talk about the incidences when Parker was forced to fight back. We listened to them tell us how Parker punched someone back or threw a girl down and pulled her hair after being provoked physically. We asked the same questions, "Did she start it?"

"No," they'd answer.
"Did she use her words first?"
"Yes, but..."
We'd interrupt, "Did the other kid hit her first?"
"Yes, but that isn't the point here."
"That is PRECISELY the point," I interrupted coldly and loudly. "School systems these days want kids to be pushed and punched while 'using their words'...you know what? That doesn't work. Sometimes you have to show them you are not weak and that is what she's doing. We're proud of her. She's teaching the bully not to bully her anymore!"

No, I reflected as I slipped on some mud along the trail, my daughter had never been a weakling and I was wickedly proud of that! I need HALF that much strength, I thought. I'd been afraid of everything my whole life. I was afraid to face life alone, by myself, with no one but me to take care of things. The world was a scary place and someday soon Parker would grow up and move away to college and then what would I do?

With these heavy thoughts, I wandered into Puenta La Reina and immediately perked up at the thought of having a café con leche, maybe a little food. Though, truthfully, food was not as appealing as one might have thought at this point in my adventures. I had been struggling with an embarrassing dilemma and had hoped it would fix itself by now. Since leaving the airport in Florida, I had been constipated so badly that my belly was becoming a hard drum and the thought of eating was almost nauseating. I decided to seek out a pharmacy.

Once in the village, the way was marked by the familiar yellow arrows or old stone way-markers; all I had to do was follow the trail. Big green blinking neon "plus" symbols hung over the pharmacies and I went straight for the first one I saw. There were pilgrims milling in doorways sipping coffees and greeting fellow travelers. I felt honored to be greeted and smiled at. I was starting to appreciate this journey and my fellow peregrinos. There was a deep sense of camaraderie that was infectious. It also served to pull me out of my self-reflections at moments like these.

I pushed into the pharmacy and walked up to the counter where a young brunette was filling an order for someone else. I waited patiently until she looked up. "Hola, habla Englais?" I asked.

"Uno momento," she replied with a finger held aloft. She filled the customer's order and rang him up. After their transaction, she held her finger up again and walked to the double doors behind her where she exchanged words with someone inside. Another woman, taller and older, came forward.

"Hello. You speak English?" I asked hopefully.

"Yes, I do. Do you have blisters?" she asked.

"No, no, not yet! I am having trouble with ...ummm...bowel movements. I need something that will help."

"BOW wells?" She was clearly confused.

"Yes, um, I'm not eliminating anything." I tried to be delicate.

"Hmmm? BOW wells..." I could see she was trying to understand.

"I need something to help me go to the toilet, the baño!" I said. Still she remained stubbornly confused.

Exasperated, I said in low tones so no one else would hear, "Pooping. I'm not pooping. For almost four days now. I am worried." I rubbed my lower abdomen for emphasis. I quickly looked up to see if there were others in there with us. Only two people. I fervently prayed they did not speak English!

"Oh!" she exclaimed loudly and with excitement. She

pointed her index finger and with a downward motion near her ass she said, "You mean SHITTING? You are not shitting?!" I thought maybe she needed a megaphone because the guy on the opposite corner at that little café sipping his café con leche had not heard her. Silently fuming, I nodded in embarrassment.

"I haven't for four...CUATRO days," I told her.

She squeezed my arm in sympathy and directed me to a shelf of miraculous things. I almost cried in relief that the idiotic conversation was nearly over!

She grabbed a glass bottle and it had some dark pills inside. The name said *Aliviolas*. I recognized the name senna among the list of ingredients. I knew what senna was and had used it before to cure this sort of thing but never after a four-day bout! She warned me to take only one, as the results could be "more than I wanted." I didn't think so, but didn't want to argue, only to get the hell out of there. I thanked her again as I paid and quickly opened the bottle outside. Someone brushed me as I took off the protective covering and my precious brown glass bottle wobbled dangerously for a moment.

"Pardona," I muttered irritably.

"Hey! Is that an American accent I hear?" I looked up at the male voice.

"Yes, I'm from Colorado! Where are you from?"

"I'm from California. I'm traveling with my mom. My name is Sam!" He had a sweet smile and eyes that looked a little sad down in the depths. He was very lean. His face was hard with deep lines running from the corners of his eyes and almost cleaving his checks down to his jaw. These weren't laugh lines. His face was tanned and mottled with brown sun spots on his flat cheekbones and along the ridge of his forehead. His ears looked red and raw along the rims and I wondered if he ever wore sunscreen. His hair was thick and full and cut short. I guessed he was about 55, but would not have been surprised to learn he was much younger based on that evidence of hard living in his eyes and lines on his face.

We shook hands—his were brown and wrinkled from sun exposure. Since we both needed more coffee, he invited me to join him and his mother. We walked to the nearest cafe, where his mother waited for him to return with her blister medication. After ordering a small latte and orange juice, I discreetly popped two of my magic pills before joining their table. I set my pack against the wall and sat at the high, round table next to her with my back against the wall.

Sam's mother, Virginia, looked like a very sweet lady. Her small smile stayed in place and she blinked a lot as though she couldn't see very clearly. She merely listened as Sam explained that she was the one who'd wanted this trip. Her husband, his father, had died suddenly and they were both there to overcome the grief. She had wanted to walk the Camino with her spouse but he'd passed before they'd had the chance to do it together. Her poor feet were already troubling her so Sam had been carrying her pack, as well as his! He didn't mind at all. He seemed in good spirits but said they were probably going to be slower than me. Virginia looked about 74 and I complimented her on her strength. Good lord! I would not be doing this at her age. I listened as she nodded her sweet smile at me.

I concentrated on their story and grief, so when Sam asked me abruptly, "Why did you decide to walk the Camino?" I was taken aback. I realized it was only natural to ask, but I was not ready to give answers.

Sam's face watched me curiously while I gathered my thoughts. "It's okay," he assured me, "we're all here for something!"

"You're right!" I'd been feeling a bit sorry for myself on my lonely quest. I looked around the cafe and noticed the barista for the first time. There were about a dozen pilgrims inside, with backpacks of every color leaning haphazardly along the outer wall near the exit. We were all pilgrims sharing this journey together. The magnitude of that realization stunned me for a moment. People talked loudly and laughter floated in the air. Beyond the windows more pilgrims lounged in plastic red chairs on the cobblestone walkways, filling doorways of cafés across the street.

"I'm here to get over a bunch of shit...you know. Like everyone else, I suppose I'm looking for more to this life. I'm looking for me...maybe." He waited. "I was recently divorced after a seventeen-year relationship, sold my coffee shop, fought a battle with cancer...just three surgeries before I lost my health insurance in the divorce....was depressed...and almost killed myself...but my daughter kept me.....He cheated on me with someone I rather liked!" Feeling uncomfortably close to crying, I looked at him almost resentfully and angrily swiped at my tears. "And you?" I choked out, hoping he would understand that was all I was capable of talking about at that moment.

He patted my right hand that held tightly to my coffee mug and I flinched. After a moment he swallowed a lump in his own throat and shared.

"I almost died from a heroin overdose. I woke up in the hospital. The daughter I never helped raise was there waiting for me to die in a hateful way. She was a woman and I had no part in raising her...but I was proud! I was so ashamed of myself. I knew she had a right to hate me. See...I'd been found in a gas station urinal. I'd urinated all over myself and there was blood in the bathroom from the needle. A so-called friend, or fellow heroin user, called the ambulance and they said I wouldn't make it.

"My mother and I lost my father a couple of years ago. I think I died, because they told everyone I was brain dead…Anyhow, I saw him. He showed me love, not anger. He said I needed to survive… for Mom." [A quick look in her direction showed her nodding and wiping her eyes.] "I went back even though I didn't want to! When I opened my eyes in that hospital bed, there was my daughter, her angry accusatory eyes were the best thing I'd ever seen. I can't make up for all of those years without her, but I can live clean and sober and hope she'll visit once in a while."

His eyes stared holes into the tabletop as his fingers gripped his cup much like mine had. There wasn't really much to say after that. As strangers, we'd shared too much too early. I shifted on my seat and looked around the bar. As awkward as it was, I felt a bit better. Something that had gripped my heart tightly seemed a bit looser. I didn't want to delve into that discovery just yet, afraid I might become inconsolably sad. This wasn't the time or the place for any of that! "Time to leave" I told no one in particular.

We sat companionably for a few more minutes. His mom reached over to hug me. I lied to her when I told her I hoped to run into the two of them again. Something about their relationship bothered me. Sam said his mom needed a little more rest before they shoved off, but she winked at me and I thought maybe HE needed the rest since he carried both packs. We smiled and I walked out into the gray morning to follow those arrows.

On the way out of Puenta La Reina, I walked over a pedestrian bridge built in the twelfth century! The stone and masonry that had been used seemed as solid to me as if it were built recently. I reverently walked beneath ancient arches as I passed out of the city and onto the bridge and over the river Rio Arga. The trail veered right and over an incline out of the city. At the top, slightly out of breath, I paused to look back at the medieval parts of the village. I loved these views. The old stone villas, balconies facing the cobbled walkways, and the steeple rising from the center of the ancient structures near the plaza where Sam and his mother sat cozily inside the cafe.

The tenuous strands of love between Sam and his mom provoked a sense of frustration within me. The invisible thread spoke of a long-suffering relationship newly minted into a shiny, silvery promise. I knew from experience, that quivering strand of new hope could either bond them together again if tended carefully or snap in two with minimal discord. I'd needed to get away from them quickly. They reminded me of the new cord of reconciliation between me and my own mother—a cord that showed many retied knots from the many times I severed my unhealthy relationship with her, only to get reeled back in again and again. Whether it was one year, two, or more, she always managed to pull me back in until the next time she whispered about me to someone.

My life had proven to be vastly entertaining to talk about—I would give them that. But it angered me that no one could let it all go even after I begged my family members to see me differently. They enjoyed keeping the pain of my past alive though I made strides my whole life to overcome and achieve happiness. Now, with the latest string of God-awful events, the rumors were circling like vultures over my head again. Would I eventually succumb to the victim mentality they wanted to box me into? *I would die first*, I thought. I marched angrily down the trail as if I could escape their whispers by walking harder and faster. I was surprised my ears weren't trailing plumes of smoke behind me, for I glared at that trail so hard my eyeballs ached with the need to blink.

I'd understood Sam's need to share his story. It made me revise my thoughts a bit. "Maybe this is part of the Camino," I grudgingly thought, "to be able to share and not be ashamed or judged for it. To accept each other on this path, no matter the circumstances and offer support!" This concept made me cringe a bit out of habit, but I pondered it more as I walked, my anger at having to feel emotions receding more and more as I thought.

Just past the Bogota Monastery ruins rain fell earnestly, turning the already slick trails to a soupy mud, thick with slippery stones. Rain poured and the mud sucked, literally. It slurped at my shoes with each step. My long toes scrunched inside the tips of my shoes in efforts to hold them on my feet. I slipped on rocks and fought to stay upright. The red mud was slick as snot and each step left an elongated, sliding footprint. Going downhill, I wish I had trekking poles for the first time. At one point, I slid forward so that my left foot became wedged in between two rocks just as I stepped down with my right. The mud successfully clung to my shoe as my foot popped out of it. I did not want to step directly into the mud with my left foot, so I paused a moment with my foot held aloft while rain promptly soaked it and the inside of my steaming shoe. It appeared surprised, the tongue pulled forward over the loose laces that lackadaisically dangled to either side in the mud.

Desperate to avoid sinking my shoeless foot into the cold mud, I tried to balance on my right foot while aiming my left foot uphill at the opening of my shoe. It would have been a fantastic feat if I hadn't slid forward at that moment. Instinctively, my shoeless foot shot forward into the muck. Now I was sliding into the splits, leaving my poor shoe farther behind. I growled, as my arms wheeled uselessly while I wrestled to stay upright. Nothing helped. I landed on my right shin where the shock of icy mud made me aware of how numb my feet had become. From there, I stood up unsteadily and turned a baleful glare at my traitorous shoe. I walked a few steps back up the hill and pulled it out of its trap. With a sigh of disgust, I planted my butt on the grassy knoll and wrung cold mud off my foot before I shoved it into my wet shoe.

A few kilometers later, my muscles shook with fatigue and curse words punctuated each forward motion into the ice-cold, slick red muck as I finally came to another medieval village perfectly perched on a hilltop. I made my way to the town square ringed by beautiful arches, also dating from the twelfth or thirteenth century. Too irritated to take much notice of the architecture, I grumpily waved to other pilgrims who yelled various things as I walked to the nearest café. I needed to thaw my hands and feet and drink something warming. I squeezed into a tightly packed bar where everyone greeted me grimly with sympathetic pats and glances at my mud-caked feet and legs. Of course, most of them were in the same condition, so I patted shoulders as I passed, too. I set my pack against a wall and pulled my wet poncho off to lay over it in a limp heap.

Pins and needles started in my feet and ankles where the numbed skin was warming up. Immediately, I shucked my shoes and changed the wet, muddy socks for a pair of clean wool ones. The mud had already caked off the quick-drying material of my pants but had left a large stain, evidence of the struggle I'd experienced. With the clean socks on, I rubbed my feet while I received sympathetic looks from other pilgrims who tended their own sore feet. The bar was so crowded that getting to the counter was impossible until a man came over and asked me what I would like. I ordered hot tea, fresh OJ and an omelet while I rubbed my hands together to warm them.

To an immense room-wide cheer of relief, I looked up to see the sun had made a weak appearance. Though it still looked beastly cold, it graciously was not raining. As I ate, I watched pilgrims passing through the town square. Many had walking sticks. They resembled funny insects clicking along with their long sticks jabbing the ground before them. Their multi-colored ponchos pulled over their packs added to the illusion, looking like exoskeletons. A few wore funny hats. I thought of the movie James and the Giant Peach and played match-up with some characters from the movie. I definitely saw the lady bug character; she had a red poncho and black sticks, black hat. She was a grumpy lady bug! I didn't blame her. I imagined I must have looked just as grumpy as I'd arrived. Her face pulled downward and she huffed as her lanky male partner strode ahead a bit. He reminded me of a grasshopper. His face was long and pointed, but his eyes looked cheerful.

The two bugs came inside as he gestured at a couple of chairs near me. He watched while lady bug huffed and gasped and clicked her way over to him, seeming too tired to understand she should put the sticks away inside the bar while people moved out of the way of her potential jabs. Her poncho puffed around her as she sat down. The grasshopper came back to her with two mugs of hot liquid. He said something in French and her face relaxed for the first time. She thanked him and it was clear she was simply exhausted. He glanced at me and I offered a "Buen Camino!" He smiled only with his sparkly eyes, the corners tipped up, as he replied the same.

I sat in that cafe until the crowds thinned again. After an hour or so, I stood, balled my dried poncho into a side pocket of my pack, and cringed at the sudden muscle cramps in my calves. Limping rather than walking, I noticed a couple of picturesque old homes with their intricate balconies and geraniums bursting from rusty blue pots. One blue shutter hung slightly askew, the dark depths of the home beyond seemed to beckon me inside to share its ancient secrets. I thought I glimpsed someone moving inside, but it was only the drapes within the dark interior. I thought if I stared long enough someone would appear to put my ghost-town fantasies to rest. Though these towns seemed idyllic from afar, I wondered where the people were. If it weren't for the traffic and business of us pilgrims I wondered if these towns would even be here at all. The thought made me indescribably sad.

After a few minutes all I could think about was putting one foot in front of the other. My calf muscles hated me. They told me so. I had almost five kilometers to go to reach the next town, Villatuerta Puenta. My original destination that day had been Estella, but I knew I couldn't make it that far. I thought if the next five kilometers didn't kill me, I would call it good for the day. I tried to focus on the beautiful countryside rather than the pain radiating from the soles of my feet up through the calf muscles. Really, above the knees I was fine. I figured that was eighty-percent good, so I ignored the other twenty-percent that screamed at me.

Those five kilometers were bitches! The mud sucked at my shoes and sapped the energy from my muscles. When I stepped on stones instead of directly in the mud, I slid. I worried that the whole way would be like this. "Don't cry, silly, don't cry." Now I'd been reduced to talking to myself. I felt I was losing it a bit, possibly. Had it happened finally? I usually didn't talk to myself nor glare at inanimate objects so it could have. "Time will tell, just move," I retorted at myself.

With sudden inspiration, I struggled up over the ledge beside the trail and walked in the tall grasses, poppies and yellow mustard flowers rather than slick rocks. The tall grass bent under my feet. I crushed flowers underfoot as I went. I only apologized to the flowers once. It was just as slow up on the ridge of the trail, but at least my shoes weren't sticking anymore. Up ahead I saw a woman walking with her poles. She was moving even slower than I.

I waited until we were abreast of each other before saying hello. She glanced up at me with sweet brown eyes and a huge, toothy smile. "Bon jour," she said. I don't remember making the decision to walk with her, nor being invited. I hopped rather ungracefully down next to her. Truthfully, I almost took her out. My hasty departure from the ledge of grass propelled me quickly onto the slippery rocks, causing me to slide toward this sweet, unprepared little lady. After a quick *swish swish* of my feet and a bit of arm flinging, I almost grabbed her out of instinct. She looked rather frail, so I stopped myself just in time.

When I stood solidly next to her, I looked into her amused if slightly startled eyes and asked if she spoke English. She stared at me uncertainly and said no. Since I'd nearly broken both our necks, I stayed on the trail. She was rather elderly and I worried that she was out here alone. She was razor thin and somewhere in her late sixties. Her hair was dyed the dull, flat brown as only gray hair disguised with a box of cheap hair coloring can be. Just plain, dull brown. But her eyes were girlish and twinkly. I made a walking gesture with my fingers and pointed at her, to which she nodded. I now had a walking partner for a ways.

I pointed to her. "Estella?"

She shook her head and with a big pout on her lips, made

disgusted sounds and pointed at the mud. She shook her walking poles in mock anger. I laughed. For the first time on this trip, I really laughed! It felt so good to have a companion of any sort; even if we couldn't really talk, we could pantomime! I walked next to her even though she had her poles. She couldn't really grab my arm but I wanted to be there for her in case something happened.

We continued in companionable silence, both of us buoyed by the nearness of the next village. I felt warm inside from knowing we'd made a connection. That knowledge suddenly made me feel lighter. I could feel myself cracking open a bit. I still didn't know what this journey had in store for me or why I'd been compelled to walk this horribly long trek. Not patient by nature, as I am a Leo, I told myself the truth would be revealed little by little.

Walking next to my little French lady, I wondered why I had suddenly felt the need for companionship. Maybe I was finally bored of my self-imposed isolation, I mused. Did I really need to make myself suffer any more for all of the things that had gone wrong?

When my marriage collapsed, some of our friends had been completely stunned. Sitting across from a friend at a table in my coffee shop, I'd opened up about the divorce. Her shocked response still reverberates in my head.

"But...you two are the perfect couple. I thought out of everyone that I know... you would never be getting divorced! He's such a great guy! I like Derek a lot. Why is this happening?!"

Loathe to make anyone hate him and still wanting to protect him, though I had no idea why after he'd betrayed me so badly, I had held in my temper and said, "It's just one of those things that happens over time. I guess we grew apart," the easy lies stuck in my throat as I nearly choked on my lemon loaf, while my head screamed for me to rage with the truth and my heart pounded in pain and anger.

How could I talk about the slow divide...the alcoholism. The nights of cold dinners waiting for him to come home from "happy hour" when he'd really been at the strip clubs? Or the absolute shock of his absence when I needed a tumor removed. That had been The Event. The day my heart broke for good and I started to see his lack of empathy for anyone but himself. Ever the stand-in mother, my sister Renee had taken me to the doctor and held me while we learned it was benign and my phone had no missed calls from "the man of my dreams." Then, waking up enough from an anesthetized coma to scream "Fuck you" in his face before succumbing to the meds and passing back out. How could I describe that ambiguous moment when the gear in the cog suddenly shifted the stable revolution of our marriage wheel to "off kilter" and I questioned everything?

How did I talk about his love affair with a near-family-member of mine, so painful the ripple effects were felt for years afterward? I couldn't bear to even think of the horrible things his online chats had said about me, the mother of his child. I had simply left the house we'd built together and moved in with friends while trying to contain the rumors. I tried to run my coffee shop as if nothing unusual was happening and juggled shared custody of our daughter. Then the panic attacks hit—but not before the cancer. This time it was melanoma and lymphoma. Still no concerned calls from him. He didn't love me at all. My heart finally shattered along all the fault lines he'd affected over the years. Our divorce was final before the last of my stitches came out.

Where did I start as I stared at this "friend" of mine who

didn't really know me at all? Why did I have to keep everything so damned private? Was it a result of trying to hide and stuff my feelings as a child? There had always been the burden of carrying secrets I couldn't talk about. Something that made me want to scream, rant and yell. Instead, I tried to contain it all, effectively protecting the guilty parties involved, hiding it behind a smile and a shrug as if to say, "Nothing is wrong. Don't worry about me." I'd earned the status of being "the good girl. The quiet one." I'd erroneously learned it was better to create the illusion of normalcy. Now all my hard work had caved in. There was no containing the mess anymore.

With a soul-weary sigh, I glanced up from the endless mud trail and spied Villatuerta ahead. We were nearly there. I smiled tiredly at my little French woman whose name I never learned. She returned it in the same manner. She must have sensed the heaviness of my thoughts when she paused a moment to look me in the eye and pat me on the shoulder. I felt a tear well up but patted her hand and nodded toward town. "It's okay," I said aloud. We limped uphill into town together. I wondered at her perception of my feelings. *Everyone here must be working through something,* I thought. I grasped the nearly forgotten Archangel Michael pendant around my neck. I prayed for the miracles to start, "Please show me why I'm here on this awful trek!" I thought with irritation. "And hurry up...please and thank you," a bit grumpily added.

Pilgrims milled around the bars and cafes as we trudged into town. We ogled their clean shoes and pant legs. It seemed their chores were done already. They were free to eat and nap, I thought jealously. My clothes stuck to my skin in cold, wet patches and I felt starved nearly to death. Tired of being upright, my feet dragged up that last hill. My backpack pulled on my right shoulder more than the left. Consequently, my right arm felt slightly numb and tingly. The albergue was tucked around the corner and up another hill. My hopes of laying my tired body on a warm bed were dashed when I found the entrance where the barn-like doors that split across the middle were open on top, showing a clear view of the entry from outside. People huddled in chairs with blankets while they waited to be checked in. It would be just as cold inside as out! I nearly whimpered out loud.

Despite the promise of another downright cold night, I pushed open the lower half of the doors and entered *La Casa Magica*, or The Magic House. Inlaid pebbles on the ground floor were intricately arranged but hard on my sore, cold feet. I limped into the waiting area. As I sat to wait my turn, I removed my shoes to rub my feet with one hand while I dug around in my pack for anything to eat. My stomach was growling audibly and I was nauseous with extreme hunger pains. Suffering from multiple bodily needs at once, I didn't know where to start as I jammed crackers in my mouth and rubbed my feet vigorously, while slightly preoccupied with the tingly sensation in my right shoulder and upper arm. I could have either laughed or cried at that moment and just barely held my emotions in check.

"Hola, peregrina! Una momento, por favor!" A woman's voice called from the wooden staircase that wound up and out of sight to another level. She was about thirty and very lean. She yelled something else that I ignored while I inhaled crackers and whatever else I had that was edible before finally taking stock of where I was. I knew this albergue was one of the oldest around at nearly six-hundred years old. I appreciated the uneven beams that twisted across the ceiling. They looked original. This entry was oddly shaped, not exactly rectangular, sort of rounded with arched doorways and another square door more recently cut out to my right, with a cheap, modern French door retrofitted into it. The walls were made of stone. A hammock chair had been hung from one of the beams and an Asian woman was curled inside with blankets. Her head lolled to one side as she slept.

The woman who'd shouted in Spanish at me came back down and I stood while my calf muscles and feet cursed at me. The stones were hard and unforgiving on my swollen feet. She watched me limp across to her with my passport and money in hand. I winced with each step but managed to ask, "Cuanto por uno peregrino, señora?"

She grimaced in sympathy pain (perhaps also in reaction to my poor Spanish accent) and pulled a chair away from the desk for me. "Ten euros. You are American?"

I nodded. "Si. Yes."

I sat gratefully and she walked back around to the other side and sat across from me. "Where do you come from?" She held out her hand for my pilgrim credentials and passport, which she took to run a background check and make copies of my paperwork. The process was irritating and a bit scary even for a non-criminal!

When she came back with a smile I relaxed, though I had nothing to worry about. "If you like, you can eat here this night. We are serving a vegetarian meal with paella, salad, fruits, wines, and breads for seven euros more. Dinner is at seven p.m. in the cellar beyond those doors behind me," she gestured without looking.

"Is there any heat in this building?"

She shook her head regretfully. "No, I am sorry. There are blankets on your beds but this building is almost six-hundred years old! We have a fireplace in the dinner room. Come. I will show you where you can wash a few items and dry them, too. It's another three euros for laundry service."

Of course it was, I thought.

I stood as she did and this time my feet behaved better. I limped with her past a kitchen with a big gas stove outfitted with a big circular electric cooking contraption. The stainless steel sink and counters were spotlessly clean. We walked outside to the patio which overlooked a grassy courtyard one story below us. Rough-looking cats roamed the patio, meowing pitifully at us. Under a roof overhang looked to be a gathering area complete with outdoor fireplace. The laundry machines squatted along one wall with a sink, complete with brushes to scrub the mud off my shoes. The hostess opened an outdoor refrigerator and held up a bottle of wine that I could purchase before dinner. I shook my head. I wanted to clean up and lay down before I fell over.

She led me up the staircase to the bedrooms and baths. With an extra little yank on my bedroom door, she pulled it open to admit me into a room painted periwinkle, one of my least favorite colors, though it looked fresh and clean. Dark wooden beams marched across this ceiling also. A single, long window with narrow double doors opened to a teeny, non-functional balcony. Eight beds waited to be chosen from—and they were not bunk beds! Joy! I chose the bed in the middle of the room, farthest from the open window and the sticky door that would surely be opened and closed all night long by everyone I shared this room with.

There was a folded wool blanket at the foot of my bed and clean sheets. The woman left and I realized I never asked her name. "Oh, I am such a rude American!" I felt a bit bad but didn't dwell on it long. I had chores. First, I needed a shower in the worst way. I limped down the hall to the common bathroom and found a long, mirrored wall with outlets and shelves so we could charge our phones while we showered. I seriously hoped that was what the outlets were for as I couldn't imagine carrying a hairdryer in my pack, nor a curling iron. *I'd like to meet that pilgrim for a good laugh,* I thought.

I gasped as a man walked out of one of the toilet stalls. He had long, dark brown hair, pulled loosely in a ponytail at his nape. He stood around six-feet tall and was lanky but had wide shoulders and strong cheekbones. His brilliant green eyes were a bit too shiny. His dark complexion enhanced his handsome features. His face was friendly enough but I backed up a step. I had known there would be unisex bathrooms at some point but wasn't at all prepared. He laughed nervously.

"Hola, chica!" he giggled and held his hands up. He was definitely high. "I'm almost outta here. Not used to these same sex baths, huh?" He wore expensive-looking wool blend clothing and his pants were the good-quality hiking kind that zipped off at the knees, probably from a name brand sport store. He giggled again while I waited in silent mortification for him to depart.

He smiled at me as he dried his hands and I broke my silence. "You're American?" I asked as I backed toward the hall and stuck my head out to see if other people happened to be around. It was silent at the moment, of course.

"Yup, Eric from Tallahassee. Where're you from?"

"Colorado....I'll shake your hand later, just not in the bathroom. Are you done in here, by chance?" I tried to make it friendly rather than panicky.

His eyes crinkled with laughter. "I am, sister! See you later." He giggled all the way down the hall in the direction of MY room. I rolled my eyes. Great.

I decided to undress inside the shower stall to be safer. It wasn't easy in that enclosed space. I almost fell over a few times. When the first blast of ice-cold water hit my chest, I screamed through my nose so it wasn't too loud. There was nowhere to escape the icy blast, so I swiped at the showerhead but it didn't swivel. There was no choice but to grit my teeth and bear the cold as it gradually warmed up. Once the water was heated, I luxuriated in it until it threatened me with cold again.

I dried off and wrapped my wet hair in the towel—one of those quick dry towels from REI and one of my favorite items I'd brought with me. I extracted my clean clothes from the bottom of my pile and dressed outside the stall, keeping an eye out for the door opening. No one came in and I dressed hurriedly, grabbed all of my stuff and practically ran back to my room.

I made a pile of filthy clothing beside my bed before I completely ran out of energy. It was all I could do to lean over and grab the extra wool blanket off my neighbor's bed and haul it onto mine. After doubling both blankets over my entire body and head, I curled into a ball with the towel still wrapped around my wet hair. Though I shivered with fatigue and hunger, I fell instantly asleep. Sharp hunger pains woke me an hour later. I still shivered. I wasn't warm at all. I unwrapped the blankets from my body as I stood up in the cold evening air. I took the towel off my head and dried my hair more thoroughly, not satisfied until my hair crackled a bit. Then I brushed it quickly. I decided to wrap one of the wool blankets around me and head downstairs to see who had checked in. I grabbed my dirty items, including my shoes.

On the way, I snatched my forgotten phone and charger from the bathroom quickly, grateful no one had taken them! I stuffed my feet into my sandals, covered with fresh, warm wool socks. Though my feet felt better, my calves tried to seize up on the way down the stairs. I had to grab the rails and gingerly step down from step to step. It was almost hilarious except it was happening to me, which made it not so funny. Eric the bathroom hippie materialized out of nowhere and grabbed my dirty things so I could use both hands on the rails. "Thank you so much!"

He smiled his charming smile. "No problemo, sister!"

I finally set both feet on the ground and shuffled toward the laundry area, for I couldn't raise my feet a millimeter off the ground. A fire was roaring in the outdoor fireplace near the Adirondack chairs. The washing machine was free but the dryer had a long line of people waiting for it. I threw my clothes in the washer hoping I wouldn't have to wait too long to dry them. We had an hour before dinner so Eric and I bee-lined for a couple of the chairs that faced the fire. Without speaking, we pulled our seats as close to the fire as we could.

I sighed in ecstasy at the heat that radiated onto my shins and face. These small things seemed like such a luxury when I thought about the fact that I was staying somewhere more than half a millennium old. I sat in wonder and thought of the pilgrims past who must have stopped here! This journey truly was significant.

I looked over at Eric. His eyes looked golden in the glow of the fire and he had a small smile on his lips. I wondered if he was blissed out on something because he always had that smile and his eyes were still a bit too shiny. "You're limping, too. Did you have a hard time with that mud?"

He turned his face a bit in my direction as he answered. "Nah, I got bit by something and it's spreading up my damn legs!"

"What?! Both of them?"

"Uh-huh." He bent over and exposed his left shin. Good God! It was swollen and purple along the ridge of his fibula and the infection spider-webbed out around most of the soft tissue to either side with tentacles of red and splotches of purple. I gaped in appalled horror. He pulled up the pant leg of his right leg and sure enough, he had it there as well, though the infected area was smaller and less purple.

"Uhhhh...Are you taking anything for that? Maybe you need a hospital!"

He giggled. "Lots of vicodin, man!" Well, that explained a lot.

I shivered again from the pervading cold. Just at that moment, one of the old mangy cats leapt into my lap and promptly kneaded my legs with his claws until he met his satisfaction and curled into a little ball. He smelled worse than a litter box full of shit, but he was warm and it radiated down my legs. I let him stay and his purring was thanks enough.

Eric giggled. "Mom has been wanting to walk the Camino for a long time"....he revealed a bit at a time as I sat in silence.... "and she asked all of my brothers and sisters to go but they all said they couldn't for one reason or another. At the last minute, she asked me and of course I could go. I had nothing going on. I was her last resort! She's not very happy about me coming but she had to bring someone and I'm glad I'm here." He smiled his cute smile but I saw something flicker in his eyes. "Do you have kids?" he asked politely.

"I do. One beautiful daughter. She'll be thirteen in July! I can't believe how fast time goes. I still miss that little baby... you?"

"Yes...I have one in Costa Rica and another in Puerto Rico.

Different mothers. I don't see them...."

"Can I ask you why not? You must miss them!" Something hard flashed in Eric's eyes. He looked like a mellow, fun-time guy but not the sort to be taken very seriously. His eyes lost some of the sparkle. His silence stretched out a painfully long time. "You don't have to answer, you know. This is the Camino and we all have things we either share or we don't. There's no judgment here, Eric."

He scrubbed one hand down his face from forehead to the tip of his chin. His fingers lingered there as if he could pull the words out. I sat in silence and stared at the fire. When his words came, I had to lean in to him to hear them.

"I have a drug problem. Been in rehab a few times and I can't seem to find the right key to staying off. I love the way I feel when I'm high and not so much when I'm not. Got myself shot over something really stupid..." He laughed. "Yeah, sister! Bet you don't know anyone else who's been shot!?" I shook my head. "I guess that's why I'm here on the Camino...huh..." He looked down at his hands and smiled sadly at his lap.

"Well, Eric, maybe there is a bigger design to this whole thing. Maybe that's why you were the one chosen to come with your mom. She has her reasons for being here and you do, too. We all do."

He looked up and met my eyes. He nodded thoughtfully. "Thanks..."

"Alesa," I said.

We tipped our heads back and watched the fire. I remembered my promise to update everyone on Facebook about my progress on the Camino. "Hey, do you happen to have the WiFi code?"

"You bet!" He dug out his phone and a scrap of paper and handed it to me. We immediately lapsed into phone mode and ignored each other while we electronically posted photos and caught up with the rest of the world. I figured it was about ten a.m. back home and so I posted a few photos to Facebook with a comment or two and with anticipation for the responses I would have in the morning. Then I sent a mass email strictly to the family members who worried the most and assured them I'd arrived in Spain in one piece and all was well. Feeling a sort of guilt over my electronic connection, I thought about pilgrims who'd walked this way without all of the modern conveniences we now had access to. They'd had nothing but a walking stick, a gourd with water, bread, and the clothes on their backs. Sheepishly I put my phone in my pocket, vowing not to use it too much.

Just then, the hostess came out to announce that dinner was ready. I slid my hands carefully under the smelly feline and gently lifted his still sleeping form. He woke before I could lay him on the stones in front of the fire. He sat up and meowed as he yawned, his thorny, pink tongue rolled out. He shook himself uncertainly as he walked his bent old body stiffly away a few paces.

"Clean yourself, smelly cat!" I ordered him. He whined a scratchy meow at me as I walked away with my blanket wrapped around me. The line for the dryer had finally dwindled so I hastily switched my clothes and loaded the change. I turned to the sink next to the washing machine and washed the awful cat smell from my hands before joining the dinner party.

Sounds of laughter greeted me in the dining room when upon entering I came nearly face to face with the largest animal I'd ever seen that could loosely be called a dog. I looked slightly down at this animal that regarded me calmly, yet I'd still made a squeal of surprise in the back of my throat and the air leaked out of my lungs in what I would have to say was a high-pitched whine that I could not control. Eyeballs larger than mine stared up at me as I paused with one foot poised to step down, uncertain if this thing was going to bite my face off. The thin cook came in, grabbed the wiry, gray fur on the scruff of the animal's neck and led him away to lie in a corner near the fireplace, out of the way. I looked hesitantly left and right to make sure there were no more beasts lurking about before I cautiously chose a chair on the opposite side of the room.

Don't get me wrong—I love dogs. I just hadn't expected to run into one in a dining room, nor would I have thought they could be nearly as large as a donkey! I sat down where I could keep an eye on the thing, not wanting to be surprised with its large face in mine. I would surely give him my whole plate of food, no questions asked, despite my hunger pains.

The Asian woman that had been sleeping in the hammock chair was already seated across from me. Her hands covered her face delicately when she leaned forward and stage-whispered that she'd been frightened of the beast as well. I laughed softly so I wouldn't startle the animal and introduced myself. She insisted that I call her Erica after I mispronounced her Asian name an embarrassing number of times.

More people filled the room and before long we forgot about the giant dog that slept peacefully in his corner by the fire. We were served a beautiful platter of paella with roasted vegetables arranged in a floral design on top. Erica did not like the food much but politely tried everything; though she screwed up her face at the olives and pickles, she tried to eat them and lied about liking them. The whole table laughed when she covered her mouth with her hand to delicately extract the bits of food she could not swallow.

My little French companion entered the room and sat on my left. Though we couldn't speak each other's languages, we were both happy to see each other. We shared our bottle of wine and baskets of bread. Despite the language barrier, I felt we'd made a connection. Slowly the Camino was revealing her beauty to me in this way. I fought a few tears. I had never felt so alone, yet not lonely. I was separate, but not apart. There was community here. I was surrounded by such love and acceptance. I looked across the room at Eric and I think he felt the same. His shiny eyes winked at me. He raised his glass to me and I did the same. My eyes teared up again and I looked down at my plate, feeling absolutely alive and yet, far, far from home.

Dessert was announced. They had flan! I was thrilled to try it, had never had it. I waited for Erica to take some. I couldn't wait to see if she liked it or not. She cautiously dipped the very tip of her spoon into her flan, barely getting a speck of it on the utensil. She lifted it to her lips and we all laughed as the relief lit up her whole countenance. She dug in with delight and huge smiles. The creamy texture was pleasant and it was cool on my tongue. I ate it all but decided it wasn't my favorite dessert on the planet.

I drank a little more wine and before I knew it everyone started disbanding and heading off to bed. I could not wait to sleep! I was shocked to realize it was only nine! This had felt like one of the longest days of my life! My fresh, clean clothes were bone-meltingly warm in my arms. They went straight into my sleeping bag to warm it while I prepared for bed. Once I crawled back into my sleeping bag, I left the clothes at the foot of my bag so my feet could warm up. With my two wool blankets doubled up, a full belly, and my warm clothes at the foot of my sleeping bag, I blissfully drifted off to sleep immediately.

I slept in a warm, dreamless void. It felt like five minutes before I was woken up.

CHAPTER FOUR

Rustling and loud whispers woke me. Thin morning light glowed in the room. People were pulling out in the same mad-hatter rush for the Camino trail as before. I've always been sluggish in the mornings and this rushing around was beginning to irritate me. What was the damned hurry?! I peeked at my phone by my bed. The time was six-thirty a.m. Most albergues had policies to be out by eight. I understood that. It's good to get most of your walking done earlier in the day if it was HOT outside. But, I felt certain today would be another dreary, overcast, rainy day and so I was in no hurry to start another agonizing walk through mud and gloomy weather. Briefly, I wondered how easily I could extract my earplugs from my backpack. Before I could act on that thought I fell back asleep for another hour.

I awoke again and this time the room was blessedly quiet. I stretched around some painful knots on my side and back. My calf muscles instantly clenched in pain. I grimaced in silence and rubbed my calves hard to release the muscles from their rigors of agony. The clothes I'd slept in were now bunched uncomfortably in certain places and I had to pee so bad my abdomen hurt. I still had not been relieved of the awful constipation and suspected this may be contributing to my lethargy. I yawned and kicked my sleeping bag off.

As soon as I stood up, I nearly screamed in pain. I doubled over and gasped with the stabbing pain that radiated up from the soles of my feet through my calves. Uncontrollably, I fell over onto the bed opposite mine, glad that no one was lying there. I felt I was going to pee my pants but couldn't walk! I finally had to go so bad that it didn't matter if I was in pain. I tentatively stuck a big toe on the cold floor. No pain signals raced upward so I lowered my whole foot. So far so good, I decided to go for it and set the other foot down and in one movement stood and swayed on my feet. Mild needles of pain now, this was okay. I shuffled through the room and out into the hallway to the bathroom. I almost peed my pants but got there just in the nick of time. I sat while tears of relief coursed down my cheeks.

After a sullen glance out the window confirmed gray skies and a light rainy mist, as usual, I dressed in layers to protect me from the constant chill but with the ability to shed clothing easily in case the sun decided to make an appearance. With a simple ponytail and my still-soggy, cold shoes encasing my feet again, I departed for the next destination.

I found myself staring at the closed sign on the café across the alley. Just the thought of going without coffee made my forehead crinkle with an early caffeine withdrawal headache. I was pretty sure the headache was fictitious, a sort of anticipated manifestation brought on by the sudden unavailability of my morning staple. Nevertheless, I rubbed my head as I vowed to get some caffeine somewhere ASAP. I would have to trek 3.7 kilometers and find some java in Estella.

Below my knees, everything hurt and my wet shoes sloshed water with each step. I sat on a rock to exchange my wet socks and shoes for dry, acrylic socks and my trekking sandals. I hung the socks and shoes from my loops on my pack so they wouldn't get the rest of my dry, clean clothes wet. There was no chance of them drying in this climate anyway.

Lacking energy, I limped through an underpass into Estella, greeted by walls of ancient villas still inhabited, with laundry blowing over their iron balconies. I wondered why they bothered hanging them outside in the endlessly drizzly air. How silly, I thought, wouldn't it be better to hang them inside where they had a chance to dry? Within a few meters of entering the town, I heard the happy sounds of children coming from a balcony above me. I heard a giggle and looked up right when the little shit spit in my eye. I flipped the kid off while swiping his saliva from my poor eyeball as I continued down the walkway looking for a place to stay and rest. I was now wet, cold and pissed—not the best of combinations.

I realized I'd passed an albergue that had said "Hospital de Peregrinos" and so I backtracked, on the opposite side of the road this time so the spitter couldn't reach me. I found the sign and went inside, feeling defeated for the day.

A glance at the clock inside the marble entry showed it was just nine-thirty. It was no surprise that I had to wait nearly half an hour for the host to come and talk to me. Most pilgrims would not be arriving for hours. We argued about whether or not I really wanted to check in so early. I'd removed my wet, cold shoes and once again exchanged my socks for dry wool.

Slowly, I set my dry feet on the man's desk and leaned back in my chair, prepared to fall asleep there if he would not check me in. He merely huffed in exasperation, his pink cheeks puffed out as he nodded and gestured for my papers. I had them ready in my hand. He left shaking his pink head with its ring of white old-man hair. As he left mumbling under his breath, I sank into a foul mood. I spied a map of Estella folded on his desk and so

I swiped it, thinking I needed to find a pharmacy soon to deal with my constipation issue. The pills that I'd purchased didn't seem to be working at all, so I needed to do something more drastic.

Before too long, the pink-cheeked, white-ringed man returned and abruptly shoved my papers back at me. I grabbed them before they fell to the ground and followed his back up the stairs to the quiet bunk room level. He gestured left and right. I chose left because I wanted a window that faced the cobbled path below the building. I chose a bed in a corner so that I'd have fewer people around me, thinking this would be a quieter space than in the middle, certainly.

With the map in my hand, I grabbed my valuables, including various pieces of identification, and left in search of a pharmacist who could help me out. Walking past bars and shops without my backpack made me feel a bit naked! I didn't have a big shell on the back and no one paid me any special attention as I walked past. I quickly found the Plaza san Martin, just a square, masoned courtyard flanked on the left by a long flight of stairs leading up to the church of San Pedro. To the right was another twelfth century building that was currently an arts and cultural museum, rather than the Palace of the Kings of Navarre as it once served.

During the thirteenth through nineteenth centuries, religious factions had developed separate living boroughs branching out from Estella, possibly why the name means "star." These religions warred within Estella for dominion over all. Warring factions destroyed the castle adjacent to the church of San Pedro, which resulted in damage to two sides of the church that I could not see from the walkway. I passed the impressive steps leading up and turned right to stay on the walkway that led over the twelfth century pedestrian bridge.

In the middle of the bridge, I paused to gape at the view of medieval three-story villas that rose above the water on both sides. The villas captivated me with their dichotomy of ancient homes fallen into ruined rubble that butted up to newly remodeled units that were clearly lived in. Some of the remodeled units looked expensively done, yet they often sat against a crumbled wall which supported an empty shell of a long-abandoned home reduced to tumbled-down stones. I stared at this gap-toothed splendor for a few minutes, feeling at once creeped out by the abandoned units and enchanted by the inhabitants grilling on their back porches by the water.

People passed me on foot and bicycle as I stayed in that spot, too lost in thought to move. A small family walked past me, pulling their handsome little boy with them. His brown ringlets bounced as they hurriedly pulled him along. His little feet skimmed over the ground a bit as they moved faster than he. His tiny fist clenched a bag of chips. In their haste, they never noticed when the bag fell to the ground. The little boy looked back at it sadly for a moment before he was pulled over the bridge and around the bend ahead. I picked it up and tossed it in a garbage can, feeling sad for the fact that his parents hadn't noticed he'd lost something.

I found the plaza listed on the map and the two farmacias. As I walked through the arches along the plaza, I noticed lots of kids running around and playing ball. One boy saw me looking and kicked the ball in my direction and, laughing, I ran over and kicked it back so hard it flew over his head. He looked back at me shocked that I had kicked it to him. He smiled and waved as I continued past. I circled around and around but none of the farmacias on my map were open! I decided to visit the hospital listed on the map instead.

I found the block where the hospital was listed, but there was nothing that indicated a medical building. There were no emergency vehicles. I looked for a green cross like the pharmacies had, but there wasn't anything. I didn't see any of the common medical signs. Around and around the block I went until I was ready to cry. I tried to ask people passing on the sidewalks but none of them spoke English. Finally, a woman with blonde hair passed by and I tentatively said, "Pardona, senora?"

She paused to look at me suspiciously, "Si?"

I held out my map and pointed to the location where we were and gestured around me. "Donde está el hospital?" I was becoming upset with my lack of progress and had noticed a sharp pain in my gut since this morning. I was afraid to let this issue go much longer. She spoke rapid Spanish, but at my confusion, she grabbed my arm and indicated I should follow though she was rather curt with me. I tried to be patient since I'd obviously pulled her away from something she was in a hurry to get to.

She led me around to a spot that I recognized for I had been standing there in confusion a couple of times. There were three unremarkable steps that led to a nondescript metal and glass door with a buzzer. There were no signs of any kind. It reminded me of an apartment building. She pressed a buzzer and we stood awkwardly looking at each other for a moment. "Hola!" The blonde woman stuck her face in the buzzer and spoke a little into it before the door was buzzed open. She smiled at me.

"Bueno! Muchas gracias!" She ran back down the stairs and out of sight as I went hesitantly inside. I still wasn't convinced this was a hospital. A tiled staircase led up about sixteen steps before I came to a landing that more or less resembled a waiting area. There was a row of five black chairs sitting against the wall to my left, two of them occupied by men about my age. To the left of the men was a receptionist behind a glass partition like a gas station would have. The walls were a light, cold gray color and the white tiled floors did nothing to lend warmth of any sort. The receptionist was now speaking to me. I walked over to her and asked to see a doctor. She looked confused. I leaned in close and tried to whisper the phrase I'd memorized on my iPhone translation app before setting out this morning.

"Por favor, necesito uno enema. Saline enema, por favor?" She just shook her head at me. Immediately, she spewed a stream of Spanish words at me, pushed some paperwork forward and pointed toward the chairs. I looked at the form and didn't understand any of it. We weren't going to get anywhere with all of that. Impatiently, I shook my head at her. Oh, how I wished for a Walgreens right then. I gestured to my extended belly and rubbed it. "Ow!" I said. She continued to shake her head.

"Um. Cinco dias! No pooping. No pooping!" I looked at the seated gentlemen. "Habla Englais?" I asked. They both shook their heads and continued to stare in fascination. Oh my God. This was so embarrassing. Tears of embarrassment threatened to spill over. My fists knotted at my sides and I took a couple of deep breaths to calm down and think. At that moment, she stood and asked me for my passport. Immediately, I slid it to her. She held her hand out for more...I didn't know what she wanted. I gave her all of my identification along with the pilgrim credential, though I highly doubted she wanted to give me a stamp.

She disappeared around a corner for a minute. She must have paged someone to check out the nut case in the waiting room because the double doors behind me swung open and Señor Doctor came in, dressed in his white lab coat. I almost ran over and grabbed his lapels in sheer desperation but I took another calming breath instead before launching into my rehearsed lines, hoping I pronounced them somewhat correctly.

Of course he had to be young and handsome. His black hair was slicked back into a wavy do. His stylish glasses perched on just the right spot on his handsome nose. His shoes were so shiny I didn't even have to look down at them to see them sparkling in the dim gray waiting room. He was the only shiny thing in the room. With his lips tipped up in a polite smile, he waited.

"Habla Englais?" That was a bit too hopeful. The receptionist made her way over to his side and whispered in his ear about me. Finally, I said "Look! I need...necesito uno enema! Por favor... uh saline?" I held up one finger. Frustratingly, he still stared stupidly. I stuck my enlarged, hard belly out for him. To me, it looked obvious that I was so constipated, I could have fit a stuffed cat in there. I drummed my hard, protruding belly with my fingers so he could hear the solid sound. "I could be in a band and I don't need an instrument! Necesito uno enema!" I was pretty confident that I had been saying it correctly and felt ready to cry for their incompetence.

"Enema?" He finally switched his gaze from me to the receptionist. I was now crying in earnest. Between sobs and feeling hysterical, I said in a not quiet voice. "No pooping!!" I held up my right hand with all fingers extended. "Five...CINCO dias!" Now I was so desperate I made the downward motion the pharmacist had made the other day. I pointed my index finger at my ass and with a downward swiping motion almost yelled "No SHITTING. CINCO dias!" I made a rude farting sound as I repeated the gesture. For the life of me, I don't know how he kept a straight face. I didn't dare look at the two men seated in the black chairs.

"Ahhhh...no shitting? No shitting!" WHY on earth they all understood that word was beyond me. The idiot was getting it and that was what mattered though! He calmly turned to the receptionist and saw that she was holding all of my personal identification. He scowled mildly at her and with a "tsk tsk" took them back from her and handed them back. I tucked them in my purse while he gave instructions to the woman. He looked at me again. "Cinco?!" He sounded incredulous.

I nodded and held up all five fingers again. "Cinco."

He cringed. The receptionist brought him a pad of paper and even though it was in another language I could tell that it was a prescription pad. My pride had taken a hit and my face was flaming red, but I was so thankful to him right then I could have kissed his face. He finally turned to me with the golden ticket of happiness. I reverently held it for a moment. I couldn't read it, but I knew it was going to help.

I refused to allow myself to look at the waiting room occupants besides myself and the doctor. Pulling myself together, I looked at them through watery eyes. "Cuanto?" I asked. I opened my purse and the doctor laid his hands on mine. His sincere eyes gazed down into my own as he shook his head no. "Gracias!" I said. Then, I turned and fled down the stairs with my prescription safely tucked in my fist. I bee-lined to the nearest farmacia, which had finally, luckily opened for business, and handed the woman behind the counter my prescription. In short order, I had everything I needed to fix the problem.

I practically ran back to the hostel. It was almost one by the time I made it to my albergue. I was dismayed to find the room half full of pilgrims. With the bathroom being unisex, I watched people for a while until I decided there would be no good time to do what I had to do. I straightened my back, walked in without glancing around and ... a short time later was a new person and didn't much care what people thought. I wanted to sing and dance, I felt so light!

    I practically skipped to the restaurant next door where I ordered wine with the lackluster salads that were a staple of the Camino. Try as I might, I just could not get quality greens. I ate everything except the half frozen iceberg chunks. Afterward, I felt better than I had in days. Grabbing my journal, I traipsed to the lovely courtyard in back of the hostel. An eight-foot-tall stone wall enclosed around us on three sides. Rose vines climbed to the top of the back wall along the crevices. Big pink and red roses exploded in full bloom in the garden. A single beam of sunlight lit up a thin cross-section of a table and chair. I made my way toward it, shivering in anticipation of warming up in the rays of weak light. My body had grown accustomed to shivering, I hardly noticed except when presented with an opportunity for warmth.

    So constant and invasive was the chill along my Camino journey thus far, in fact, that this weak beam of sunlight will forever be scorched in my memory. My body immediately melted into a relaxed posture. I threw my head back to let the sun warm my face. I would have purred with pleasure were it socially acceptable. I controlled myself. People were lounging in chairs near me, speaking in different languages with their friends. A couple across from me smiled at my reclined posture. I nodded at them and greeted them in English. I laid down my journal and let my hands flop on the table in the patch of light. I wished I could draw that sacred heat deep into the core of my body and hold it there. Shivering in my sleeping bag at night had become extremely tiresome. I dreaded it daily now.

    The pleasurable warmth had saturated my muscles with such

complete lassitude that I'd nearly nodded off when a loud, male voice startled me awake. A short, wiry man near my age had entered the courtyard with a much younger, pouty teen male. I had the urge to grab his lower lip and pull it out farther to tease him as I would my daughter. It was apparent they were father and son, and the son wore a pained "I would rather eat my shorts than be on the Camino with my dad...where are the hot chicks" look. Dad went over to a small group near the door and began speaking so loudly at them, it could really only be called yelling. He held a paper bag from the market and seemed to be asking if they were going to cook a meal together. I sighed and wondered why he had to be so loud about it. Just then, the group turned as one and pointed to me and said something to the man. His eyebrows went up as he looked my way with the kind of interest that made my stomach drop.

Feeling somehow exposed, I waved hesitantly in their direction since they all stared at me. The little man took this for a friendly overture and immediately headed my way. In three long strides he held out his hand. I looked at it for the briefest second and cautiously offered mine.

"I hear you speak English! Are you American, by chance?" he nearly shouted.

"Mmmhmm. You bet. Colorado....yourself?" I was trying not to bite my words out in utter rudeness, but was trying to seem uninterested. He didn't get it.

"Oh! It's great to meet another American! I'm from Cali!" I was relieved. I'd thought for one drastic moment he was going to be from Colorado—then he'd be harder to shake. "My name is Aaron. I'm traveling with my son." He gestured to the young man whose shoulders tried to swallow his ears as he hunched in embarrassed shame as he watched his father hit on another

American woman.

"Aha! Good for you, Aaron. Wow, traveling with your son. That's brave of both of you. Are you enjoying yourselves?"

He sat down though he hadn't asked if he could. I sighed in irritation, yet still pushed up into a less-slouchy position, giving up my complete enjoyment of the sunlight. I hated the side of myself that couldn't be rude to this man. I envied that ability in others. It sometimes sucks to have manners.

"Oh, you know. How much fun can you have with a sulky eighteen-year-old? He doesn't really like all of the walking and would rather be in Barbados with the babes on the beach than traveling with his divorced dad. But, hey, he gets a free vacation, right? Are you traveling alone?" He looked at me intensely with bluer-than-blue eyes behind his glasses. He oozed desperation. Did he really expect to find a Camino Honey? I wondered as I instinctively pushed my chair back a few inches.

I nodded. "Yup." How MUCH fun could an eighteen-year-old have with his newly divorced father flirting rather desperately with every available American woman on the Camino. *Not much*, I thought.

A look of outrageous concern immediately overtook his face. I watched his salt and pepper head draw closer. He leaned toward me as far as his slender frame could manage without completely lying across my table. I moved my right forearm out of his breathing zone and moved my body as far left as my chair would allow.

"That's not safe for a woman these days, you know! Do you have something for protection? Why would you go by yourself?!" He was completely oblivious to the daggers my eyes threw at him now.

In cold anger, I imagined pummeling him to the ground and

stomping on his head. Okay. Maybe a little dramatic, but that's where I go in my head when I feel backed into a corner.

"The Camino is, in fact, one of the safest trips a woman CAN make by herself. Plus, you have no idea what I'm capable of so don't assume I can't take care of myself. And there are extra police along the Camino for the reasons you are hinting at." I especially hated defending myself.

Obstinately refusing to understand, he insisted, "Well, I'm not entirely sure that is wise. You'll join us for dinner. How about it?"

"Sorry, I'm meeting friends," I bit out.

"Really? We can all go! Where are you eating dinner?"

Pushy man! "I don't know. They are going to find me after their siesta and we'll decide from there," I lied, the blush giving me away.

An angry flash in the blue lake of his eyes was so quickly replaced by wide-eyed interest that I thought I'd imagined it. Seeing no way out of refusing the hand he held out, I took it cautiously. He put his other hand over mine, trapping it as he bent down to kiss the back of it. Then, he kept my hand prisoner while he tried to make an impression with his eyes. They lingered on mine for the longest moment until I broke the spell myself. I pulled my hand away roughly and rubbed it on my pant leg as if to get the feel of him off me.

"Buen Camino, Aaron. I hope you find what you're looking for. Have a great night." At this, he got the message. He strode off without a reply.

He'd left his paper bag from the market. I opened my journal and pushed his forgotten sack to the far side of my table. He would remember it eventually. I tried not to laugh at the idea of him striding back to retrieve it. I was no longer in the mood to write so I pretended to read. His friends gestured and talked while Aaron faced me. He glared. I simply pointed at his bag. His face tightened.

The son walked softly over to claim the bag. I watched as he slowly picked his way over to me. He grimaced in shame.

"Sorry about Dad. He's been trying to meet a woman and is really upset about the big D." I took that to mean the Divorce.

I nodded, infusing some sympathy into my face. "Fun trip, huh?"

He rolled his eyes and whispered, "You've NO idea..."

"I think YOU will be the one to find a honey on this trip." He laughed and winked at me before he walked away with his dad's paper bag loosely gripped in his fist. Aaron still glared like a spurned lover so I turned my chair at a ninety-degree angle to fully enjoy the sunshine again. The sun had slowly grown stronger so I concentrated one-hundred percent of my attention to the heat and light behind my closed eyelids. I focused on my breath and tuned everything else out. Soon I was so relaxed again that I would have melted onto the ground were it not for my legs propping me up. I'd always been good at tuning out the world around me, a handy tool in less-than-savory situations.

Before I could burn, I went inside to seek my bed. I didn't want to sleep, merely catch up with friends on Facebook and listen to music while I journaled and sent messages. I furiously texted a message to my very good friend Laura, thanking her for her support, ignoring tears of gratitude that slipped out to punctuate my feelings as they fell between my hands. With her skills as a psychic medium, Laura had put many of my fears to rest and encouraged me to take the time I needed to heal. I'd gone to her at the lowest point when I knew with certainty that I was not meant to have a normal moment in my life. These were the days I could hardly stay out of bed longer than to make my daughter breakfast and get her to school. Now a year later and somewhat settled into a home of my own, I was loathe to leave my daughter for fear that it would be too hard after the calamity of the previous year. Laura had insisted I would find myself and come back able to be the mother I ought to be.

With a shudder, I remembered the days I'd driven to my favorite scenic overlook down a steep and deadly cliff with a river just a silver thread below. During the drives, I felt my mind empty itself of everything, every worry, every care. With the emptiness came an oddly peaceful feeling that seduced me to flirt with death. I sometimes stood at that rocky ledge with my arms out as my steady heartbeat swayed me rhythmically forward and back. Moaning winds rushed through the trees to ruffle my hair and caress my back, as if offering to help push me over. Leaves rustling below me invited me to jump. Images of my daughter flashed at just the right moments when I teetered too far forward, almost letting gravity take me. Each time, her image pulled my body the other way at the last crucial second, a cosmic tug of war. The game became more dangerous as I began driving there nearly every day. Something within me, that part of me that would not stop fighting no matter how I begged for release, made my hand reach for Laura's number. I'd called her not really believing she could help me.

As soon as I heard her familiar voice, I'd broken down and cried, "I'm just done fighting. I can't take one more thing. Don't want to do this anymore. I don't want Parker to become this depressed. I need help... (Oh, how that hurt my pride to ask. I'd been solitary from the time I was seven.) I don't know if I can take one more day," I added hoarsely.

"Sweetie! Come see me right now!" As my last recourse, I

did so immediately. I showed up thin, pale, grubby from not showering for days. She hugged me like she didn't mind my filthy state and told me she would give me a reading. We'd connect with guardian angels and people from my past who'd passed on. It sounded nutty to me, but who was I to judge? — I'd just driven straight to her door from the proverbial and literal edge.

I followed her into her candle-lit living room. Everything was spotlessly clean, no dust anywhere. I couldn't remember the last time I'd cleaned anything at home. I shrank a little inside my filthy, black Matchbox 20 t-shirt that I'd slept in for two nights. We'd seen two trips to the overlook together and it was starting to feel like a second skin. I scratched a little self-consciously at my collar bone while I waited for her to begin. She looked beautiful as always, her long platinum blonde hair brushed to perfection and a black scarf tied loosely around her neck in a whimsical knot. The long black boots she'd pulled on over her jeans looked crisp and smart. Most arresting were her large, sparkling blue eyes that regarded me gently. I'd glimpsed the hollows under my own eyes in the rear-view mirror right before I turned the engine off and had turned the mirror away.

She sat in a soft gray chair facing the corner of the couch I was trying to hide in. I noticed the box of tissues on the coffee table and impulsively grabbed one to have something in my hands to fiddle with.

She spoke softly, "We've known each other a long time so I want to explain how this works. I'll close my eyes; you might see them roll up in my head. That happens when I focus with my third eye. I don't want that to surprise you. I'm going to just do a reading and we'll start soon, but is there anything in particular you need to know, Alesa? I've also set a notebook there if you want to take notes."

I picked it up dutifully. "I'm not sure what I want to know or why I came...only that I need help," I whispered. "I thought my life was going to turn out all right...you know? This divorce, the affair...it's all too much right now."

"It's okay, sweetie. Let it out."

I stared at her, unsure of where to start. "How...how do I go forward for Parker's sake? I can't face this girl. She was my friend and is the sister of someone in my family. We are related by marriage now. She comes to family gatherings..." My heart lurched at the thought of how gullible I'd been in thinking Derek took her to movies as an uncle might...What uncle had ever taken ME to a movie? God, I hated my blind-trusting nature! When would I learn? I continued, "How do I not beat the hell out of Derek on Parker's birthday in two days? I want her to have a normal day! I don't know if I can do it. I can't. I would rather die. I'm so depressed."

Laura leaned forward and patted my knee. "Hey! I am your friend. You are going through a lot. I'm so glad you are opening up to me now. I had no idea you were in so much pain, Alesa! This reading will really help you." She took a deep breath and I copied her. She told me to relax and be "open." I wasn't sure what she meant, yet I imagined dropping an invisible barrier from my heart. I was surprised to feel an electric pulse of something I can only describe as energy connect the two of us. I was more shocked when she said, "That's right, you feel that? Okay. Let go of your disbelief for the next hour, okay?" I nodded stupidly.

As she spoke about my guardian angels that were ever-present, waiting for me to ask for their assistance, I tried not to become impatient. There were apparently all kinds of angelic beings just waiting to assist me. After a few minutes she finally mentioned something that made me switch gears. Her lips twitched up in a smile when she told me a woman was coming through who needed to give me a message. She described a woman with short blonde hair and laughing, blue eyes. "I know this isn't your mom because I've met her several times, but she says she is your mom!" Laura laughed, her eyes opened as she looked at me, waiting for me to say something. "She loves you so much!" I cried then, thankful for the tissue in my hand, though I'd already shredded it to ribbons. "My mother-in-law," I choked, "my regular mom." She'd passed away suddenly the year before. There had been nothing anyone would have been able to do to save her.

"Well, she knows about everything between you and Derek and she is sad for you both. She loves you but also wants you to know it is all okay in the end. She wants you to know she is also happy in the afterlife..." Laura turned her head sideways as if listening harder, "Hang on, she's showing me something..." Finally, with her eyes still closed, she said, "She drew a picture of a heart...and says the heart is now healthy." She looked at me. "Does this mean something?"

It did. I nodded and replied, "She died of a sudden aneurysm in her heart." I sobbed. I hadn't realized how very much I missed her.

Laura continued, "She wants you to know that no matter what, you are going to be okay. You will be happy again. Now...... your dad is here, too." That's what I'd been hoping for. "He's been gone a long time, so he isn't pushing to come through as hard as your mother-in-law is...but he is happy now, too. You don't need to worry about him...did he take his life?" She opens her eyes to see my nod. "Okay...that makes sense. He said he is no longer sad. He checks on you a lot, just so you know. He is always around you."

At this point, I took a few minutes to cry while Laura got up from her chair to retrieve glasses of water for both of us. When I was composed, she continued and said we should look at whatever messages the angels had to say about my future over the next few months.

Apparently, they wanted me to stay in the shade. I was confused about this and so Laura asked them to clarify. I was supposed to eat a lot of mushrooms. I didn't get that, so she again asked for clarification. She told me I would become very ill at the end of the year, it would be a struggle, but I would get through whatever it was. At the same time, the house Derek and I had decided to put on the market would sell.

Both of these things turned out to be true. It was September when I sat down with Laura and in December of that same year, our house finally sold, our divorce was in progress, and I was diagnosed with melanoma and lymphoma. On New Year's Eve, while recovering from the last surgery, I wrote a Fuck You letter to 2011 and burned it to ashes in Renee's backyard, despite her screeching like a harpy that I was intoxicated and dangerously ignorant of how to work a pastry torch properly. I suppose I'm lucky I still have my eyebrows as I've never made crème brulee in my life.

The last message Laura had left me with that day was that I'd be taking a significant trip. She'd laughed and told me it would be a long, arduous, hard trip and certainly not one she would ever choose to make. She saw a long path through woods and over hills. Me with a backpack. I still shiver when I remember that prediction, and then I remember that I am finally here!

I was still in my bed, completely ignoring the pilgrims all around me as they milled about, talked loudly, tried to nap, or made other noises. Most were utterly exhausted. I wondered for the hundredth time why I'd been drawn to make this trip. I certainly thought there must be more relaxing places where a person can get in touch with the mess her life had made. Why couldn't I have gone to the tropics or something? No, not my style. Here I was torturing myself for a lifetime of torture. *Idiotic*! I thought.

I'd asked Laura once as we sat in a bar enjoying cocktails if I should take someone on this trip. "No, you're going alone. It's very green there and I see lots of flowers. This seems like a spiritual walk for you." She smiled a little sadly and said, "You need to go and have fun. I'm definitely getting the message that you don't have enough of that."

As it turned out, Parker did have an okay birthday. I was able to be present and had even showered, fixed my hair and worn a dress. She'd had many friends to distract her so that the occasional hateful glares I directed at her father were completely missed. He, on the other hand, was utterly mystified by the switch in my attitude. While not perfectly peaceful, I wasn't screaming and threatening to rip his throat out either, as I had been the day before I had seen Laura. When he tried to hug me, I stepped back and stuck my hand out to stop his approach. "Don't come near me," I hissed low in my throat so Parker couldn't hear. I'd left the party shortly after that to return to the coffee shop where I could focus on work for a few hours.

Without warning now, a pair of feet in wool socks swung down from the bunk above me. I stared at these huge, obviously male feet dangling toward the floor. I stuck my head out and peered up. An older man sat hunched in the midst of a huge yawn. His brown wool button-down sweater matched his large wooly socks. He glanced down at me and blinked rather blearily like a scruffy owl behind his oversized round glasses. He flopped a weary hand in greeting and fought another yawn. I waved and politely ducked back inside my space underneath him.

The bed rocked as he slid onto the floor and muttered a low curse at some pain. He ducked down and stuck his hand out. That was how I met Andrew from Australia. I sat up and moved so he could sit next to me. He promptly did so and bent to rub his feet as he continued asking me questions. When he found I was traveling alone, he merely raised a brow in surprise but patted me on the shoulder and said, "Right brave of you, girl!" I liked him right away. He was on holiday for only a week and had wanted to try the Camino after he'd watched the movie *The Way* with Emilio Estevez and Martin Sheen. He'd met up with a "couple of blokes" who were sleeping in bunks across from us.

The man across from me turned over and gave Andrew a baleful glare. "Can't sleep with all this chattering. Shall we go eat then?" I knew he wasn't irritated by the teasing banter in his voice. With that, the top bed above him rustled with its occupant's activity. Rick and Ross were brothers, also from Australia.

Andrew turned to me, "You're comin' with us." His tone said he would not take no for an answer. He stood and cringed, "Damned blisters!"

"How bad are they?" I asked and wished I could take it back for he was not shy about showing me. He peeled back his sock to reveal the meanest blister I had ever seen. It spanned the whole width of his heel and stood out a solid half inch from his foot. I nearly gagged at the yellowish color of fluid inside.

"Eeee-yuck. How far did you walk today?"

"About twenty-five kilometers. We're going the same tomorrow." I gaped at him. "I only have a week and can't fall behind or I'll miss my train back to the airport. I can't do the whole Camino. I need to get something for these blisters though!" As the conversation turned toward the treatment of blisters, I tuned out. Rick must have noticed the green pallor in my face for he suddenly interrupted with demands to eat dinner. I heartily agreed and stood to throw my jacket on.

We decided to keep things simple and walked to the restaurant next door for their pilgrims' dinner. We were seated in the back dining room where the wine started flowing before we could decipher the menu. Our waitress glared at us as we howled over the menu. One entree read, "Ham with man sauce and walking peas - bery good." This one had us almost rolling on the floor. I ordered that for the sheer hilarity of the description. Turned out it was a soup of green beans in a heavy broth and a few very small pieces of ham. It was NOT "bery good" but worth the laugh. Everyone snickered when I ordered the "lambs with skinny corns" for my second course. Thankfully, it tasted much better than the ham with man sauce.

Throughout dinner everyone was curious about me and my choice to travel the Camino alone. My answers started in my cavalier sort of way. With self-deprecating humor, I said "You know the story... American woman, divorced, single mother, here to find peace on the Camino...maybe I'll finally find Mr. Right. You know...same as many." I tried my best to blow off their questions, but these were three older men with children my age, and they all had grandchildren, too. I sensed they were concerned for me but they let me redirect the conversation.

Andrew needed a vacation from work and other stress in his life. There was trouble brewing at home with his grown kids and his marriage was growing sour. Andrew and I shared a meaningful glance, both with tears in our eyes.

He hadn't known Rick and Ross who were related by marriage to two sisters. He had met them in St. Jean Pied de Port and they'd been an inseparable trio ever since. Although he was due to leave in a week, Rick and Ross would continue on to Santiago. Rick was considering giving up preaching at his local church but walked the Camino to see if he couldn't get a clearer answer. He asked me if I went to church. I'd been waiting for that and I glibly replied, "No. I study witchcraft and Satanism on a regular basis though." I waited. He and the others blinked at me for a moment in shock and then the laughter started again. We all laughed until we cried. Rick raised his glass to me and said "My dear, I have no doubt that is not true. Good one! So, ARE you Christian?"

"Way to press on like a true Christian!" I quipped.

He shrugged. "Hazard of the job." Then he winked at me but clearly expected an answer so I gave him one.

"I don't believe in categorizing what I am. I believe that Jesus existed much like Buddha and Mohammed...If a person were to break down all the religions and all of the messages imparted by these individuals, they all seem to convey some of the same messages. Be good to your neighbor. Don't lie. Don't steal and cheat. Don't murder people. They are the same rules of governance that make communities livable and safe. They keep us out of harm for the most part or there would be bedlam, right? When God said, 'Build me a temple,' my belief is to do that in my heart, not build a mega-church or some other behemoth at the taxpayers' expense. I spend time praying for those that need it, including myself. I wear a St. Michael pendant. I believe these angels are there to protect and help us and yes, Jesus existed. He had powers to heal by the 'laying of hands.' From what I have researched there is an ancient Asian practice called Reiki that is close to what Jesus did with HIS hands. I'm not saying we are all God, but I believe that we have the ability to overcome a lot of things with our minds and energies...more than we realize. I meditate because it calms my mind, and God knows I need that! I know Christians that go to church one day a week and sin like no one's watching the other six. The ones that I've encountered just want to judge me or my gay friends. I don't believe I'll go to hell for not being a Christian." I took a breath and another swig of wine, afraid to see if I'd upset anyone. When I glanced up at Rick, he merely nodded with acceptance of my little speech.

"This is an issue with today's people, yes. There are a lot of passages in the Bible that people take exception to, so what does the church do about it? It is also my dilemma as numbers in my church are dwindling. Thank you for being honest." This was not what I'd expected. It was refreshing.

Andrew leaned toward Rick, "Is the inquisition over?" We all laughed and enjoyed a lovely evening. These men drank like fish! After we'd each finished nearly a bottle each, I had to tap out and insist on water. Rick and Ross started to carry on about the church again when Andrew turned to me and asked me why I was so sad. This took me by surprise. He kept an arm around my shoulders while I filled him in on a few things. He asked about my family and I couldn't help crying. When I told him how my dad had taken his life when I was a young teenager, he cried too.

"You poor dear. No wonder you are here by yourself. Let's get ourselves to sleep now! These two will chat on and on about the church." We stood and nearly yelled our goodnights to Rick and Ross. They couldn't be startled out of their debate so we left. Andrew and I swayed arm in arm to the hostel. I can't say who held up the other. We made our noisy, drunken way to the bunk room where I bumped into several occupied beds before landing heavily on my own with a loud curse. After struggling with my laces, Andrew assisted in removing my shoes. The last I remember was being nearly thrown into my sleeping bag and a blanket tossed on top before he struggled up the ladder to his bed. I laughed a bit too loudly as the whole bed threatened to topple and was shushed from somewhere in the darkened room.

Briefly, thoughts of brushing my teeth interrupted my drunken stupor before I dropped into a dream:

In the middle of the night, I walked alone down the cobbled streets of Estella, now a desolate city with sepia-colored stone walls that leaned precariously toward me. I hurried past sections of hollowed-out buildings, their yellowed stones tumbled to the ground around the husk of their remains. Long, lonely howls rose from the dark recesses as I hurried past these stark reminders of human mortality. Fear rose up my spine. I expected ghastly beings to leap out at me any moment. Dressed in the clothes I'd fallen asleep in, I crept slowly down the road without my backpack. I could not go back. Brief glances behind showed a veil of darkness crept with me, it swallowed the trail from where I'd come. The only option was to go forward. Ratty bedsheets and other forgotten yellowed, stained laundry blew in a breeze I couldn't feel. Rusty balconies bent and warped with age, squeaked their despair as they threatened to fall. Oddly hanging shutters protected windows with broken glass. There was no sign of life within the darkened windows, though I knew I wasn't alone. My shoe crushed something underfoot. A raised-shell marker had rusted through. An eyeball winked at me from down inside! Fresh fright ignited within me as I walked around them in a continuous S shape to avoid more blinking eyeballs. Up ahead someone walked around the corner just in time for me to glimpse his profile. I was sure it was Derek. He hadn't wanted to come here with me. He'd told his mistress that! Angered, I ran to catch him. We ran the same pace, first right, then left around the rusty shell markers. Stone walls squeezed closer and closer until I nearly panicked and turned back. Just when the walls were about to touch me, everything opened up to a small walkway over a bridge. The edge of town faded behind me as I raced toward Derek. He'd paused in the middle of the path at the crest of the bridge. Moonlight illuminated half of his face so I could see one large hazel eye watching me, shiny blue tears running continuously from it. I reached out for him as he said, "I am so sorry. It's all okay." With that he blew me a kiss and jumped over the side of the bridge. I ran to the railing, afraid to look over and see his broken body, but he was standing on the ground far, far below me. With his face turned up toward the moonlight, both of his eyes sparkled with blue pools that trickled ceaselessly. He cupped his hand around his mouth and yelled at me, "You have every right to be here. You belong on this walk. I never did." With a sad smile and a wave of his hand, he turned and walked under the bridge below me and out of sight. Wind blew through the trees when he disappeared but did not rustle my hair. I ran to the other side of the bridge to catch a glimpse of him on the other side. Estella rose from her rusty yellow ruins to my left while the trail opened to my right into verdant green hills. Dark silence from below. He was gone. A river flowed like a wide silver ribbon away from me. It wound down a steep ravine toward Denver. I knew that's where Derek had gone. Rather than follow him, I turned to continue my journey alone. I noticed another man waiting for me at the end of the bridge. Andrew stood there calmly. Something about him seemed odd. I looked at his feet. He had no shoes. His blisters bled small pools underneath his feet. "It's really fine, Alesa, it's just the Camino," he assured me.

CHAPTER FIVE

With a start, I awoke to complete darkness, convinced I'd fallen into one of the ruined buildings. My heart raced frantically for a moment as I waited for a howl from the depths of this hollowed building. My rational mind took a moment to fully awaken from the dream as I stopped fighting the smothering blackness. It was merely my wool blanket suffocating me. I was completely entangled, uncomfortable yet pleasantly warm. My sleeping bag twisted round and round my waist, making me distinctly aware of how much I needed to pee. I peeled the blanket off my head and shoulders as I inhaled cool air.

Unprepared for the stench of multiple unwashed pilgrims first thing in the morning, I gagged on the foul air. Instinctively, I coughed the air back out as I rolled out of bed. I took small sips of air to acclimate to the stench, which was a rather devastating combination of beer-sweat combined with various filthy body parts. The French people in cots to my left seemed to be the worst offenders as the stench was strongest that direction. Hung over just enough, I was on the verge of vomiting on the bunk room floor.

With one hand plugging my nose and my iPhone in the other, I sat on the toilet, relieved that the bathroom air had not been befouled. I sat there and checked my Facebook page. This was the only way I could stay connected to people back home. As I read their posts and comments on my photos, I wept with sudden longing. I longed to feel like I belonged there…anywhere. Their concern for me almost made me feel like I belonged. Almost. I wanted to feel like I was home, finally. Really home for the first time in my life. At home within myself. That was what I yearned for. When my legs became numb from sitting on the toilet too long, I stood, washed up, and brushed the fur off my teeth.

I packed my meager belongings as the guys grumbled about me forcing them to drink too much wine. I chuckled and threw my pillow at Rick, forcing him to laugh and groan simultaneously before he turned his back to me. Occasionally, I giggled when an unsuspecting victim woke in the same fashion I had and made the awful stench discovery for themselves. Andrew's pack lay in wait on his bunk. *I must have sat on that toilet a while,* I mused. Just then he made his limping way toward me. As he drew close to the French pilgrims, who still slept blissfully unaware of their impact, he gestured at them and looked at me in horror as if to say, "How can ANYONE be that smelly?!" I laughed out loud at that, grabbed my pack and clapped his shoulder on the way past. "I have to get out of this cloud. See you at the cafe."

Andrew joined me as I started my second coffee. He limped badly. I asked him how his feet were and he shrugged and said, "You know, they hurt but there isn't a thing I can do about it now." This reminded me of my dream! I looked at his profile out of the corner of my eye. It was odd to think of the people I'd met on this journey so far and how much of an impact they'd made on me even if we'd only spoken a few words.

"I guess it's just the Camino!" I spoke the line from my dream. He nodded and said, "You're right. No big deal."

We all walked out of Estella together and my heart lightened at the signs of life. No sepia-toned walls. No rusty shells, not even a moan or howl to follow us out. I looked behind me once and half-expected to be greeted by a black veil. Light shown on the plaza behind me. As usual, the trail led through the heart of the medieval section toward the more traditional apartments and businesses that all the Camino cities had. It was always a shock to leave these old sections of town where I felt a tangible connection to the history and livelihood of centuries past and then get thrust into a modern city with cars and horns and crosswalks. Then, the pilgrimage would plunge us back into nature for hours on end, passing vineyards, olive and cherry groves where we would again begin the meditative processing of our own thoughts and feelings and connections with the earth and other pilgrims. It felt like being thrust back and forth through a time machine at times, from the twelfth century to the twenty-first and back again.

After walking up the rather long hill past the apartments and busy intersections of Estella, we veered onto the trail and soon came upon a fountain built into the side of the Bodegas winery, just outside of Estella. The first travel guide ever written regarding the Camino was the *Calixtine Codex* from the twelfth century, and it lists this region of Estella being known for its bread and wine, among other interesting tidbits, including what it was like to be a pilgrim in the twelfth century. For hundreds of years, pilgrims have lined up to drink from this Bodegas fountain, using their scallop shells to cup the wine. There is an inscription on the fountain wall in Spanish. Of course, I can't understand it so Andrew translates it into the following: "We are pleased to invite you to drink in moderation. If you wish to take the wine with you, you will have to buy it. Pilgrim, if you wish to arrive at Santiago full of strength and vitality, have a drink of this great wine and make a toast to happiness," Andrew read as he tried to untie my scallop shell from my pack. "How many knots did you need for this damn thing anyway," he teased.

"Forget it. I'll just use my water bottle. Take it out of the side pocket." He handed me the small metal bottle I kept as an extra, though truthfully I wanted to throw it away somewhere to lighten my pack.

I held my bottle under the fountain of free wine, feeling a bit silly as everyone else had filled only their shells.

"You know there's a video camera pointed at your head."

I glanced up and there it was. Guiltily, I turned the tap off as he laughed. Rick had taken two shells full of wine, with a wink in my direction as I held out my bottle in a mocking toast. Ross conservatively took a sip from his shell before tossing the rest. We all gasped. He shrugged. "Not my thing in the morning! Ugh!" He shuddered.

As one, we all turned and headed up the hill again. We walked past an empty monastery perched on a hill with flowering trees. The building was now a museum but wasn't open at this time of day so we continued on. The guys were all quite a bit taller than I and struck a rather vigorous pace for their age, I thought. A little peeved that I was being paced by a few sexagenarians, I swallowed my pride and turned to Andrew.

"You guys go on ahead and don't feel bad about it. I like to walk on my own at my pace anyway. Catch you at lunch?" Andrew nodded and patted me on the head. I worried about his physical shape. He was obviously a bit out of breath. I felt like hugging him. I worried about him as we walked abreast for a while but he slowly outpaced me and pulled farther ahead. He waved at me before disappearing down a hill and the image glued itself into my mind. I immediately missed my father and looked toward the heavens. Sometimes I saw unicorn or horse shapes in the clouds when I thought of him, but not today.

Though it had been twenty-five years since my father's death, I still miss him greatly. He was not my real father, but the father I was meant to have.

My mother had just suffered a cruel separation from my biological father. She'd moved back to Wyoming from Illinois and set us up in an apartment close to her parents. On a trip to the grocery store, with my sister and I loaded into a cart, she ran into an old flame. She'd had a crush on him in high school but he'd been a senior when she was a freshman so he hadn't paid any attention to her. Suddenly, there he was! The story goes that he immediately fell in love with me and Renee; we were only two, still in diapers. Before long he married her with the condition that he could adopt us. My real father did not hesitate. He signed over paternity to the new guy without a quarrel and within a couple of months they were married and we were legally his.

Dad had a halo of wispy blond hair that framed his face and light-greenish blue eyes. Dad was a barber and owned a shop called The Unicorn. We spent many hours there listening to him softly laugh and as he gently washed and cut people's hair. He seemed to love everybody and we became used to him kissing everyone he knew on the cheek or forehead in farewell. We entertained ourselves quietly in his shop by counting the various unicorns hiding in pots and peeking out of corners. They ranged around the shop in various poses. Dad was casual about his business. He treated people with kindness rather than greed. Sometimes customers paid him in home-made cookies, instead of money. He had a generous heart, which made it easy for people to accept him when he worked in bare feet. He detested shoes.

His demeanor was sweet and made my sister and I confused as to why he and Mommy yelled so often. Sudden screaming and yelling often interrupted the sweet innocence of early dusk or late night dreams. We now lived in a small house in the country just a mile from our grandparents. One night I awoke sharply to the sounds of screaming and glass breaking. A crack of light from our bedroom door showed Renee already hunched on her knees as she peeked out at the scene. I crept behind and joined her. Our twin breaths were ragged and loud to my ears. I subconsciously snaked my hand over my sister's mouth to quiet her, but she smacked it away. I hardly noticed.

Mommy seemed to be upset about her hair. She wanted Dad to give her a haircut. I had no idea what time it was, but it seemed pretty late for that. I thought maybe she should make an appointment. Her hair was long and dark, almost black. I liked to run my fingers through her wavy, silky mass that fell almost to her waist. People told her she was the prettiest woman in town. She was proud of that.

She threw a plate straight at Daddy's head!

Just in time, he ducked and it smashed into the cabinets. He tried to grab her hands. She ran around him and grabbed the biggest knife from the cutting board. Now we were scared, sure that she was going to stab Daddy. I started to cry. Renee turned and pulled me down to my knees next to her. We held tight to each other but couldn't rip our gaze away. Mommy ran outside with the large knife held high over her head. Daddy immediately hopped to the door and slammed it shut. He locked Mommy outside with her scary knife. He turned toward us, saw our door open and ran to us.

He reached us in two long strides and scooped us up while we listened to Mommy screaming outside. He tried to cover our ears but the best he could do was one ear each. It sounded like she was crazy-mad. She was yelling mean things and howling like a wild animal. We all trembled and cried, even Daddy. He put Renee and me in the same bed, knelt next to us and whispered, "It'll be okay, girls. Just let her scream it out. We won't let her in until she calms down." He kissed our cheeks and dried our eyes as we calmed down, too. He held us in his arms for the longest time and kept one eye on the bedroom door. It seemed to take forever but when she finally stopped, the silence scared us more than her animal-like screams had. My heart beat too hard against Daddy's arm, the weight of his bicep was crushing me. He was sweating. His armpits smelled terrible. I didn't want to cause more trouble so I wrinkled my nose in the other direction and breathed through my mouth. He waited another minute and I must have grunted and wiggled because he said, "Sorry, honey!" and moved to a more comfortable spot. I relaxed my nostrils then.

He stood up and we both grabbed at his pant legs. "Don't go out there, Daddy! Don't go! Stay with us!" we screamed. He gently pulled our hands off him and explained he had to check on her to make sure she was okay. My lips quivered in fear as Renee and I grabbed each other so tightly I could feel her heart beating with mine. We waited and waited with our twin breaths mingling, like our heart beats. We stayed frozen together. We didn't dare get up until we heard soft talking from the living room area.

I almost peed my pajamas when Renee got out of bed. She was always the adventurous one. I didn't want her to leave me alone so I crept after her, begging her to wait. We quietly cracked our door open and peeked out. I almost gasped aloud when I saw Mommy. She was standing in the door that Daddy had opened. Her hands hung down limp by her sides. The knife was on the counter and Daddy was sitting on the floor in front of her in shock. I grabbed Renee's shoulder in fear. She'd cut all her hair off. Shiny pieces of her scalp showed where the hair was very short. There were longer pieces here and there. The scariest part was her face. She looked calm but very pale, as if she was going to be sick.

Before I could scream in terror, Renee closed our door very quietly. She pushed the knob and turned it to lock it. Neither of us wanted to go out there. We climbed into the same bed again and wrapped our arms around each other. Our twin hearts beat the same frantic beat until we slowly relaxed in the comfort of each other's arms. I had dreams about Mommy's gray face hovering over me and kitchen knives hanging from her hands.

The next morning our grandparents came very early to rouse us out of bed. Grandma threw coats over our pajamas as we blinked at her in sleepy silence. I was grateful to see her calm face and smell her comforting perfume. She didn't bother to brush our tangled bedheads as she softly explained that we needed to stay with her and Grandpa for a little while. We didn't dare ask questions. Grandma grabbed me in her arms and Grandpa took Renee. Very quickly, we arrived at their home and were gently laid in the guest bed. We both shed tears for Daddy because we hadn't said goodbye to him.

My steps slowed as I remembered Mom arriving a week later at Grandma's doorstep. She waited in the entry, wearing stylish new clothes and a red beret jauntily tilted to hide the worst bald spots. I'd been afraid to look her in the eyes, but when I finally raised my eyes to hers, I could see that my Mom was there inside. Not the wraith-like creature I'd glimpsed in the doorway nor the woman with knives that haunted my dreams.

Her eyes shown with unshed tears of apology as my sister and I hesitantly hugged her and allowed her to shepherd us back home. Dinner that night was enjoyed with forced gaiety. During dessert, Daddy announced we were expecting a baby brother in six months or so. Mommy's brightly painted lips quivered as she held on to her tight smile.

....

Drinking wine along the trail was not as much fun as you might expect. Andrew and the guys had taken off ahead of me and I've always had an issue with drinking alone. Plus, every time I became thirsty, the wine sat like sour vinegar on my tongue. My head pounded from the drunken episode with Andrew and the guys the night before, so I discretely poured the wine onto the ground at my next resting place and drank copious amounts of water.

Feeling my hangover recede after a short break, I stood again and tried to walk faster so I wouldn't miss the guys for lunch. Long breaks in the cold weather did not help much because my sore muscles tightened in the cold if I didn't move. Though the terrain was beautiful, the monotonous walking soon lulled me back into the past again.

Mom finally divorced Dad a year after my brother was born. It seemed to break Dad's heart. He'd been inconsolably sad as he wept on the floor in a corner of the living room. He sat hunched with his arms over his head and cried more than I'd ever seen a man cry. Renee and I hugged him repeatedly to cheer him up, but nothing helped. Days later, Daddy had moved into a small house across town and we were allowed to see him once a week. It wasn't long before Mom's new boyfriend was staying over at our house a lot. He was loud and younger than Mom. We resented him for his good looks and big, loud mouth, but he soon married Mom and became our new stepfather.

Along with his boisterous mouth, larger than life personality and huge black wolf dog, named Bear, he brought strange friends. Mom began throwing late night parties. She cooked large quantities of excellent food and when she thought we were asleep, smoked some "herbs" to calm herself. When we caught her, she said it was medicine for relaxation but I didn't like the way her eyes looked when she said it. My mom wasn't in there at those times. She reminded me of the woman with knives in her hands. During these parties, she let our stepfather's creepy friend, Jim, take us for rides in his truck and didn't seem to care that we hated his tickling and that he lived in his vehicle. Soon, there were things I couldn't share with anyone, even my dad.

Though I wanted to tell him what was happening, I could never find the words. We were shuttled to his house once a week and things continued like this until we were fourteen and Dad took away any chance of confiding anything in him ever again. We'd gone on a huge family trip to Hawaii—me, Mom and Renee. Sis and I were excited to be leaving Wyoming for such an exotic trip. We had never been anywhere like it. Though we had a wonderful time, we remembered on the return flight that we'd forgotten to call Dad and wish him Happy Birthday. Hours later, we wrestled each other to the front door, fighting to be the first one to call him. Renee beat me to the phone.

Daddy wasn't sad; he arranged to pick us up the next day. He took us on a picnic at the waterfalls in Sinks Canyon. As we competed to fill him in on our trip, two teenage boys came running down the trail laughing hysterically about a fire they'd started. They were pushing each other excitedly. We paused in confusion. Laughing over a fire? They didn't see us until they were right in front of us. They shut up but kept laughing as they disappeared down the trail. Daddy told us to wait while he ran ahead to put out the fire. Instead of staying behind, we followed as fast as we could.

When we caught up to him, he'd put the fire out by himself. We had no idea how he did it by himself. He yelled at us to look for more sparks, or "hot spots," to step on. It looked like it was out, but we walked around and stomped just to feel like we were helping. Once we were certain the fire was out, we didn't know if we should head back and alert the authorities or keep going. Daddy took our hands and told us he was a volunteer firefighter and he would report it later, but today was our day. So we continued to the falls and ate our picnic.

He was our hero that day. When he took us home that afternoon, he became quieter and quieter the closer we got to home. He pulled over slowly to park Agamemnon. We turned to hug him. I was sitting in front so I saw him crying.

"Dad...? What's wrong?" I asked with rising alarm.

"Nothing, honey, I just love you." His voice was tight. He hugged me hard to his chest and cried. Then he twisted in his seat and wrapped his big hands around us both. He crushed us in one gigantic hug. He kissed my eyeball, then Renee's forehead.

Renee was scared. Her usual calm was replaced with worry frowns across her forehead. She pursed her lips in the way she did when she was thinking hard about something. I knew he acted strangely, but he often did, so I thought maybe he was just being extra emotional, like maybe he just missed us and was happy to see us and feeling bad that he couldn't go to Hawaii. However, looking at Renee's face, I felt scared, too.

"Daddy! What's wrong? Why are you crying? We love you, too!"

We were all crying now. He gently pushed us away with his

hands on our shoulders. We sniffled uncertainly. He dried his eyes and told us that whatever we found in the car we could keep. He'd planted dollar bills in his car and photos of us with him. It was the strangest treasure hunt we'd ever had. He had hidden money bags stuffed with cash. It seemed like something that was meant to be fun, but there was a choking desperation in the air that made the game feel strange.

We sat confused with our treasure troves in our laps, uncertain about what to do next. "Okay. Now remember that I love you very much! Go inside, your mom's waiting for you." He waved to her. She stood in the window watching us; she waved back. We clambered out of the vehicle and stood watching him drive away. I felt a little wave of pain pass through me, then looked at my sister. She must have felt the same. Her honey blonde hair lifted from her shoulders in the breeze as she stared after him as well. The bridge of her nose was burned and peeling. I had the urge to pull a loose, triangular piece of skin but knew that would annoy her. We went inside to tell Mom and our little brother about our strange day.

A week later, Mom came home early from work. I saw her headlights and knew she was home early to tell us some bad news. Her face confirmed my fears when she emerged from her white town car. She glanced behind her and swiped at her tears with one hand as she shut the door with the other. She leaned heavily against her driver's side door. She was crying deeply now, bent double and clutching her middle. Grandpa's large GMC truck pulled in behind her car; my grandfather had followed her to the house. I turned to look at my sister's wide, scared eyes.

"I think Great-Grandpa passed away," she whispered. A gush of sorrow preceded our mother as she came in the house like a hurricane of emotion. She saw us waiting. Renee's hands gripped mine tightly to her chest. Mom's face screwed up into a ball of pain. She tried to tell us but her hands kept covering her mouth as she doubled over as if in pain. Though she was obviously very upset, we didn't yet know if the situation was really that serious. I tended to retreat from her when she cried; having been subjected to so many of her tantrums and crying jags, I was nearly immune to them. Renee took her customary lead role as she dropped my hands, walked over and calmly took hold of Mom's shoulders just as Mom collapsed in her arms and sobbed, unable to speak.

Grandpa's frame filled the doorway then. He hesitated before walking through the door. He held his hat in his hands. His blue eyes sparkled with unshed tears. We waited in the horrible gloom for someone to break the news but they seemed reluctant. Renee finally asked, "It's Great-Grandpa, isn't it? We've been sort of ready for this..." As soon as the words left her mouth I knew something much more dreadful had happened.

My ears rang as I stared at Grandpa's cowboy boots. They were planted at an angle and he stood stiff as he said, "No...," he cleared his throat. "Kids, I'm afraid to tell you that your father... ahem...your father has died. He sent a letter to your mom. We received it today at the car dealership. It appears he's taken his own life. He shot himself. His body was found this morning in Green Mountain in his car..." Mom was still sobbing but had managed to pull a letter from inside her purse. She was opening it. My heart raced as it unfolded. Daddy's handwriting scrawled across the top.

I stood up quickly and raced to the phone. I operated solely on instinct and quickly called Daddy's number. The phone rang until his answering machine picked up. It was his usual message. I closed my eyes and imagined he was fine. He was maybe sitting in his chair, drinking his green bottle of beer. The machine beeped at me.

"Daddy! Daddy! Pick up your phone. Please! Call me back!" My voice was high pitched and scared. I felt dizzy. This couldn't be real. It couldn't be. My grandfather came around the corner and stood next to me. He very calmly pulled my fingers off the phone and turned me into his hug. I stood there stiffly, fighting my tears. I covered my ears. If I didn't hear it maybe it wasn't true. I shook my head and refused to look at anyone.

"I'm sorry," Grandpa whispered. I didn't want to hear it. I pushed away, turned and ran out the door, not sure where I was going.

I ran with tears blinding my eyes. I bounded down Capitol Hill, which was so steep I was afraid to ride my bike down it without the brakes fully engaged. I ran as though I couldn't feel the ground. I skidded a few times and almost tipped over onto my face. When I got to the bottom of the hill, the road evened out so suddenly that I tripped. I landed on my right knee and rolled onto my hands. I righted myself and kept running with gravel and dirt embedded in my palms and knee. At Main Street I barely slowed for traffic. The light was red but I kept going. I ran to Daddy's store and beat on the front door. No one came. He should have been open! I pounded again and still no one came. I stepped off the concrete steps and into the bushes along the front. They scratched my legs. I didn't care. I pressed my nose to the windows. I could see all the unicorns in there. Daddy's sinks were shiny and clean. There were no piles of hair on the floor. He always swept the cut hair to one side and made a big pile for the day. It was a good day when the pile was huge. The store felt empty and I could tell he hadn't been there in a while. I was screaming now, "Daddy! Daddy, I need you! Daddy, don't go…" I gasped, "Don't please don't please don't."

My breath came in gasps. I had a crazy idea that this could somehow be undone. I had to be able to rewind this and make it not be true. I sat down on his store steps and bent over my knees. I cried until big, fat saliva bubbles ran into strings and touched the ground. I couldn't breathe with all the mucus in my nose. I blew my nose in my shirt, there was nothing else to use, and wrapped my arms around myself and rocked. I rocked back and forth, my heart hammered in pain as I whispered, "Daddy! I'm sorry, I'm sorry," over and over.

Grandpa's car hadn't made a sound but I finally noticed his tires parked in front of the walkway. His car door shut softly as if he didn't want to disturb me. A few seconds later, he quietly sat next to me. He didn't say a word. I liked that. I leaned into him and cried more before he could lift me up enough to get me to walk to his truck. He pulled a clean cotton handkerchief from his shirt pocket. It sported his initials in blue hand-stitched knots. I almost laughed at his old-fashioned ways. We pulled up to Mommy's house in silence. I sat in his truck and thought of the last time I'd been sitting in that spot in a blue and white car. My face crumpled and Grandpa said he was sorry again. I nodded at him. I couldn't speak. What was there to say?

That night family members came over and tried to console us. Aunts and uncles tried to hug me. I'd been withdrawn before, but now it was worse. I had hated to hug people since I was little. They always commented on it. Secretly, I had my reasons, and that reason was thankfully divorcing Mom and taking his gross friend with him. I shuddered at the thought of his friend and the secrets I kept from everyone. My stepfather didn't even know. I wondered briefly what he would have done if he had. I looked around the grieving people in this room. They had no idea why

I couldn't hug them and I wasn't about to tell them. The only person I safely hugged was Daddy and now he was gone.

It was a few days before I stopped trying to call Daddy. I walked around numb and barely responded to people. Everyone commented on how quiet I was. I didn't make any waves, didn't cause any trouble, didn't feel a thing. Renee couldn't even connect with me. The pain in her eyes pushed me further into my cocoon. People eventually stopped bugging me about it, for the most part, and accepted me as withdrawn and quiet. Their worried frowns only served to anger me and cause me to pull inward. I retreated to my own private world, drew my invisible shield tightly around me so that no one could penetrate it again.

When my dad left like that, he left a hole in my heart that could not be filled. Even further, I lived in fear of losing everyone I cared about. Realization dawned. I kept myself from feeling too close to people because of him. Sometimes I wanted to beat him up for his thoughtlessness.

CHAPTER SIX

Bright pink and red poppies along the trail cheered me up when my thoughts became too heavy. I wished for a little sunshine to brighten the landscapes' hues and warm my skin for a while. The cold drizzly weather was depressing! I looked forward to some warm food and friendly conversation to break up this lonely trek. I looked forward to sitting next to Andrew again and realized he reminded me of Dad. It had to do with his sparkling blue eyes and the Fatherly way he was doting on me. I had a sudden, out-of-character urge to hug him. Though we'd only met the previous night, I was starting to care for the big guy.

As I trudged into Villamayor de Monjardin, annoying whistles and cat-calls furrowed my brow with anger until I realized it was just the guys. My scowl fell away but not before Rick saw it. He was standing inside a doorway waving to get my attention. My hands already moved to unhook the latches on my straps as I moved toward him. He quirked a brow at me as he said, "'Bout time, grumpy pants." I managed a weak punch on his shoulder as he hustled me inside out of the cold. I set my pack in the line of others by the door, hurried over and hugged Andrew.

He kissed me on the cheek and pulled out a chair. They'd already finished their lunch. Andrew patted my back and told me to sit. We were offered the full pilgrim menu, a three-course meal, of course, unless I wanted tapas from the bar. I closed my eyes and grudgingly imagined the selection of omelets and croissants that were habitually offered. I would kill from some fresh fruit and maybe a nice soup. I told Andrew as much. He quickly got up and told me to "stay" like a dog. Rick and Ross sat across the table already deeply entrenched in a deep discussion over the definitions of "church." Bored with that topic, I looked elsewhere in hopes of avoiding another discussion about religion.

Two minutes later, a glass of fresh-squeezed orange juice materialized in front of my face. Andrew set it down with a bowl of Campbell's vegetable soup and a small piece of bread! *He must be a great dad*, I thought wistfully. For the effort he'd gone to, I didn't tell him I detest canned soup. I ate the light meal with no complaints and, as I did so, Andrew joined the debate across the table. He must have sensed that I was in a funky state of mind and didn't wish to talk. It was odd and comforting to have made such a close friend in such short time.

There were the usual assortment of pilgrims coming in and leaving. Some were limping along like me, others looked as if they could go another twenty miles. Cyclists pulled up in front and clamored for space among the foot traffic in front of the bar. They searched for spots to lean their bikes. The two baristas behind the bar never even looked up to greet the newcomers. They simply waited for people to push their way to the counter and order or simply ask for the nearest bathroom.

Some languages were loud and harsh on the ear in comparison to others. I decided I liked the Australians and Germans I was meeting. They all seemed to know English and were friendly as could be. The French were hit or miss. Sometimes they were nice, but distant. Others were plain rude....or smelly as warmed three-day old garbage—I grimaced at the memory. I relished sitting next to someone new each night. Their stories were always intriguing. Each person would have something to teach me. I hungered to know more.

Andrew paid for my meal and would not accept the money shoved in his direction. To our mutual surprise, I hugged him fiercely again, quickly before I could change my mind. I let go of him awkwardly and didn't say anything. When I turned toward the door, Rick and Ross were standing with their arms out as well. I laughed them off and stepped outside, adjusting my pack again to even the weight between my shoulders.

Castle ruins sat squarely above me on top of a mountain, directly in sight. "Hey! Where did that come from? I didn't notice it on the way in."

"You were glaring holes in the ground, silly girl!" Rick shot back.

I gaped at the castle that rested atop the cone-shaped peak in front of me. "I wonder how they got up there on a regular basis," I mused aloud.

"How would you like to deliver his mail?" Rick shot out.

"Yeah, what if you just needed milk for your porridge?" I asked.

"You'd milk your goat, or your cow...or your... whatever... milk something." We all snickered.

After just half a kilometer, I noticed a hot spot on my left heel. I worried it might be becoming a blister. *Why now? I haven't had one until today!* I thought with irritation. Andrew was limping as well from his blisters, but I could tell he wanted to get going faster. I told him to go ahead again and I'd see them later. I wanted to crank my music anyway to block the pain. My feet were acting up today, first with the inflammation along my heel and now this blister. Just to make things even jollier, the rain started again. Andrew and I helped each other with our ponchos before he limped hurriedly after Rick and Ross. As soon as he pulled ahead a bit, I turned up my music to drown everything out. Memories, cold, rain, blisters…everything.

Andrew dwindled in size on the horizon as I followed. The trail was hilly and a bit twisty but it took a full kilometer before he was gone completely from sight. It was a gradual leaving and that's the way it should be for a father figure. This thought made me trip over my feet. *Was that the lesson here with Andrew?* I wondered, as I nearly fell down. I certainly had formed a connection pretty quickly. He had entered my dreams. "It's just the Camino…" Was it really? These thoughts occupied my mind most of the afternoon.

I stopped once to sit to drink lots of water. So far, I had not needed to urinate on the Camino trail and was thankful. Other people had; I could see the evidence they left. I had a plastic bag dedicated to my paper products that I planned to use if the need arose. Littering was one of my daughter's big concerns in life. She's been known to yell out of my open car window, "Hey! Pick that up, litterer! That's not nice!" while I cringe in the driver's seat and quietly roll up the window. I love how opinionated she is. I knew she would make a wonderful lawyer or salesperson someday. She won't take no for an answer, no matter the answer I give, until I put my foot down and say, "Because I say so and I'm the boss and you are not." She usually laughs unless it's something she wants very badly. *She is so unafraid of the world, unlike her momma,* I thought with pride.

Sharp pain grabbed my heel when I stood up to shake water off my poncho. I wanted to yell in pain but there were a couple of pilgrims coming toward me; it would have scared them. So, I whimpered instead. I decided not to make any more stops until I got to Los Arcos. It was tougher to get started again each time I stopped. The tendons tightened each time I rested and the inflammation flared as soon as I stepped on the foot again.

The terrain helped to distract me with its great beauty. I was still traveling through the Pamplona province, so the vibrant green hills were stretched ahead and rolled all around me with farmland and olive trees manicured into arrow-straight rows across hilltops and valleys. There was a beautiful mountain ahead in the distance, past Los Arcos. With the deep chill of rain, the pain in my foot, and a new friend in Andrew, who had unexpectedly brought my past to life, a pervading sadness wouldn't leave me alone today. Each step felt heavy. The way was tough going. You never knew when the Camino would smack you with something you had to face. I filled my head with music and tried to blast away the painful memories for the rest of the day.

Four hours after leaving Villamayor de Monjardin, I arrived in Los Arcos in a worse mood than before. I was now shuffling toward the town center. I had no idea where the guys found beds, and for a second I wanted to cry. Self-pity filled my soul. I needed a foot tub, a hot shower (though chances were slim on hot water at that late time of day) and lots of food. I especially needed a nice, quiet room to sleep in. I grabbed my St. Michael pendant as I thought about all of the items on today's wish list—they all seemed reasonable enough.

Though I knew I would not like the place, I wandered into an albergue to my right, all the while telling myself to keep searching. The ceiling was low and the entry room was tiny. Three doorways led off in different directions and I could see beds directly ahead of me. It smelled mildewy in there. In the room behind me, a young man in blond dreadlocks was sitting cross-legged on a table and strummed a guitar rather badly to a grungy woman with black hair. She was not wearing shoes and her filthy, callused feet were propped on the table next to the young man. I rolled my eyes and left. If I wanted to hang out with that, I could just go home to Boulder!

The next albergue I came to was full, sort of. I'm still unclear on that. A man barked in English, "It's maybe full! People called ahead and reserved. Their backpacks were taxi'd here, you see? I haven't seen them yet, though, and so it is MAYBE full." He looked overwhelmed and shrugged his shoulders at me. I hadn't given him any indication that I was upset so I had no idea why he was so animated.

I passed a bar/cafe on my right, the town square on my left. Yellow arrows led me under an arch that led to end of the plaza where I crossed a street to see a large blue and yellow sign with an arrow pointing to a large municipal building on my right. The sign read "Albergue Municipal de Peregrinos Isaac Santiago." Pilgrims lounged there so I cut across a green lawn in front of the library and made my way to the entrance. It was made up of two concrete rectangular buildings contained within a chain-link fence. It looked rather sterile like any institution rather than the charming old buildings I was accustomed to. My heart sank when a small group came out with their packs, shaking their heads. Didn't look like they had room. I tried not to be discouraged as I walked up to the pretty brunette behind her desk.

She sat up straighter when she saw me. "Uno, peregrina?" she said hopefully.

I nodded. She smiled. "Bueno, bueno. Completo." I hesitated at that but she held her hand out for my credential and passport, which I happily handed to her. She stamped my credential, noticed that I was from America and reverted to English.

"Come on, dear. You look tired. I have saved the best bed for last!" She took me around the corner from her desk and there were only two bunk beds in here, a window and a radiator by my bed. I touched its cold surface. She leaned in and said, "I will turn heat on when you are sleeping. This is women's room only. No men snoring!" She winked at me. Then she showed me the bathrooms. "You will shower now. Everyone else is taking some sleep, so you will have warm water, if you hurry! Eighty people stay here, so hurry, peregrina! Your feet, they need warm water." I did as she instructed after dumping my pack and snagging my toiletries. I was so filthy and damp that when I removed my ponytail holder, my hair stayed in a ponytail shape. Now that is *hot*, I giggled at my image in the mirror.

The water was on the warm side of hot, but not nearly hot enough for all the people who were going to need it. I was glad the woman had given me her advice! I still shivered when I stepped out of the tub and decided it was because I was starving. I dried my hair with my towel and combed it enough to look halfway presentable. I thought about applying mascara but was, frankly, too lazy.

My calves were cramping so I shuffled to my bed. My legs refused to lift in steps. I wasn't the only one; most people my age and older were shuffling as if they were afraid to fall and not get up. I called it the Camino Shuffle. I dug to the depths of my pack to find crackers, cheese and fruit. It was only five p.m., so there were two hours before dinner. While snacking on food, I shook so hard I almost bit my finger and the thought made me laugh. I wished someone was recording me attempting to eat and shaking too badly to hold my cracker properly. I wanted to laugh. I wanted to cry. I thought about journaling but was too tired for that, too. Mental and physical exhaustion would not let me do anything but grab a pile of blankets, heap them on my shivering body and attempt some rest.

As I lay there trying to stop shaking, a wave of emotion came over me so strongly that I wrapped my arms around myself and curled in a ball inside the layers. I suddenly missed my ex-husband with an intensity that surprised me. My rage had become a palpable thing when everything had fallen apart. I had been on the brink of madness when it all happened. I convinced myself it was all going to be better than okay once I left him. I had at one time loved him with my whole heart. I'd spent the last year overcoming pain, regret, illness, and tried to rediscover myself as I dated men who weren't good for me just to prove to him that I could. In retrospect, I hadn't wanted, nor needed, any men—I simply hadn't realized it. I mindlessly thought I wasn't alright if I didn't have someone.

It had hurt my pride that he'd moved on so quickly. How could he do that to me? Who was he to get over ME so quickly, my pride wanted to know. I had given him everything, my whole life, my whole heart. How could he not be there when I got sick? My body suddenly clenched in a circle around a sob so that I could not breathe or make a sound as my muscles tightened around the air trying to escape. It felt horrible. I felt like I was going to break or die from lack of air, whichever came first. The sarcastic-asshole side of my brain remained aloof and unattached, watched the scene as if apart from me. *Thank God no one's in this room, huh?* I thought sarcastically. *Good Lord, pull yourself together before someone sees you.* I convulsed against the sob that rose up out of my throat and with horror clapped my hands over my mouth to hold in the awful sounds that were sure to follow. I had such control that only a high-pitched whine emerged with a small stream of air. I hissed like a balloon, taking comfort from the fact that only a werewolf with extremely sensitive ears could hear this tone. I gripped blankets in a wad against my stomach as I fought the tsunami inside me. Small whimpers made it past my lips, but that was all. Just then I relaxed, too exhausted to fight, and a great gasp of air moved through me, loosening the sobs. There was no choice now but to let it all out. I lay in a heap, heedless of anything except that I was mortified at my loss of control. I couldn't stop. Ludicrously, I put a hand on my belly as I cried to make sure I hadn't pulled any muscles. I cried myself to sleep as I thought of all that should have been and now would not be.

The alarm on my iPhone woke me an hour later. My room was freezing and I hated the thought of getting up. If I hadn't been so hungry, I would have stayed. I'd washed some underwear and other items in the shower and hung them over the radiator to dry, thought they were stone cold and no heat was coming from the heater. I decided to join the pilgrims for dinner. I washed my face at the laundry sink since there was a huge line now for the showers.

"Peregrina...Alesa?" Taken by surprise, I turned slowly toward the pretty woman who'd checked me in. I hoped my eyes weren't too red-rimmed. She smiled shyly. "The Camino....she never gives you more than you can handle. Si? You understand?"

I did. I nodded and murmured thank you as she came forward and gently hugged me. We both had tears in our eyes. I turned before I started crying and walked out without looking at her again.

By the time I made it back to the town plaza, a festive sight greeted me! I walked toward a cluster of people sitting in groups and as I drew close, I heard my name being called from two directions! I looked left and saw Andrew and the guys so I ran over and hugged him. They were already enjoying wine and snacks. I snagged one of Andrew's calamari so he thrust the bowl at me.

"Sit down and eat!" He pulled out a chair. I grabbed his wine and chugged some of that, too. I heard my name again and looked toward the restaurant that everyone had ordered food from. "Ohmagosh, Andrew. I have to go say hello to some people. I'll order food and come back. Save my seat!"

"Hey-y-y, sister!" Eric the bathroom hippie called. I shuffled over to him as fast as I could. He laughed at my pain. I smiled ruefully and shook my fist at him. "What's goin' on?" He pulled me into a hug. I was happy to see he hadn't perished from his leg infection or whatever the hell it was.

"How's your leg, Eric?" and turning aside, "hi, Sandy," I said to his mom, though we'd had little occasion to talk. She smiled and waved at me.

"Aw, sister, it's no good. It's not any better." He pulled his pant let up and he was right. It looked no better.

"It looks worse!"

"No worries. We're not stoppin'!" I looked worriedly at his mother. She shrugged apathetically.

"He's had worse. We've been to the doctor and they don't seem very concerned. As long as he takes his meds at night, he is fine to walk in the morning."

I looked nervously at Eric. He was guzzling wine. "Uhhhh..." I pointed at the wine.

His mom leaned in to me and stage-whispered, "He'll be fine. He's done a lot worse. This is good for him."

"Oh," I said weakly.

Just then, I spied Sam's weathered face as he and his mother walked over to us.

"What?! How did you guys get here? I thought you were behind me!"

Sam winked with a wide grin, "Taxi! We had a hard day yesterday, so we took a taxi to here and we're going to walk a lot tomorrow! Do you know Eric and Sandy?"

A warmth spread inside me. These two were supposed to meet each other. I nodded and excused myself so I could order food. *Funny how the Camino works to bring people together,* I thought, *and never gives us more than we can handle.*

I placed my order at the counter. The woman didn't even try to speak to me, rather pointed at me and then outside. I nodded. It was so great to be able to communicate without speaking. She also pointed to a wine glass and I nodded my head. Sure, why not? I grabbed the wine and sat by Andrew. He'd saved me his calamari.

That night we feasted on lightly fried, breaded calamari and shrimp, pasta, and wine. It was so cheap to drink the regional wine that I felt like I *had* to drink. As dinner wound down, someone pulled a stereo out and placed it on the stones of the plaza. Dance music started. People Camino-Shuffled out to the square and moved their bodies around without moving their feet. It was hilarious. The Macarena played and everyone went nuts over it. Andrew had never done it, so I pulled him out to the middle of the crowd to show him. He got the hang of it but refused to move his feet so he got trampled with each turn. We laughed so hard that tears streamed from behind his glasses and down my cheeks as well. I adored him.

Rick and Ross came over to tell us that the pilgrims' mass was starting. This was a special mass that was performed in the town squares on certain nights in specific towns along the way, but pilgrims had to catch them on the right night or risked missing out completely. Andrew was still humming The Macarena as we joined the masses inside the Santa Maria cathedral. Murals and carvings on every wall and surface were so ornate they took my breath away. The gilt-gold was painted liberally over most of the carvings of saints and angels.

Most of the service was in Spanish, of course. However, since this was the blessing for the pilgrims, many of the regular parishioners turned to us and wished us a good journey or "Buen Camino." They shook our hands and looked us in the eye with smiles. This hadn't happened before. The preacher then gathered all of us pilgrims to the front of the church and passed out cards in each of our languages so that we could follow along with his blessing. I looked around at this crowd and felt truly blessed to be there. I saw Eric's tall frame at the back of the crowd. The sleeve of Sam's green jacket was next to him. I felt blessed to witness whatever miracle had brought them together. I sent a quick prayer up that Eric would listen to Sam's story and become inspired by it.

The blessing only lasted a couple of minutes and we filed out to the church steps. Andrew and I sat inside a bar enjoying one more glass of wine before we tucked in for the night. He asked me tough questions. I liked that he didn't put his arm around me to console me or act condescending. He just listened. Every few minutes he brushed at his face or sniffed a bit. He finally looked at me with misty eyes and grabbed my hand. I bent my head to the side to lay it on his wide, soft shoulder. We talked about his trouble with his wife and the distance between his daughter and grandchildren. Both of us were silent for about ten minutes after that.

"I am going to take a bus tomorrow. I may not continue the Camino, Alesa. I need to see a doctor for these feet."

"You're really leaving because of your feet?" I asked.

"Yes, that and I feel the need to go home. My blisters hurt a lot, yes, but I am missing my wife and it doesn't feel good to be gone from her so long. We need to fix things."

"I understand, Andrew," my voice grew hoarse... "I will miss you." Everyone had their own journey on this trip and I knew that I would have probably chosen to go on without them sooner or later anyway as I needed this time alone.

He walked me to the albergue steps. "Coffee tomorrow at 7:30?"

I rolled my eyes. "So early? Fine," I said slightly grumpily.

He patted my head, "Off to sleep with you now."

I hugged his large frame. His body wasn't made to walk this far, I knew. "Good night, Andrew."

The other three beds were occupied with softly snoring women. I chuckled to myself. Women thought it was just men who snored, huh? The radiator finally emitted heat. I crawled into my sleeping bag and with the two blankets was truly warm for the first time since coming to Spain! I would have purred if I could have. I slept peacefully and did not move a muscle nor dream strange things.

Donna DeLory's *Bathe in These Waters* woke me gently. Light filtered in the slats of our shuttered windows. The women were already up and gone! I almost felt lazy. Reluctantly, I left my warm cocoon and padded to the bathroom gingerly since every muscle below my knees ached. My left heel had a blister across the heel that I hadn't noticed the night before. I glued a blister pack to it and hoped it would stay put for a while. Today's walk would be nearly twenty miles.

Before heading out for the day, I quickly assessed the items in my pack, looking for items to toss in order to lighten my load. The only item I thought I could do without was the pack of six fruity flavored condoms my roommate had tossed in as a joke. She had only been half teasing when she suggested I get laid on this trip. She sure wished I would stop my moping. God, I did too, but seriously doubted I would need these here! I missed her at that moment. I pictured her laughing blue eyes and blonde ringlets bouncing as she talked. Before I became emotional again, I shoved the condoms deep into my pack. I wasn't going to get caught crying over fruity condoms.

Once on the road to the breakfast cafe, pilgrims converged on me in the opposite direction. I dodged people as they marched forward along the journey. Multi-colored backpacks bobbed and dipped in the human tidal wave. The energy swamped me as they passed. I felt a pull to go the other way. Most people were smiling and chatting to their comrades. A few looked seriously dedicated to finishing their day ASAP as if they already worried about finding a bunk at the next major stopping point.

I arrived to breakfast a few minutes late, per my usual style. I didn't apologize; this is the way I am. I am not a morning person at all, so I felt they should feel lucky I'd made it at all. I sat when Andrew pulled out my chair. I settled in and my café con leche materialized out of nowhere. He had even ordered me a *tortilla con potata*. On the side there was a croissant, orange and banana for the road. I gave him a kiss on the cheek.

"You didn't have to do that! But thanks!" I grinned at him.

His eyes were shining when he said, "The three of us are idiots. You trusted us. Be careful on the road, okay? I'm leaving today. I want you to be safe and take everything you can from this experience." He winked at me to let me know he felt a connection, too. My chin wobbled and I couldn't speak for a minute.

"I'm so glad I got to say goodbye, Andrew. You're very sweet. Your wife and girls are lucky to have you. Truly!" My eggs swam in my vision and a big tear plopped onto my plate before I could stop it. I had to excuse myself to the restroom and cry for a minute. I was feeling more and more lost. I wasn't sure that this Camino was turning into what I'd thought it would be. When I got everything under control, I joined my table again. We ate and talked a bit, but the mood was sad. I stood to go. Andrew held my backpack in his large, sun-browned hands. He'd packed the other food items inside. He checked my water bladder to be sure it was full. Fresh tears threatened again. I had to get out of there. I was being driven by my honed instincts to run away from uncomfortable feelings. I grabbed a handful of napkins and stuffed them in my pocket to use as tissues. Andrew raised my pack so I could easily put it on.

"Do you know these straps are uneven?" he grunted at me.

I shook my head, paused and then nodded.

"Doesn't feel right, does it?"

I shook my head—my right shoulder often felt tingly at the end of the day.

He adjusted the strap for me on my right shoulder slightly, just enough to notice that the pressure now seemed evenly balanced. I quickly turned and hugged him tightly. I listened to his heartbeat for a second. Thoughts of my dad floated in front of my face and I knew he was there, too. This is why I'd run into Andrew. I had the chance to say goodbye this time. I gave him a rather tearful kiss on his cheek and turned to Rick and Ross's concerned faces. I offered a watery smile and handshakes. They rolled their eyes and patted my shoulders.

With quick hugs to both of them I took a step toward the door when Andrew stuck a note in my left hand. I grabbed it and left without looking back. I nearly ran. Once outside, my thoughts cleared a little. My focus came back. I could see backpacks heading out of town so I simply followed. I drew a long pull of air through my mouth and held it for a second before letting it out slowly. I drew another. The familiar pace settled into my bones. A feeling of belonging enveloped me now on the trail. This is where I excelled. I was great on my own. I took strength from pounding out my steps on the ground. I followed the tracks of pilgrims who had trekked this way for at least a millennium. I imagined their energy pulsing through me as I walked. I thought maybe their spirits still passed along this trail like the breeze that moved through my hair and dried my tears.

CHAPTER SEVEN

Today's walk was relatively mild with the exception of two climbs where no more than 170 meters were gained, but the declines were steep. With the tightness and pain radiating up from the bottoms of my feet to my knees, I had to focus on not losing control down these hills. It was too bad I hadn't felt enough energy to practice a little yoga during the trip—I was too exhausted at the end of each day to stretch! Before I left Colorado, my friends told me I should teach yoga in the mornings to my fellow pilgrims since I'd become a certified yoga teacher the year before. Sounded great to me! Until sheer exhaustion at the end of each day slayed those thoughts.

I thought back to December of 2011 when I'd been separated from Derek for a few months and living with a friend, whom I had met through the coffee shop. I juggled business ownership, half-time with my daughter, and tried to keep a happy front for my customers. It took all of my energy to erect a happy facade over my depressed state so that my business would not fail. I'd never taken my problems to work with me and I was not about to start now. By the time I left work, it was all I could do to walk to my friend's house and collapse, wrapping my depression around me like a blanket and falling into bed again.

My assistant manager stepped up to the plate when I called in tears to tell him I would need surgery to extract a tumor. I'd had an unsightly spot removed from my wrist before I could lose my health insurance benefits from Derek. The divorce was about to happen and I wasn't sure I could afford insurance on my paltry salary. My dermatologist had told me it was nothing, but the surprise in her voice was evident when she told me she wished she'd taken photos of my mole for research purposes. Turns out the sneaky tumor had grown down between my left radius and ulna. To add insult to injury, it had spread to a few lymphs under my collar bone. Derek overheard the call and agreed to halt mid-drive to the courthouse to file our paperwork so that I could have peace of mind that I was covered for those surgeries. I thought that was nice.

Two months later, given the all-clear, our divorce was finalized and my stitches freshly removed. My staff still picked up my slack at the shop. I slept all day when I didn't have Parker. On a Thursday in mid-February of 2012, my friend Debbie dragged me to yoga one night when I lacked the brain capacity to form another argument. Seizing the moment before a few brain cells could fire, she grabbed my uninjured arm and bodily yanked me to her car. She was lucky I had been lounging in yoga-like sleepwear or I might have fought a bit. After a sluggish attempt to whine and complain, I gave up and realized I'd been taken prisoner and to just go with it. I could go back to sulking in a little over an hour anyway once she took me back to my cave.

We sat in a darkened room with candles glowing. It seemed like a nice place for a nap, so I flopped backward on my borrowed mat and sulked there instead of at home. The instructor came in. HE was hot. I hadn't expected that. I sat up with energy I hadn't known I had and looked askance at my haggard appearance in the mirror. Funny how I hadn't cared when I'd been certain the instructor was female. A glance at Debbie's smirk told me she knew exactly what she'd done.

Paul sat his beautiful, lean-muscled body on his mat. In Lotus, with his hands rested and relaxed on his knees, he took a deep breath in. Everyone else copied him. I readjusted my ponytail and smoothed some errant strands that stuck up. He closed his eyes while I took the opportunity to sniff my armpits and wished I hadn't. Every other woman in there sighed before closing theirs and waited for his sage advice. After a couple breath cycles, his deep voice softly read a poem about accepting ourselves and "coming home to the seat of our souls" before closing with "dedicate tonight's practice to yourself and let go of what's not serving you." This, of course, felt like the deepest moment since the history of deep moments! Truthfully, I fell in love a little bit.

The lights were turned off and candles lit around the room. It was magic. We flowed through our poses with the gentle guidance of his voice. I lay in Savasana at the end, feeling my heart beat with a bit more enthusiasm than it had in a while. Did I feel different? Maybe not so uptight. I wasn't mad at Debbie anymore. Lying there, my fingertips brushed hers in gratitude. She turned her head and regarded me with her patient, knowing smile. The hard wall around me had developed a crack somewhere. Yep, there were no arguments with Debbie the next week. Showering started to happen with regularity as well.

One day after class, Paul told us he was teaching a course in Costa Rica for five weeks. I jumped on the opportunity to explore all facets of yoga, not just for the ability to teach. Plus, it was the chance to travel outside the U.S., which was another first. That's how I found myself secluded in the jungles of Costa Rica with twelve other people from all over the world as we submerged ourselves in the learning and practicing of yoga. They formed their friendships and cliques. I watched it all happen as if I wasn't fully present. Anytime there was an opportunity for free time, I was invited to join in on fun excursions but I held myself apart. During those times, I journaled and drew pictures of my daughter or the wildlife I came across as I journeyed through the jungle alone. It was only toward the end that I started to crack the shell around me and by then, I was truly isolated emotionally from the yoga tribe. They'd yearned to know me toward the beginning, even in the middle, but I couldn't reach out in time. I felt I was the only stranger on that trip. I had been successful in my own processes but still unable to cry over the loss of my marriage. Though I had spent time trying to cry over him, that's when my emotions went cold and my tears dried up. I would rejoin the group for class, feeling frustrated and desperate to break out of my invisible cage but unsure how to do it. I hoped this time to shatter it on the Camino.

    I brought my focus back to the trail and focused again on the beauty of the landscape. It never failed to amaze me with lush green colors and amazing wildflower fields popping with color amongst the green-velvet of the wheat and grass.

    Lonely, monotonous stretches along the trails left me plenty of time to pray. Each time I asked for guidance or answers from my guardian angels, I would see shapes in the clouds that pertained to that certain question. When I asked if I would be able to return a man's love in the near future, I saw as clear as could be, a woman's figure in a dress and veil floating behind her. Next to her was a heart-shaped cloud. *Well, I think that is putting the cart before the horse, but thanks, Angels.* I thought.

    I'd gone about ten kilometers and so I decided it was time for a break to eat the snacks Andrew had given me. Flat rocks provided a seat by the side of the trail and the sun had made a shy appearance. Unsure how long the sun would last, I sat quickly to take advantage. The ligaments and tendons around my knees creaked in protest. Like all of these aches and pains, I tried to tell myself it was just a little bit of the Camino. As positive as I tried to be, I knew the Camino could be a downright bitch when she wanted, too.

Pilgrims passed with their walking sticks. There were a couple of boisterous Italian guys coming by bicycle. They announced their arrival as they pushed foot traffic off the trail. I patiently munched my croissant as they came into view. They were both good-looking in that typical Italian way. Their cycling outfits matched in white and green. They smiled charmingly. I couldn't help responding to the flirtation and smiled in response to their manly Buen Caminos, watching their perfectly round, muscular buttocks cycle away from me as they rode past. How did they manage to wink at me and watch where they were going, I wondered. Their huge quadriceps pumped up and down in perfect unison. They soon disappeared. An older couple came around the corner huffing and complaining in British accents about the rude cyclists. I held Andrew's note and waited for them to pass.

He'd folded it hastily and I'd jammed it into my pocket—now it sat in the middle of my palm like a squashed, white butterfly. Inexplicably nervous, I just stared at it wondering what secrets it revealed. I felt ashamed to admit that I was afraid it was a love note. I shook these thoughts away and opened it.

Dearest Alesa,
Thank you for sharing your stories with me. I value your trust in me, a perfect stranger. You've had an unfair amount of pain. I admire you. Not for

overcoming these "weaknesses" you confess to have, but rather for the strength of your spirit. You amaze me, though you hide your sadness with smiles and funny stories. You are strong. You really don't have to handle it all by yourself, you know! Let others help you on The Way, like you have allowed me to. I hope I have anyway. Be open to this process. Most of all, trust yourself because you are beginning to understand some monumental things that will change you along the way. I sense a great shift coming for you.

You are powerfully strong. I felt it the moment we met. I can't wait to hear how you come through the other side of this adventure. If you ever need anything, please contact me. Don't hesitate. I hope you don't think this is a love letter, though it is, in a way. You remind me very much of one of my daughters. I'd be honored if you thought of me that way.

Take care of yourself. Remember that you can dance through the incandescent light of the moon with power, strength, grace, and love. You are amazing!
Love Always,
Andrew

A small stab of loneliness went through me, though he'd scrawled his contact information at the bottom. Slowly standing as my knee ligaments and tendons groaned in pain, I grimaced at the thought of more walking. Blah. I wished fervently for a riderless donkey to happen by. When no such thing materialized before my eyes, I popped a small handful of ibuprofen with plenty of water. Groaning in pain, I hefted my pack once more and set off, adjusting the straps as I walked stiff-legged for a few paces. Before long, the beauty of the landscape stretched out as far as I could see before me, helping take my mind off my physical pain.

Going downhill in such condition proved to be much slower than uphill. Rocks slid under foot. My ankles took turns rolling one way and then the other. With each misstep, curses flew from my mouth, reverberating out over the valley below me. Dislodged pebbles rolled before me down the path with each step. My muscles shook by the time the trail evened out so I stopped to drink more water and eat some fruit. From here the trail would be relatively flat. I still had to be a bit cautious as it was slick with rain and mud, but at least it wasn't the deep, sole-sucking mud I'd experienced near Villatuerta!

After a few more kilometers, I came upon the only viable option for lunch, according to my guidebook—a somber, grim town called Viana. Of course, the Camino trailed passed through the preserved medieval town center. Though this town was larger than many I'd passed through, with a population of 3,500, I wouldn't describe it as bustling. People walking the sidewalks wore such long frowns their faces imitated the great arches and carved porticos along the building facades. Older gentlemen leaned in bar doorways smoking cigarettes and staring at passersby with expressions of hopelessness and loss. The economy here was so terrible that even the splendor of its ornate centerpiece, the Iglesia de Santa Maria with its handsome carved porticos, couldn't lift these people's moods.

With the gray skies overhead lending their sad energy to these depressed people, I ducked into the nearest café to eat and get out of here as quickly as possible. No pilgrims greeted me in this hole in the wall, so I ate quickly, freshened up and headed out fast, eager to get to the next stopping point. I still had ten kilometers to go before finding shelter in Logrono. Though fatigued throughout my whole body, I refused the thought of finding a bed in Viana. An oppressive loneliness settled around my shoulders as I shrugged under the weight on my back and in my soul.

My playlist seemed to feel the same, for only the saddest songs were shuffled one after the other into my earphones. A great hollow feeling took hold. I already missed Andrew and figured maybe I hadn't been quite ready to say Goodbye. His letter lingered in my mind. Was I really as strong as he thought? Sometimes, I wasn't so sure. I wished I could stand up for myself when it really mattered. Time and again and I had frustrated myself by not taking action when I needed to protect myself. It was only after, when the damage had been done that I became enraged enough to stand up for myself. I almost had to be angry, otherwise I had no backbone at all. But make me angry, and I came roaring to life with a vehement fury unlike anything anyone's ever seen. *There has to be a middle ground*! I mused.

Just like The Creep, I thought. Why had it taken me years to tell him to back off? He came to our big house parties and got my parents high so that he could rob me of my innocence. His name was Jim, but we secretly called him The Creep, or any variation of that name, when the adults were out of range. Before long, Creepy Man spent more and more time at our house, slept on our couch and ate our food. His glass-blue eyes were so light they frightened me, for they appeared almost white. He smelled like dirt and hay. We sometimes hid from him when he visited because he liked to poke us in the ribs and ask us to sit in his lap. He was strange but I didn't know why until the first time he touched me. I was just seven years old. Mom sent me with him in his filthy truck to pick up a pizza. Instead of going right to the pizza parlor, he drove to a dark lot and turned his truck off.

It was then I noticed he had curtains rolled up above all the windows. When he rolled them all down and reached for me, I didn't scream. I was too scared. An hour later, he casually walked in our house as I stood outside not sure of what to do. He stood in the light of the entry, his glass-blue eyes regarding me coldly. He thrust his hand out as if we were friends and told me not to be silly. He moved a few steps inside but kept his eyes on me as I walked hesitantly into my house, careful to keep out of his arms' reach. My mother's half-hooded, stoned eyes told me she didn't realize we were late, nor was she worried. I ran to the room where Renee sat playing with her Holly Hobby oven and locked our door. She looked up, brightly hoping I'd want to play, too. I felt sick with shame and pain. I crawled in bed, turned away from her and told her I was tired.

On nights like these he slept on our couch. There was never any fair warning about when he would visit. When his girlfriends tired of his lackadaisical lifestyle, they kicked him out. He came to our house. On the days when I could prepare for his visit, I stayed glued to Renee or my mother and refused to be persuaded anywhere alone with him. He winked at me as if to say, "Next time, kiddo."

I spent many hours finding hiding places in the yard, our neighborhood, underneath our house. He found most of them. I feared revealing these secrets to anyone, especially my mother. I didn't know what she might do to me if she found out. I only knew that I should be able to stop him but I didn't know how. I became a very quiet, shy girl who no one could seem to "bring out of her shell." Before too long, everyone seemed to accept that I had just become a bit withdrawn and quiet. I was the good child now.

Mom found me in the bedroom closet one day, quietly sitting in the darkest corner hugging my pillows to my chest. "What are you doing in here all alone, Little Mouse? Come outside and play." I shook my head. "My little day dreamer," she sighed and ran her fingers through my hair. Then she knelt and tried to hug me but I cringed farther into the corner to escape her groping hands. I looked steadily back at her as I gauged her hurt reaction. A frown passed over her face but cleared quickly. She wasn't going to fall apart this time. She had company to prepare for. "Well, we're having friends over tonight. It would be nice if you came out to say hi, you know. Everyone wants to see you."

"I'm fine in here," I replied softly and firmly.

One evening, when I was eleven, a profound shift took hold of me during dinner time. Mom had made my favorite dinner. Homemade tacos. With this act of love, I felt the urge to spill the secrets right then and there in front of everyone. Scarily, the words seemed to float toward the front of my mouth so that I almost blurted them out. Horrified, I grabbed my milk glass and swallowed it all in one long, painful gulp to push the words back down. My heart pounded with the need to say something. I fought the battle by stuffing nearly half a taco in my mouth. I couldn't breathe for a moment and that was just fine. Sis looked at me oddly. I chewed and swallowed, coughed and chewed some more. I asked for more milk. Mom and Bruce were talking loudly and hardly noticed the odd scene across from them. My sister poked me. "Slow down! You'll choke, stupid!" I nodded at her as tears rose in my eyes. Nobody had poured me more milk so I stole hers. "Hey!" I drank it all down. The cool liquid splashed in my belly before she could punch me in the arm. I pictured the words swirling in there like water in the toilet bowl. Sis grabbed my hand and leaned dangerously close. I knew if she asked me anything I would start to cry. Panic rose with the crest of my tears.

An eruption across the table saved me and snapped Renee's head around. A tiny squeal escaped from Mom. Inexplicably, she crumpled the remains of her taco in her hands and sprinkled them on Bruce's head like confetti. She flicked her rice at him with a dainty swipe of her long hand. Sis stifled a gasp. My little brother dropped his fork. All eyes riveted on the lettuce that floated in Bruce's hair and dangled over his eyes. Silence descended with a heavy thump. The kitchen clock ticked loudly while Bruce stared at her with a strange, wide-eyed look on his face. I had never seen his cheeks flame red like that before. I couldn't tell if he was mad or embarrassed but something brewed beneath his peculiar expression—perhaps it was rage. His large, tanned hands hovered over his plate. Mom's eyes flicked down once and we all did the same. He had three tacos remaining amongst a pile of gooey, cheesy refried beans. Horror opened Mom's eyes wide as she started to rise. He calmly scooped his dinner into his hands, crunching it as he too rose out of his chair.

Mom made it to the kitchen doorway before the back of her head blossomed with an arrangement of taco meat, tomato chunks, lettuce and sour cream. She screeched to a halt and half-turned toward him in rage before he grabbed her arm and yanked her out the entry door to the patio. He slammed the door behind him. Their voices rose as they fought outside the kitchen window where we'd all pressed our noses to spy on them. Seeing us, Bruce moved her around the house to the back so we all moved to the bathroom where the window was already open half an inch. We hovered below the window and listened in hushed awe. "Calm down, Katherine!" Bruce hollered. She screeched some more. My little brother had climbed into my lap and clung to me with big eyes while they fought. His breathing was loud and panicked. I shushed him right before Bruce's voice came through the open window, "Kids, go to your room. This is between your mom and me." We stood and hung our heads in shame for eavesdropping while he watched us shuffle out of the bathroom.

Food had splattered and dripped all the way to the entry. We slunk back to the kitchen like silent thieves. I sat at my chair while Renee started to clean the mess. "Leave it for them," I told her. She shrugged and continued picking pieces of taco off the molding around the door and scooping up handfuls from the floor. I shrugged at her sense of duty. My little brother climbed uncertainly back into his chair and looked at me with tears in his little eyes. I patted his hand and shot a wide grin at him. "That was great. Everything is going to be fine," I said, and for the first time in a long time felt it really would. Unexpected happiness filled me as my brother and I finished our tacos. An appetite I usually didn't have took hold. The tacos tasted like the best thing I'd ever eaten. That night filled me with hope—if they divorced, it would mean the end of my personal hell. I wished with vicious glee that they would continue to fight. "Please hate each other. Please divorce, please divorce...please GOD." I prayed with a ghost of a smile.

That night Renee and I read stories to our brother. He clung to me, his little arms strangled my neck, while Mom and Bruce continued to fight. It was music to my ears. I had a new idea about how I would treat The Creep. I would be openly hostile and didn't care what anyone thought. I hummed to my brother while he fell asleep in my arms. The weight and heat of his little body soothed me as I schemed. I drifted toward sleep satisfyingly content, sure that a guardian from heaven had intervened for me tonight. Things were going to be alright. With new resolve, I decided I would not let The Creep get his hands on me again. As I held my brother's warm, sleeping form I fantasized about the many ways I could be strong against The Creep. He would not win ever again, I vowed to myself.

As the landscape of vineyards and farmland along the Camino came back into focus, I marveled at the strength I'd grown in that one significant moment. At only eleven, I had figured out a way to stand up for myself. It hadn't been easy from there but the anger became an integral part of my life. It kept me going, provided a weapon. I hid it well, didn't show it, but it resided inside me just the same. Sadly, this anger, I realized, had grown over the years to become an impenetrable but necessary shield. At least I'd felt it was necessary. I realized I was tired. Not from walking. Tired from carrying that imaginary shield and sword. They were heavy. I wanted peace more than anything, yet could not seem to cultivate those things in my life. What was I doing wrong?

The city of Logrono looked very large in comparison to what I'd been visiting the last few days. The travel guides promised a mecca of culture and food. Now in the famous Riojan region, renowned for its wine, I was looking forward to a Riojan red with dinner tonight and maybe some good company as I was sick of reliving the past. I needed a respite! I prayed to meet some cool people to hang out with that evening. I needed a shower, dinner, good conversation and lots of WARM sleep.

I wandered into town and off the Camino trail, but didn't care so much at this point. I knew I'd find it tomorrow. As if by magic, I found myself standing at the rotating doors of the Hostel Logrono. This was a modern building, painted in a soft creamsicle orange color with white accents. The modern living room housed pilgrims already lounging in various chairs and couches. Some surfed the internet, others watched television, which I hadn't seen since I'd left the airport in Madrid. I stood staring stupidly at the moving pictures for a minute before shaking myself out of the tele-trance.

"Uno habitación, por favor," I muttered to the woman who sat merely watching and waiting for me to wake out of my trance. She smiled and led me through everything. With a quick stamp to my pilgrim's booklet, she led me out and up some marble steps to a large white paneled door. My room had a tray ceiling, was painted a nice peachy color with white trim. There were only eight beds in here and I was thankful for it! I laughed to think this was a nice upgrade. There were separate common areas for laundry and bathrooms.

In a haze from the long walk, I arranged my sleeping bag and unpacked for the night. Lockers had been provided, so I locked things I didn't need for the shower and took off down the hall. I almost dropped my bundle when I walked into the bathroom to see an old woman walking without a stitch on. Her skin draped on her bones like creased satin, her breasts swung like rope. She showed no shame whatsoever. She smiled a beautifully confident smile at me. I was ashamed of myself for noticing her wrinkles. I quickly claimed a very tiny shower stall of my own and stepped inside to undress in private.

After showering quickly in the ice cold water, I tried unsuccessfully to dry off and dress inside the little cubicle. I fell out the slightly open door and nearly hit my face on the wooden slats that served as a place to hang dry clothes. It sounded like an elephant had lost the battle in the tiny space. No one came running, so I gathered my dignity with my soiled clothing and met one of the women from my room in the laundry area. She introduced herself as Sara from England. She had traveled the Camino three times before now. She spoke animatedly about her experiences and great love for the Camino. I secretly hoped I would last to the end and not hate it. I accepted her invitation to dine with her.

We stepped out onto the mall together and had only gone a few limping steps when a charming group of Italian men asked us to join their group for dinner. With hopeful faces, they sadly told us they lacked females in their group tonight, would we sit with them? They seemed harmless so we agreed. They took us to a nice restaurant unlike the bars I'd been eating in. This place offered a more upscale menu. The men kept the wine flowing and we laughed so much my stomach hurt. None of them tried to flirt overly much, just enough to flatter us. They shared platters of food. I admired the passion with which they enjoyed everything. The man to my left had dimples that cleaved both cheeks and he offered me bites of everything with a sexy smile hovering in the corner of his mouth. They wanted to take us to a dessert and coffee bar for after-dinner nightcaps, but I insisted on going to bed, feeling languorous after such a long day and satisfying meal.

My feet were dragging from fatigue when the dimpled man came running back to me. He held my arm and said, "I assist you, bella!" He walked me back, me leaning on one arm and Sara on the other, to the hoots and hollers of his companions. He walked us all the way to our door and with a gentlemanly flourish, took the key from my hand and unlocked the door. Sara discreetly stepped past me. He grabbed my hand, bowed and kissed it. Then, he stole a kiss from my lips. Before I could say a word, he laughed and bowed again and left. I watched his retreating form as he walked back down to the lobby. With a dreamy smile I turned back to see Sara laughing behind her hand.

"That was too cute! He could be your Camino romance! Go get him!" I shook my head. "It's not time yet. I'll know when it's time." I grabbed my toiletries and dreamily walked to the bathroom to brush my teeth again.

That night I dreamed Derek and I watched Fourth of July fireworks on a patchwork quilt laid on the grass by the lake near my house. There were blossoms exploding in brilliant colors. The sparks fell on us and burned holes in our clothes. We weren't afraid. They didn't hurt. I turned to him and told him I would always love him. He grabbed my hand. His eyes lit up with hope.

"That's not what I mean," I said. His face fell with sadness.

Just then a firework exploded close to us and his face lit up in bright yellow light for a moment. Crystalline tears formed in his eyes. Every facet of his face was revealed in that second and I saw how much he'd aged. It made me sad and I touched his cheek. I rose up and kissed his lips.

His tears fell to a pool on his chest while my dress was burned in spots. The holes grew larger. I had to go or risk no clothing.

I walked away, aware of how much he still loved me, and yet felt free. My hips swished with the fullness of my skirts. I felt beautiful. I looked back at him. He laid with his back to me as he watched the fireworks over the water. His clothes flared with sparks now and then, but he didn't seem to feel them.

CHAPTER EIGHT

Sunshine caught at the corners of my eyes the next morning. I glanced at the time and saw that the alarm was set to go off in ten minutes. I growled softly and rolled over. If I fell back asleep quickly, I could get nine more minutes. I lay there pretending to rest more when I noticed something odd taking place. I actually wanted to get up! That couldn't be right. I stubbornly lay there and tried to close my eyes. They popped open. I rolled over onto my back and stared at the bottom of the top bed. It flexed toward me now. Someone had arrived very late and I hadn't heard a thing.

I decided to join the silently packing women in the next row. They were so quiet as to almost be inaudible. Their concern for the sleeping pilgrims touched me. Sometimes, people flipped lights on and talked in normal voices with no concern for those slugs like me who wanted as much sleep as possible. I slid out of my little sleeping bag and nearly fell out of bed as I tried not to shake the person above me. With my usual graceful exit, I stood on both feet and tried not to cry out as the stabbing pain in my left foot made me grimace. I shifted my balance to my right foot as I slowly allowed my left heel to acclimate to the hard floor more slowly. My foot wanted to remain arched.

After a few minutes, my weight was bearable again. I dressed without falling over, counting it as a small success. I tied my jacket around my waist. Though today was sunny it could very well be cold and miserable, too. I packed away the photo of my daughter that I looked at each night and my iPhone went into a pouch that was easy to reach. My purse went deep into my pack so it couldn't be easily stolen. I slapped a bit of sunscreen on exposed areas and before long was ready for coffee and croissants.

With a heavy heart, I prepared quickly and quietly to leave my cozy room. Why were these dreams weighing so heavily? He'd been such an ass about the affair, leaving me to deal with the aftermath, never facing it with me. He faded into the background while he pushed for the divorce, though I had just been out of surgery for one month. I still had stitches. He hadn't even bothered to check on me during my recovery in the post-surgery pod, a room where the beds were arranged in a circle with curtains between us. As the anesthesia wore off, some woke up laughing and others cursed and kicked. I had been calm but shed tears without knowing why. How could I still care about someone who'd treated me so coldly? I chastised myself. "You'll be fine, let's just get out of here," I muttered irritably to myself.

That had been a year ago. It made no sense, except that he'd finally apologized for his affair the night before I left for Spain. I'd had a bad day and things had naturally escalated with him on the phone. I was spouting hate and resentment at him. Exasperated, he finally said, "Would you please come over? I have some things I'd like to talk to you about." Face to face with him, I watched in disbelief as he actually cried a few tears. He admitted regret over the way he'd treated me, things he had done and not done. He acknowledged he hadn't been present for me during our marriage, nor understanding what I needed from him when I was sick the first time. He seemed absolutely sincere. I grudgingly forgave him. Oh, how I had needed that apology for so long!

So lost in thought, I nearly got sideswiped by a car as I crossed a busy intersection. Logrono was a larger city than I was used to so I yanked my attention back. I had no idea if I was on the trail—the Camino was difficult to follow sometimes when it went through cities. Traffic whizzed by. Parents walked their children to school. Some of them pointed at me and smiled. I wanted to ruffle their dark hair. A man walking his daughter stopped near me and pointed to a yellow arrow nearby. He smiled kindly as I thanked him, once again back on track.

City sights and sounds competed for my attention and pulled it away from the arrows a few times. Past the city park, there was a nice lake to walk around and a nature preserve area, though I felt like I was still in the city as many people continued to pass by on their morning walks. Everywhere I turned, no matter how fast or slow I went, my heart ached with memories. Thoughts of Derek washed through my mind no matter how I tried to push him away. Tears fell from my eyes as I walked.

Much of today's trails ran on asphalt roads, which were harder to walk on for prolonged periods of time versus the dirt paths I'd grown accustomed to. Hot spots formed on both heels now and I had to stop to remove my shoes and apply blister packs. My feet had swollen from walking on pavement so long and swelled with blood when I removed each shoe. Now my shoes felt tight when I thrust them back on. The physical pain made me more vulnerable. I felt alone. I missed my daughter. I missed my ex.

Finally the trail led me past some medieval ruins, but I was too emotional to peek inside, before I came to the stone steps that led up to the town of Navarette. I was gasping with the effort to breathe through my nose and mouth. After crying the whole morning, I had more than my fair share of snot mucking things up even more. The church in this town square looked similar to every church I'd passed on the Camino. But this one called me to go inside. I couldn't resist. I headed straight for it. I felt a great need to go there.

I left my music on as I walked in. There were the gaudy gold-gilt monuments of priests and saints. I walked across the wide, dark wooden floors and sat in the middle of a pew in the middle of the room. A few pilgrims milled. With an overwhelming need to weep, and lacking the time to unbuckle my straps, I doubled over my knees just as great, gasping sobs seized me. The sarcastic side of me was horrified at this emotional debacle. I cranked my music higher so I wouldn't have to hear myself. At first I cried for Parker and everything we'd put her through. My heart hurt more thinking of her face and the sadness she'd endured. I cried for having cancer and a selfish jerk of a husband. But yet, I then cried for him. How I missed him. Holding his hand, cuddling at night, the little things. I cried like I hadn't allowed myself to cry in years.

Eventually, I gave in and let my forehead be cradled on my forearms. Air was wrenched out of me so forcefully that my ribs ached. It seemed my body wasn't happy until every last shred of air was pulled from me. When the air was allowed back in, it came in waves. I couldn't take it all in fast enough. I forced my body to relax and as I did, I felt another wave of deeper, older sorrow following the waves I'd thought were nearly done. This time, images of myself as a young girl arose in my mind. I saw myself walk to her as an adult. I hugged her as I finally cried for myself as I hadn't allowed myself to do. Ever.

I cried until there were no more tears. When the sobs

subsided, I stayed weakly leaning my head on my arms. My pack laid over my back like a comforting shell. I was exhausted now but the pain in my chest was still there.

"God, help me!" I whispered out of desperation. "I thought I came here without Derek. I really did. I thought I was alone. Everywhere I look I see him. I dream about him now. I wasn't dreaming about him until I came here! We were together for so long and the divorce was so fast. I just want to let him go. Let him be happy. Let me be happy! I want to be free of this pain. Help me let him go. I do want to be his friend. Parker deserves that." My heart hammered as I waited for the pain in my heart to go away. Without warning, a gentle heat warmed my heart and chest. Someone laid one gentle hand on the back of my head and another at the base of my neck, just above my backpack. I didn't have the strength to lift my head and thank the kind stranger, and plus there was snot everywhere.

I'm guessing that the hands were there for no more than four or five seconds. During those precious seconds, the knot of pain in my heart grew smaller and diminished completely. The hands lifted and I gasped, forgot the mess my face was in, and sat up to look at this person. No one stood there. I twisted quickly in all directions as I swiped the last of my tears away. It seemed my sobs had cleared the place out. I looked under my bench, half expecting to see some boots or a person hiding. Thinking quickly, I took my earphones out to listen for footsteps. Nothing but silence greeted me. Not a living person besides me was in the church at that moment. I felt the lingering presence of a divine love, though, and I can only describe it as the warmest feeling I'd ever experienced.

It was cold in the church, but I stayed for a few more minutes bent in prayer. I am not a person who prays. I never seem to do it well. I forget what I'm praying about very often and my mind wanders to other things. I have a wicked monkey mind. Today was different. I thanked Jesus and all of the angels for hearing me and lifting the pain from me. I felt invigorated and extremely thirsty. My face felt like a leaky balloon.

I stood shakily and wondered peevishly why my blisters hadn't been healed as well. I quickly turned toward the sculpture of Jesus. "Not that I'm not grateful! I am! Thank you so much! It's just with the blisters....nah, never mind, not important. Thanks again!" My voice was thick with mucus. I limped out of my pew and toward the nearest escape route as I held a small tissue to my nose to keep the snot contained until I could wash my face and blow it properly.

I found a bar and scurried in past a man who looked familiar. "You are very beautiful when you cry this way." He looked so sincere I tried hard not to raise an eyebrow at him in reaction. I couldn't really converse with him since I had sinuses full of mucus and other nonsense, so I nodded ever so slightly with my hands holding the tissue tightly to my face and trying not to leak all over anything. I was glad he thought so. One look in the mirror proved he lied. Once I'd washed up, I found a table near the window that was empty but crowded with discarded packs and poles on the floor near it. I set my pack on a chair near the window and squeezed through the throng again to order another café con leche. Once I had it in my hands, I sat in my seat by the window to stare at the church and ponder the miracle that had just happened.

I felt different. Lighter. Hopeful. Strong. I smiled at the church across the street and watched pilgrims come and go in the square. They were all completely oblivious of my little miracle. I wanted to laugh.

Derek's face swam into my mind again, this time I knew a reconnection needed to be made. As friends. I longed for that now. For my daughter's sense of well-being, an effort needed to be made. I posted an update quickly on Facebook about my adventure and sent him a small note. With gladness in my heart, I left the bar to continue the journey.

If you think I skipped merrily down the trail after that, you are mistaken. My blisters grew throughout the day so that I nearly cried with each step. I had no choice but to exchange my shoes for the walking sandals so that my heels could stop their angry pulsing against the fabric of my shoes. Curses flew and the pain became nearly unbearable. I don't know how I made it to my stopping point that day. Again, loneliness invaded my soul as I felt sorry for my feet and aching muscles. I felt nauseous with the pain. I wanted to give up. Go home. I'd lie, I thought, and say I did the whole thing. Who would know? Frustrated with feeling weak, I clenched my fists and intentionally remembered one of the moments in my life that I'd proven how strong I could be.

Since the food fight incident, I started to realize I could take back control, though I didn't know how. Anytime I thought of reaching out to Mom, my stomach clenched in dread. I could only imagine her dissolving into a crying heap in inconsolable despair or hysterical acts of self-blame. I definitely didn't want that. If there was a way out, I didn't see it until one day when I faced a nasty surprise visit and made an extremely hard choice. It happened one day when I was home alone. The sound of his truck in our driveway set my heart pounding with repulsion and hatred.

Renee was at a slumber party a town away. I'd been feeling "blue" so I stayed home and drew pictures and read Nancy Drew books. Mom had taken my brother to the neighboring town and would visit with her friends for a while. She was supposed to be home by dinnertime. The house was pleasantly quiet so I heard the truck's engine like a roar in my head. I dropped my book with nerveless fingers and cursed when it hit the floor with a thud. I pulled myself up to sit up on my knees and listened harder.

The clock by my bed told me Mom had only been gone three hours, she wouldn't be back for a few more. His truck door squealed on rusty hinges as he slammed it with a loud bang. It didn't latch so he banged it again. It was definitely him.

"No! No! No! Enough of this. Think, Alesa." I mumbled aloud as I scrambled off my bed, kicked the books underneath and pulled my blankets tight to hide my body imprint. I ran lightly on bare feet to the bathroom, opened the window, pushed the screen onto the ground but didn't go out the window. He'd caught on to that trick and caught me around the corner last time. I'd locked the front door when Mom left so he couldn't come in that way. He knew he could get in through our bedroom windows, though, since the latches were broken. Panic rose, threatening to freeze my thoughts and trap the air in my lungs. I pushed it down forcefully and pushed my hands through my hair to grip it in painful handfuls. The pain centered me and I focused as a beam of light caught the silver edge of the trap door on the floor of the bathroom. Out of time, I whimpered in fear but slid softly across the linoleum to the door. I grasped the silver handle of the trap door with my right hand and crouched as I lifted it slowly. A musty odor wafted up my nose. It was pitch black! I hated the cellar!

"Ale-esa!" His voice came from my open bedroom window. I almost dropped the trapdoor. To keep from screaming, I put my left hand over my mouth and lifted the door a little higher. "Guess who I saw-w-w at the gro-cer-y store!" He sounded giddy. "Your momma told me you weren't feeling well. Oh, sweetie! I came to check on you-u-u!" He grunted like he was lifting something. My bedroom window creaked faintly as he raised the sash higher.

It was a matter of seconds before he would find me. I grabbed the edge of the opening with my left hand. Swiftly and silently I swung my feet down into that great, gaping black hole. My fear of The Creep was marginally larger than the cellar so I stepped down two steps into the blackness. My insides quivered in fear. I pictured lots of things down there ready to devour me. My horribly vivid imagination conjured images of zombies scraping toward me, eagerly waiting to get a mouthful of my soft, young leg or arm.

I heard a scrape and for a moment thought they were really coming for me before I realized it was The Creep! He was sliding over my windowsill into my room! I'd hesitated in indecision when I heard him grunt as he landed on my bed. I'd almost run back up the two steps but I forced myself down into the cavernous hole. I lowered the door above me now as I descended. Before I closed the door that last inch and lost my ray of light, I scanned the storage room below quickly with my eyes. I didn't see any monsters in front or to the sides.

Then I heard his boot steps in the hall. At that moment I also felt the air stir through the open, wooden steps at my back. I was shaking madly as I lowered the door all the way to the floor above my head and lost the ray of light. Though I tried to shut it quietly, to my ears, the door hit the floor with a bang. I kept my right hand connected to the door above my head as I flinched soundlessly away from the imagined zombies behind me. My back arched away from the steps as I waited for something awful to happen. My breathing was beyond my control. It sounded loud to my ears. I imagined The Creep could hear me from up there.

Where was he? I couldn't stand being confined in the dungeon and was afraid I'd launch myself out and right into his waiting arms. Cold sweat broke out everywhere on my body. Little lines of sweat ran down the backs of my legs, tickling them like spiders. I thought of the black widow warnings Bruce went on and on about. He'd found a nest of them down here somewhere. I lifted my feet up a step closer to my body. I listened harder, trying not to think about the dangers that lurched toward me in my imagination. "There's a bigger and very real danger upstairs in the light," I whispered to myself.

Floorboards over my head creaked suddenly. He was being quiet, too. I held my breath. My heart pounded heavily against my drawn-up knees as I tried to exhale as slowly as possible. He walked in two steps to the other side of the bathroom. I pictured him looking out the window at the screen on the ground. My body fought to fly out of that dungeon while my mind fought to control my body. I cried big fat tears into the blackness as silently as I could, heedless of where they fell. I barely thought about them. "What is he doing?!" my mind screamed.

"Al-e-esa!" He called in his singsong voice. Did he really think that would work? I wondered. He was taunting me. He knew I was here in the house. He wouldn't give up. "Go away, go away, go away!" my mind screamed. My traitorous mind tried to reason with me, "Get out of here. He won't kill you." My stomach churned. No. I couldn't. *I would die in the basement first*, I thought. With that grim thought, I felt calmer. I'd made a decision. I breathed in a little bit of air very slowly through my mouth and wiped my nose on my t-shirt with my left hand. I never took my right hand off the door above me, my only way out.

I suddenly missed my mom and brother. I desperately wanted to see them. The feeling surprised me. I usually didn't miss them or feel much of anything. The strength of my sadness threatened to make me bawl so I squashed it instead. I made a fist with my left hand and dug my nails into my palm to gain control of my feelings. The pain helped. I dug harder. I listened for noise. I hadn't heard him leave. My hand itched to push the door up and peek out for a second. It was too quiet up there. I knew he listened as hard as I did.

My heart skipped a beat. I tried to hold my breath for fear he could hear the ragged, small sounds. Before fear could overtake me again, a wonderful warmth invaded me. I heard a voice in my head warning me to stay there. I imagined an angel. He stood inside the bathroom on my trap door, his wings fully extended and his sword ready to strike. He wore armor and looked fierce with long, brown hair. This image stayed in my mind as I simply listened and tried to be as still as possible. I felt myself shrinking into a calm center of nothingness. I pulled my thoughts inward. The mental image of my guardian helped calm me considerably.

A minute went by and then two. I noticed faint rays of light seeping in from cracks in the foundation just enough to make out the boxes that Mom sometimes made my stepdad sort through. Edges of shelves that held our camping gear came into view. There was the shape of my kindergarten ballerina costume hung on a corner of the shelf. That ballet seemed like a lifetime ago when I was young and innocent. A new sadness settled in my heart. I missed my five-year-old self. I'd been very cute with brown hair, smaller, darker eyes than my sister and a pointy little chin. I remembered feeling happy.

My arm was tiring so I switched hands slowly, placing the left hand near the right before lowering my pained right arm in relief. I couldn't bring myself to look through the wooden stairs behind me. My back arched in a cringe as I thought of a face caught staring back at me, just waiting for me to look. I once again thought of my angel upstairs and felt warmth flood me again. I laid my head on my knees, welcoming the scent of my laundered pants. The fresh clean smell reminded me of Mom and everyday things that usually drove me crazy about her. As dysfunctional as they were, they were normal things for me.

Thump! The Creep's foot shook the door above my left hand and I jumped enough to almost fall off the steps. I instinctively grabbed it with my right hand as I pitched a little to the side. Slowly, I righted myself as he stepped again. The next slow step landed right on the trap door with a hollow thump. He passed over me and the next step brought him to the door leading into the hallway where he paused again. He slowly turned left and walked back into my bedroom. I leaned forward to rest my head on my knees and breathe the clean fabric and just listen.

He laughed wickedly, the sound muffled a bit. "Did I find you?" My closet doors squeaked open. I heard a rummaging sound as he searched through the pile of clothes and toys we had thrown in there to fool Mom into thinking we really cleaned our rooms. We sometimes had contests to see how fast we could throw everything in there and slam the doors shut before it all toppled out. Something heavy fell and rolled a short distance. He cursed and continued to sift through our pile of closet rubble that included clothing and plastic toys, army guys...oh, those were probably my Olivia Newton John roller skates that fell. They were just like the ones she had in *Xanadu*. I'd begged and begged everyone to pitch in a dollar here or there so I could get them.

"Well, you're not in here....maybe you ran into Mommy's room again? Well, come on, chicken! Come out. I won't hurt you. You know that! Come he-ere!" He sounded a bit impatient now. His steps clunked down the hall and past the living room to my mom's room. I couldn't hear what he said. Once he searched Mom's room he came back out into the living room. He became silent. I waited and waited for an eternity on the stairs and listened as hard as I could.

This was a battle of wills. I felt sure he was testing me as he sat on our couch or rummaged in our kitchen. I couldn't hear him but I was sure that he was still in the house. I hugged my knees and rocked a bit side to side to ease the numbness in my butt from sitting on the hard wooden steps. My legs shook badly now. I was damp from cold sweat. I waited and waited.

Every few minutes I thought I felt spiders on me and brushed spasmodically at my back and shoulders, hair, arms and legs to swipe them away if they were really there. I could see more of the room now and so I bravely lowered my head a bit more and peeked between my legs for a split second to the room displayed between the safety of my calves. No one stood behind me. I breathed a sigh of relief. I could see the vague gray outlines of boxes beyond the stairs and lined up against the back cinder block wall.

Sparkles showed dimly on the skirt of my ballet costume. My tiara was somewhere on the hanger with it. I had messed up that dance routine. When the other little girls had stepped forward to spin in slow pirouettes, I shook my butt at the crowd; when they shook their hineys, I did a slow pirouette. It was all okay though, I'd seen my mom's face and she was smiling behind her hand. I had skipped off stage, though we were supposed to walk slowly, and yelled, "Hi Mommy!" Nobody seemed to mind very much; in fact, they laughed. So I clowned around on stage for a minute before my teacher dragged me off.

Lost in that happy memory, I'd forgotten to pay attention. I felt like I had been down in this dungeon forever. My stomach growled in agreement. It seemed ridiculously loud. I didn't understand why he didn't throw that trap door open then and there! Thoughts of hunger disappeared when our front door slammed shut! Bang! I thought it might be a trick. I pictured him waiting outside the bathroom doorway. I swore to myself never to stay home alone again. This would NOT happen again, I berated myself. Just then I heard a wonderful noise.

His engine roared to life. I cried out at the sound and clapped a hand over my mouth to prevent more sounds from escaping. Miraculously, he sped down the dirt road past our house and continued until he rounded the curve that dulled the noise. I pushed the door up very quickly and would have shot out as fast as a bullet but my legs still shook and I couldn't stand up very well. I had no idea how long I'd been down there. I used my arms to leverage my body out of the hole. As soon as my legs were clear I swiped at the door to let it fall in place with a loud BANG!

I walked on numb, tingly legs to the door leading out of the bathroom and paused. The house felt empty. I knew he was gone yet all of the hair on my body stood at attention as I stood silently in the doorframe of the bathroom. I slid on silent feet, avoided the creaky board on the left, and made a determined line for the front door. I paused, about to lock the door, when I made myself open it instead. I stepped out on the porch. The late afternoon sunshine assaulted my eyes. I squinted. I could see no sign of him up and down the street.

Seeing spots in my vision, I turned to go back inside the house. As I did, I spied my stepdad's tool box on the porch. A hammer leaned against the siding of the house near the door. I opened the toolbox and found a box of nails, grabbed the hammer and went back into my house. I locked the door again, walked determinedly to my room, and promptly slammed the stupid window shut. Then, I nailed the bottom of our bedroom window frame to the window sills. I moved to the window over my brother's bed, too.

When I was satisfied that every window and door was securely locked and/or nailed shut, I relaxed and sat in the middle of the living room floor on the Persian rug with the hammer between my knees. When Mom came home, her face told me she was aggravated so I jumped to help her with groceries before she could nag me. My brother's dirty little face looked happy as he ran to me. "Give me a hug, little bro," I said. He jumped into my arms carelessly. His head butted me on the chin. I hugged his sweaty, boyish frame to me for a split second before he squirmed away. His overalls were too baggy and one shoulder strap forever slipped down his little arm. Right then I didn't love anyone as much as I loved him. His sun-bleached curls bounced as he giggled and ran up the stairs and inside the house.

I set a watermelon on the counter and walked up behind Mom. My hand reached tentatively for her shoulder. Her hair covered her face as she bent over to put cheese and milk in the fridge. When my hand landed softly on her shoulder she turned questioningly with a soft smile in her eyes.

"Hi, LeLee! Did you have an okay day, honey?"

She was smiling a very real smile. It wasn't forced. Her eyes looked sharp and lively. My mom was here. I shook my head.

Tears popped immediately into my eyes. I melted a little.

"No, I didn't, Mom." Her pretty brown eyes lit up in concern.

"Honey, what's the matter? Did something happen? We need to open some windows...get some fresh air in here. Are you still not feeling well?" She asked too many questions, too fast.

I shook my head. "NO... I was sick today. I.......I..threw up," I lied.

"Then there was...a man....and he was yelling and he was in our yard."

"What?! What do you mean in our yard? Oh my God. Yelling? Yelling at you? Did he hurt you? Let's call the police!" She started toward the phone.

"No. I have no idea what he looked like, Mom" I grabbed her arm, thinking fast. "He's gone now... I just... I kind of freaked out. Some of our windows wouldn't lock and so I just...uhh.... nailed them shut."

She stared at me as my lies sunk in and after a long moment nodded and put her hand on my forehead. She sent me to my room to lie down since I was "obviously still not well." To the comforting sounds of rustling grocery bags, I listened to her talk to Bruce on the phone while my brother whined for her attention. She woke me sometime later. Shadows stretched long fingers across the room. She merely tucked a blanket around my shoulders. I fell asleep again.

The Creep didn't visit for another six months. Bruce had decided to re-plaster a few walls in our rather old home. The Creep came over to help. He leered at me grossly. This time I sneered as if he grossed me out. My stepdad never noticed our exchange. When he walked by, I stepped wide of him and made sure to look him in the eye. Interestingly enough, I noticed we were almost the same height now. This made me feel less afraid instantly. I started to become vocal about how much I disliked his dirty clothes, his rusty truck, his old dog. I hated having him around and let everyone know it. At one point, my sister had asked me why I hated The Creep with an odd light in her eyes. I couldn't bring myself to tell her. By taking this stance, it seemed to scare him a little. His visits became less frequent until they tapered off completely.

If I'd thought Viana was a grim town, I was unprepared for the slums of Najera. Boarded up businesses and concrete apartment buildings with line after line of drying laundry spooked me. Grass grew in ruts in the roads. Blue arrows tried to lead less wary travelers to desperate businesses stuck between abandoned offices and businesses. People in doorways leered and smoked cigarettes furiously as if it would be their last. I took my headphones out so I could pay more attention and watched the shadows on either side of me. I walked along a grimy sidewalk over a bridge and finally into the main square where the familiarity of lounging pilgrims and bustling cafes was evident.

I turned down a dark alley and found myself walking past men who smelled like booze. They stared at me hard so I stared harder. Just when I began to think I would have to turn around and pass them again, I saw a blue tile on the side of a building with three stars. This meant a hotel was close! There would be no crowded albergue for me this night, I gleefully decided. I found the entry around the corner and walked in through a screen door and faced a man behind a glass partition.

"Hola, como está?" I asked.

"Bien! Are you American?"

I sighed. "Yes! I'm sorry my accent is so bad!"

He laughed. "It's okay, miss. How can I help you today?" His English was stiff and formal.

A few minutes later, I'd paid sixty euros for a private room, with bathtub, and a "free" bottle of wine. I couldn't wait to soak my body in hot water finally!

After settling in, I found some bubble bath in a basket placed near the tub and luxuriated in a long soak. Despite these efforts, my legs almost buckled from the pain in my feet—they were bright red like the rest of me from the heated bath, but they looked a full size bigger. The indentations on my toes were gone. I lifted one chubby red foot and placed it on the hard tile outside the tub and grabbed the counter for balance as the crippling pain nearly sent me head over heels. Then, I bravely set the red, pulsing foot next to the other and grimaced in agony as my bloated feet grew accustomed to my weight.

I dried off with one plush towel and wrapped it around my head. Of course, the hostels on the Camino didn't provide any toiletries or housekeeping items besides toilet paper—if that—so I took an extra bar of soap and toothbrush, just in case. I towel-dried my hair and dug out the knots with my comb. When I was tangle free, I lay in the middle of my bed to elevate my legs up the wall. With my blood flowing the opposite direction, I watched the plump blue, bulging veins drain into faint lines. As they did, some of the swelling in the other tissues seemed to ease. I fell asleep naked with my legs vertical.

I awoke later to find my legs still up the wall. I shivered with cold. There was a pounding pain in my heels. I investigated to find three-inch-long blisters stretched across the back of both heels. They were huge and puffy. It hurt to drain them but was necessary if I was going to walk in the morning. I punctured them with some sanitary tweezers and drained them. The pain was relatively mild as I pressed the fluids out.

Later that evening I limped to the plaza in my sandals because my feet were still swollen a half-size larger than normal. Also, the blisters had filled with fluid again and pressing on them hurt, so I decided to leave them alone until morning. As I left the hotel lobby, I was careful to avoid the dark alleyway with the smelly guys and safely ducked behind some other pilgrims as they made their noisy way to the square.

Upon entering the first restaurant I came to, I ran into Rick and Ross! I hadn't expected that. Both pairs of eyes widened at the sight of me and they waved me over to their table. Someone got up to make extra room for me. New introductions went around the table. I was impressed with the variety. I met a young woman from Hungary, a couple from Sweden, another from Germany. There was a handsome older couple from Nova Scotia who wore matching red polos and wire-rimmed glasses. We started with the usual conversation starter. Why are you walking? Immediately, the table became quiet when the wife explained that they were walking The Way for a miracle. He suffered from stage 4 melanoma. He didn't have long to live. He hoped to be cured along the walk to Santiago long enough to see his grandkids grow a little more and be remembered by them. After that story, I could not tell them mine so I made something up about a bad breakup and needing a long vacation.

Aside from his cancer, the couple laughed a lot and shoved more food at me. Since I'd arrived late, no one came to take my order so people fed me from their plates. I loved that. The food wasn't particularly good on the Camino but we found ourselves to be so ravenous that we'd eat almost anything. Rick and Ross walked me back to my hotel when I told them about the depraved-looking men lurking about in the alley. I felt grateful to have seen them again, but they made me miss Andrew.

"I thought you guys would be WAY ahead of me by now!" I said in amazement as we walked.

"We thought so, too!" Rick joked as he elbowed me in the ribs. I stumbled into the brick building we walked past. He laughed and righted me on my swollen feet.

"I'm sorry," he wheezed with laughter so that I glared at him with mock anger. "I got sick with a flu bug and couldn't walk yesterday," Ross informed me. "Much better now, though! Thank God!!" he laughed. "We'll make up for lost time tomorrow, don't worry."

"Well, it was great to run into you guys again." We'd arrived at the entry to my hotel. "Goodnight, you guys. Safe travels!" I hugged them both. They left me to walk into the entry alone. I staggered a bit drunkenly but made it up to my nice, cozy room with my very clean sheets. The unopened bottle of wine made me almost gag. There was no way I was going to haul that around in my pack, I thought. I had a funny thought that maybe that bottle had been gifted a few times and never drunk. I giggled at the idea. I realized I would not have to sleep in my sleeping bag tonight! The room was warm enough that I didn't need the extra blankets laid at the foot of my bed. I delicately peeled my sandals off my pounding feet and let them fall to the floor before I curled under the sheets in bliss.

I awoke to a dark room with an intense pain pounding in my feet. It hurt to even rub the sheets with my toes. To top it off, my heels burned where they pressed into the mattress. I gasped and sat up to pull the sheets out from under the mattress so they didn't put pressure on my feet. Once that was done, I gingerly touched my heels. The blisters had filled with fluid again and were hot to the touch. I hissed with the pain of setting my feet gently on the hard floor but stood carefully to shuffle my swollen feet to the bathroom. After soaking them for a few minutes, the blisters leeched their fluids again. Feeling better, I blotted my feet gently with a clean towel to dry them and settled into bed again.

CHAPTER NINE

THE NEXT MORNING, I TRIED a meditation exercise to get rid of the thoughts of pain. I inhaled a huge breath and let the air out as slowly as I could, trying to feel the pain recede. I repeated this exercise until I felt lightheaded. *Good enough*, I thought. Limping and sliding my way down the hall to the bathroom, I rinsed my face with very cold water, applied sunscreen to my tanned forehead and other exposed parts, pulled my hair into a ponytail and packed up.

No one attended the lobby desk, so I left my key in the mailbox as instructed and hit the pavement. Or, I'd like to think I hit the pavement. I staggered stiff-legged marionette style down the steps at an excruciatingly slow pace. People grimaced at the spectacle I made shuffle-walking to the bar. I needed coffee in the worst way and thought, *so what if I take a long time to eat breakfast*? I did not really look forward to starting my walk today. A cliff face loomed over the city, promising a long climb ahead.

As I sat observing the people coming and going from my little corner of the coffee shop, I grew nostalgic for the community and coffee shop I'd sold just before the trip. I hoped the new owner was doing well and pleasing everyone. I'd promised my customers, my community, that he would. It wasn't easy to walk away from all the wonderful people there who had touched my life. I stayed in contact with many of them through Facebook and was receiving texts from some of my best patrons. Their unwavering love and support throughout my trials the previous year had been just as strong as their support of me now, on my journey. Many said I inspired them. I didn't see how, but thought they were very kind. The mayor was known to come in late mornings in her slippers as she lived down the block from my store. In the early days when the shop hadn't been very successful, she often helped me wash dishes. I missed her greatly just then.

I'd grown fond of the people who inhabited my store on a daily basis. Many customers had been staunch supporters of the store since the day it opened, no matter that I was its third owner. We lovingly referred to them as "townies" because they valued my tiny community-centered coffee house in a busy tech world of Starbucks and name-brand everything. They stood up for the local businesses and supported me even more when I switched to a locally roasted coffee and offered ninety-five percent locally sourced products and food items. Though I'd come from the corporate world of new home sales, they had trusted me. I'd jumped in with both feet, thrown my suits away and bought t-shirts and jeans to live in. It had been bliss for a while.

They'd shown me what community meant. I hadn't known. Life had been busy. Previously, I commuted an hour each way on an average work day, sometimes farther. Then there was dinner to make and homework and chores. I rarely had time to breathe. These people were the salt of the earth types. They worked hard for their money. I made the rash decision to buy in the fall of 2008 when the economy had just crashed. Several of the die-hard regulars ate breakfast, lunch and dinner at the store in attempts to keep me afloat. I thought it was a beautiful gift they gave me and it made me more determined to last out the recession. I worked even longer, tougher hours that first year, typically putting in sixty to seventy hours. I did hang in there, but barely, and then in 2009 things became a little easier as, little by little, we gained more business each year.

This was also a community of artists and they made sure I appreciated it, too. They played music or taught art classes. Many were artists who drew pictures or painted and sold them in my store, gave massages, or tarot readings. Whatever they wanted to share at the store, I tried. They made sure I came to the music nights and game nights. I loved that they needed me to be there, wanted to talk and get to know me. They had grown fond of me and so selling the place had been a tough decision. I missed them all.

I took that moment to stand and shuffle my way out of the bustling café. The yellow arrows pulled at my psyche. I followed them out of town very slowly. My feet felt like they were still a bit swollen so I promised myself that I'd massage them at every stop today. Since things were already off to a rough start, my earphones were immediately stuffed deep into my ear canals and music blasted at near top volume. Muse's *Madness* came on and it was perfect accompaniment for my mood.

The trail was damp and slightly muddy now. The dirt was bright red, just like some of the red canyons in Wyoming I'd grown up around. I took a few pictures of the beauty around me. The road wound up and around and through a small canyon before dumping us out into more vineyards. I never tired of the view. This was enough to take my mind off my feet as I walked steadily for a while. A little over five kilometers later I made it to the tiny town of Azofra where I paused in a plaza with benches near an albergue. I threw my pack on the bench and immediately knelt down to loosen my sandals and sat to extract my feet. I lifted one foot to the opposite knee and immediately began to massage the whole foot from back to front and back again. I switched feet and repeated. Digging out my ibuprofen and, with a snack of yogurt and chocolate, I took four more of them. Now my knees tightened up every time I stopped and sat for a few minutes. I groaned out loud as I stood.

I don't remember much more of the walk that day except that I did everything in my power to forget about the pain by blasting my music and conversing to people who passed me, which was often and continuous since I was moving so slowly. By the time I'd gone ten more kilometers I knew I wouldn't make it to Santo Domingo where most of the pilgrims were aiming for that day. I shuffled up a long and steep hill before I spied a golf course.

Something seemed odd as I stared at the golf course that appeared like a mirage. Beyond the parking lot were rows and rows of nice-looking, recently built, modern apartment buildings. The whole picture shouted "civilization!" from afar. However, as each painful step brought me closer, I noticed the empty strangeness. There were no cars in the parking lot except for one yellow sports car. Other than that, there were was rows upon rows of vacant parking spots. I gazed carefully at the empty golf course greens.

Not one golf cart moved on the lawn. I slowed as the emptiness invaded my senses. No sounds emanated from the concrete blocks of apartments. Grass grew higher than my knees in the lawns, except one that had replaced the natural seed with AstroTurf. Windows, grimy with neglect, lacked draperies or blinds. Their dark sockets stared at me with despair. For-sale signs flapped on fences and glass panes. Such an apocalyptic feeling descended over me that for a moment I pictured slobbering zombies lurking behind bushes and fences. Not a single car passed as I followed my precious yellow arrows past these abandoned complexes. I took my headphones out of my ears to absorb this absolute desolation. No dogs barked.

Around a corner, I was led to a more familiar sight where the historic part of town now stretched before me. The steeple was humble and crumbling, but I thought surely there would be townspeople near the church. The arrows led me past medieval abandoned apartments instead of modern. Crumbled stone walls and shutters hanging askew greeted me with profound neglect. With a sinking feeling I found my way to an albergue that looked like the only inhabited space in a row of dingy ruins. The building's bright blue exterior popped out amongst the walls of crumbling stone that surrounded it. I raised my hand to knock despite a terrible feeling in the pit of my stomach.

If it hadn't been for my sore and achy feet, I would have kept going. I knocked one loud rap on the door before I could stop myself and flinched in reaction. The hair on my neck stood up in a warning. I waited for a long moment and was just about to leave when a window was flung open and a man's voice yelled, "Si!" I looked up reluctantly. This man glowered at me. His toupee seemed slightly small for his head. It sat up higher than a normal crown of hair. I stifled a nervous giggle and said, "Si... uno habitación?"

"Ah! Si! Uno momento!" He slammed the window again. The white door in front of me was flung open so quickly that I just blinked. He impatiently waved me inside. I hesitated at the rancid smell that wafted over me. The odor emanating from the entry reminded me of cat piss and mildew. I took one step in and told myself I would just look. The owner told me his name was Julio. His toupee leaned precariously as I shook his hand. He then asked me where I was from and demanded my passport and thirteen euros. I could tell that he quickly wanted to get this done, but the bad feeling in the pit of my stomach stayed.

I held up my hand. "Uno momento!" I gestured around the space. "I want to see it first." It was as cold and damp inside this place as it was outside. From the smell, I thought I'd rather take my chances out of doors than in here! I hadn't packed a tent but this seemed like a miserable place. I looked back at him. He still held his hand out for the paperwork.

"Do you speak English?" I asked impatiently.

"Muy poco...a little." he said.

"Do you have heat...fuego?" I asked as I wrapped my arms around myself and shivered. He shook his head and gestured impatiently at my shoes for me to remove them. I didn't.

"No, I want to see first..." He didn't understand that. He gestured to my pack and walked to the stairs and flung his body side to side, indicating a pilgrim walking up and scuffing his pack on the walls as he walked. Was he kidding? The place was in disrepair! Plain cinder block showed in patches in the kitchen and it was so cold and damp that the floor was slick with moisture. Rather than follow him, I impulsively took steps backward toward the door. I couldn't stay there. He started to follow and now he tried to smile, but it was too late. I apologized and backpedaled out the door to take a big gulp of fresh, cool air.

I stumbled on my swollen feet as I made my way over a little bridge toward the heart of Cirueña. Unsure if I would find better accommodations, I kept going determinedly. A few meters later, a more welcome sight greeted me, though this one was also surrounded by ruins—a nicely renovated building and a sign, Casa Victoria. I knocked on the new white metal door and waited anxiously. It wasn't long before a kind older man opened the door with a friendly smile and warm eyes. He gestured for me to come in.

It smelled clean. I relaxed. Their home had been remodeled with friendly earth tones. Dark wood beams sparkled with a coat of thick varnish on the ceiling. The Spanish tiled floors were immaculately clean. My host smiled and gestured to me to follow him up some stairs. He shook his head at my limping gait. We walked up to the next landing where he led me down a hallway to a real bedroom with carved wooden doors with lead handled knobs. On the way, we passed a room with small fridges and laundry machines. I nearly swooned. This place was cozy!

He opened the door to my room. I gasped at its beauty. Two wooden-framed twin beds were the only beds in there. More wooden beams ran across my ceiling. Pretty lamps stood on each nightstand. A tall wardrobe held lots of wool blankets. The best surprise was the private bathroom in this room. I was now grinning at the host. He only wanted to charge me ten euros for a private room and it was far better than the hotel I'd stayed in the night before, except for the tiny shower. I had wanted to soak my feet again. I turned to pay him but he waved me off and gestured around the room and at the bed.

"Siesta, peregrina!" he insisted. I felt funny about using the room before I paid, but he insisted. He quietly exited the room and shut my door firmly. I sat on the bed in wonder. This was a small paradise in the middle of hell, I thought. Where had this guy come from? The room was warm! I felt so thankful for listening to my intuition and leaving that other albergue with the nasty odors and odd host. I threw my pack on the bench in front of the bed and lay back admiring the room. The walls had been done in a warm lavender, which was a handsome contrast to the dark wood accents.

I walked back to the laundry room and grabbed a couple of snacks and a Sprite. I understood from the sign that I was to leave a donation, so I left a couple of euros and retreated back to my room. I loved these trusting people! Once I'd showered, I collected my dirty laundry and placed them in a pile with my other dirty items and fell into bed completely nude. It was the best nap I had on the Camino. I awoke two hours later feeling guilty for not paying yet. I reluctantly dressed and gathered my laundry bag and grabbed some money to pay the man. I didn't even know his name yet!

As I walked downstairs, I peeked into two more rooms and was happy that mine was the prettiest. I stepped carefully down the stairs and made my way to the proprietor's suite, knocking gently on the door. The sweet man opened the door and gestured me inside.

Francisco and Maria greeted me warmly. A toasty fire glowed from their hearth in the living room. Maria led me to a long farmhouse style table and told me to sit. They must have known I was up and about as Maria set a pot of coffee and cookies in front of me. When she saw my laundry, she took it from me and told me it would be two euros. I gladly paid her for the service and my room.

"Do you serve dinner?" I asked. He looked puzzled but never lost the smile. I made a gesture of eating and he shook his head and said, "Jacobeo" (referencing a local restaurant, I assumed) and pointed out the front door. He then held up seven fingers to indicate the dinner hour. Just then a big group of pilgrims came in. I was content to watch the newcomers interact with the owners. He took their money right away, stamped their credentials, and did not offer to let them have siestas first!

I felt special. He looked my way when the deals were done and gestured that he would be back.

Francisco was humming when he reentered his apartments. He had a plastic tub in one hand. Winking and pointing at me, he set the tub on the counter and rummaged in his cupboards. He located a jar of something that looked like dried orange peels and other herbs and placed a handful in a foil packet and placed this in the tub. Then he walked to me and held it out. I was confused as I took it from him. He gestured to my feet and held out his hand to help me stand up again. I heard him "tsk-tsking" me as we walked toward the hallway again.

When I got to my room, I opened the packet and found dried chamomile and other dried flowers inside! I filled the tub with warm water and sat on the side of my bed soaking my poor feet. I lay back sideways across my bed as my feet soaked and I fell asleep again. I awoke lying on my side with my feet curled up on the bed, dried flowers stuck to every inch of my feet. They actually felt better! I carefully drained and washed the tub and rinsed my feet before going back downstairs. I'd slept another hour and it was nearly time to eat. I was ravenous!

This time, I could hear lots of laughter and loud talkers in the room so I didn't knock but went straight in. Everyone paused to look at me. I recognized a few Italians with whom I had not had the chance to spend any time yet. I nodded at them, unsure if anyone spoke English. One of the men spoke up, "You are the woman from Colorado?" I nodded in surprise. They'd heard of me? His name was Ignacio and he was delighted to speak English! He'd been wanting to practice for a year since his lessons. He had a habit of licking his lips a lot and his nose was rather long and pointy. It tended to move when he talked. His brown eyes rounded and he leaned toward me with an intense energy. He didn't notice that I shrank back in my chair to create space between us.

I listened to his boorish ramblings, hoping that someone else would come in and divert his attention. Maybe he would sit by someone else or eat somewhere else, I hoped, and knew the chances were slim. I overheard a woman mention there were only twenty-seven people left in that town. Of course, Ignacio insisted on sharing a table with me at the single restaurant in town, Bar Jacobeo. The owner, who looked fatigued and worried, took our orders with hardly a glance at anyone. I looked toward the local barflies and counted four sitting with their backs to us. Their shoulders hunched over the bar as they drank. So, I'd now seen thirty percent of the total inhabitants in this dwindling town. I looked out the window at the bright beacon that was Casa Victoria, a haven in this forsaken place.

Surprisingly, my dinner was so delicious that I completely ignored Ignacio's ramblings while I dug in. I enjoyed succulently roasted chicken, roasted poblano peppers, tomatoes, and squash! I hadn't expected to eat so many vegetables in this squalid hole of a town. Of course, there were French fries. I focused on my plate in the hopes that Ignacio would stop talking to me. It didn't help. I moved my plate a bit rudely to the right as he sat on my left and I'd seen food bits fly out as he talked. Whenever he took a breath for air, I tried to engage someone, anyone else, in conversation but he appeared to be the only person who spoke fluent English, though I knew I had heard a woman speaking English in Francisco's living room. I became anxious as he talked and leaned toward me more. He moved his chair slyly toward me a half inch at a time. I knew there was little chance that he was a bad person; there was just an element about him that made me fear him. He'd taken overpowering control of our conversation and didn't pick up on the clues of disinterest I tried to throw at him. I felt myself growing angry, mostly at myself for lacking the ability to make him stop his obvious advances. Finally, as he attempted to put his hand on my shoulder, I stopped him with a glare.

Halfway through dinner, Maria arrived with a knit wrap in her hands. She placed it around me gently and patted my head before she winked and walked back to Casa Victoria. Yes, they were lovely people. She had done my laundry and so she knew that she was washing all of my cold-weather clothes! I sat here in my hiking skort and long wool socks pulled up to my knees for warmth. I smiled at her retreating back. I turned and was taken aback by the proximity of Ignacio's face. His pointed tongue flicked over his lips as he smiled. Disgusted, I stood to go.

"You can't leave, yet, my lady. It is not time to go. We have dessert and wine to partake of!" Ignacio protested. With a firm tone, I told him, "All of this talking has worn me out. I'll finish my meal in my room. Goodnight!"

"Stay, please? Just a moment more. I enjoy talking English to you!" He actually whined. A forty-five-year-old man whined at me. I hid my disgust as I gestured to the owner that I was ready to leave and threw my money on the table. My leftovers were boxed hurriedly.

"Ciao!"

"I'll walk you to your room!" he announced gallantly.

"NO! You will not. Goodnight." I left quickly. Once at my bedroom door, I breathed a sigh of relief. Remembering the gleam in Ignacio's eyes, I turned the deadbolt and, with the solid thunk of the iron bar, I sagged a bit against the door. I sat on the end of my bed and greedily ate the rest of my dinner. Afterward, I journaled for a bit before I watched television, hoping to soak up more of the language. I don't think it helped at all.

Surrounded by strange languages and circumstances suddenly made me extremely lonely and sad. I couldn't quite understand the forces that had driven me here to this strange place, strange journey. Right then, I wanted to go home. I couldn't even tell a pesky Italian I wasn't interested in his unwanted attention. I just wanted to feel normal and like all of the strong women in my life who I looked up to. Would I find love again? Some days I wanted a partner more than anything else in the world, other days I was glad to be single and free. I was so confused.

I knew that part of the fear was based on the past. "Ignacio was probably a very nice guy," I told myself, "it's just the past haunting you again!" I turned my eyes up toward the ceiling. "What do I have to do to become whole again? I'm tired of feeling inadequate. Tired of proving myself. Please help me here." I punched my mattress for punctuation. I was frustrated. I'd thought I was over the past, put it behind me. The recent events in my life had blown everything wide open again. My family members felt sorry for me. Sorry for me! I hated that victim mentality and strove to prove that wasn't really me anymore. But was it? Something always seemed to provoke my anger again. I had to get away from everyone. Was that why I'd come here? To be alone? I didn't want to be alone...well, maybe I did. A tear of frustration leaked out for not knowing myself better than that.

Why did it always take me so long to stand up for myself? I tended to trust people to the detriment of my own well-being. I rolled over on my bed with a growl, angry at myself again. I ran my hands through my hair in frustration as the examples of abuse in my life ran like a never-ending movie. I allowed myself to be taken advantage of until my anger grew to a point where I finally snapped and brought "judgment day" down on the person's head. Was there no middle ground for me? I didn't want to be living with such hot anger inside me.

In regards to The Creep, I did something they told me I couldn't do. Years had gone by since the last incident of rape when I finally stood, rather sullenly and feeling manipulated by my mother's intervention, before the local police as they begged me to testify. They told me their hands were tied as far as litigation because the statute of limitations said too much time had gone by. The most we could hope for was a "raised awareness among the community." I'd be helping other kids. That did it. I shrugged an agreement. They didn't know they were dealing with someone whose memory would recall incriminating evidence with minute detail despite the passage of time.

I woke up one dreary, unimportant winter morning shortly after Mom divorced Bruce. Renee and I had just entered high school. We were fourteen. We'd moved into a different house again and I had my own room. The chill of winter invaded my bones so I nestled down in my blankets, not looking forward to getting up. In fact, I spontaneously decided to feign illness. I wasn't sick—just uninterested in doing anything that required energy that day. I barely applied myself at school anyway, did just enough, but still received "good enough" grades. I couldn't become excited over anything, even the winter dance. My friends wondered why I wasn't more thrilled to be invited by a gorgeous high school senior named Mark. Mom was letting me go because she knew his parents and he was "a nice kid." The dance was a week away and I hadn't taken Mom up on her dress-shopping invitations.

On this particular morning I listened to Renee as she bustled around with her motherly duties, making sure our brother was up and getting dressed for school. I heard him complain loudly to her but his feet thumped on the floor. I pulled the covers over my head as she opened my door.

"Sissy! You're not up yet? Get up, lazy bum, it's time to go." She always called me lazy and she was right. I hated mornings with a passion and I was lazy. So what? There were enough people who rushed around and got things done to make up for my lack of effort so I didn't really care what she thought. She walked over to the head of my bed and yanked the covers off my face. I hit her on the arm.

"What's wrong with you?" she asked? Her hair was cut in an asymmetrical style that was longer on her left side. I wanted to laugh, though it was the current style.

"I'm not going today."

"Are you sick?"

"No. Yes...not really, well sort of. I just don't wanna go today." I thought maybe I was. I didn't feel quite right, maybe a bit more blah than normal.

She set her left hip on the bed and settled in. She leaned over me and I tried not to cringe from her nearness. She laid her warm hand on my head.

"You don't have a fever. Come on. Let's go. You're gonna miss the bus."

"You go. I'm not going today. Tell Mom for me." I turned over. She hugged me briefly and kissed my cheek. I wiped it off instinctively. She huffed and kissed me again and held my hand to my side. I felt the saliva drying on my cheek and nearly gagged.

"Take it...you meanie! Why can't I ever kiss my own sister on the cheek?" She sounded agitated.

I shrugged and wished I could let her kiss me without being

grossed out. A part of me longed to be normal like that. In my mind, I reached out and hugged her hard but couldn't bring myself to actually do it.

"Okay, silly, I'll tell Mom. You lazy bum." She said this tenderly. I heard her leave and softly close my door before I wiped the kiss off my cheek. I closed my eyes and listened to her and my brother leave the house. His voice was always so loud. He was complaining about walking and eating his toast at the same time as my sister hustled him off to his bus. The house was quiet. I was wide awake. I lay completely still.

Half an hour later I heard the sounds I'd been unconsciously waiting for. My mom moved around the kitchen. Instead of grumbling to herself like she always did in the morning if she wasn't downright yelling at herself, she was humming! I pushed my blankets off and belted my second-hand robe on, quietly opened my door and waited. I took one step down and sat on the landing just so I could listen to the sounds she made as she got ready. She sounded happy for a non-morning person. I worked my way downstairs until I glimpsed the edge of her yellow robe at the stove. She was making scrambled eggs.

She turned to me as I walked into the kitchen. Her eyes were clear and aware, calm without the frenetic energy they often had. She was here today. She came toward me and held her arms out. I sidestepped.

"Not feeling well, honey?" I shook my head, not sure of what to say. I couldn't fake being sick, obviously. I still had no idea what to say and so I stood mute. She swiped a hand softly down my arm before I could move away.

"Want some eggs?" She turned back to her pan. The moment hit me. This was a relaxed morning. Instead of a mom screaming at me about wearing too much makeup or making her late for work, she was being a mother! We usually ate a bowl of cereal for breakfast. I stared at the back of her head. I was so lost in the surreal moment that I blurted, "Have you ever known anyone that was sexually abused?"

As quick as they left my mouth I wanted the words back! I waited with my hands clenched very tightly at my sides. Her spatula stopped moving the slimy eggs around and hovered over the pan. She must have needed time to think because she paused like that for the longest moment. Then her other hand moved to turn the burner off. She turned with the egg-slimed spatula still in her hand, her eyes searched mine as she said very slowly and carefully, "No, I haven't. Have you?"

My heart lurched heavily. I put one hand over it and pressed, making sure it wasn't stopping on me. My throat wouldn't work and so I couldn't get any words out. My eyes filled with the long-ago unshed tears of my seven-year-old self. I gasped for air and nodded my head twice. I was horrified at the force of emotion that doubled me over in pain. My arms twined around my waist to hold it all in. Mom grabbed me and held me to her. I didn't have the strength to fight it. I sobbed one very long, loud and intense sob before falling to my knees with Mom holding tight to me. She tried to gather me closer but I shook my head as I fought for air and control of myself.

"You?! Honey, it was you?! Oh my God! What happened? When? Should we call the police? Oh my God! Talk to me, honey! LeLee, please." She was now starting to rock my rigid body. I cried harder and grasped her robes only to keep from falling over. She was starting to moan now in a low voice. The sounds disturbed me and I pushed on her harder but she wouldn't let go. Between moans she begged me to tell her more. "When? Who? Where?"

I couldn't speak yet and so we stayed locked in our half hug/half struggle while I waited for a bit of calmness. I finally shoved away from her and sat back on the floor.

Her hands groped to pull me in again. "Mom! Stop! I don't want to be touched!" This seemed to make her cry harder but she sat on the floor also, her eggs forgotten and spatula now stuck to the floor. She covered her mouth in an attempt to quell the sounds she knew I hated. With a deep breath I told her. "Jim. You always got mad at me for calling him The Creep..." She started to interrupt. I snapped, "Just shut up for a minute. I am trying to tell you!" She held her hand over her mouth and nodded at me. Her eyes were beginning to lose the consciousness that I prized. Afraid that she was going to her crazy place again, I quickly said, "When I was seven. Many times on and off over the years until I was almost twelve. There, that's it. I just needed to tell someone."

We stayed on the floor for almost an hour. I was relieved at first but watched in regret as her anger and sorrow transformed her. She began to wail and tear at her hair. She ranted about my stepdad being a prick and bringing that asshole into our home and hurting HER daughter. She screamed while I mentally gathered myself. She grabbed the phone in a white hot rage and told me she was calling our ex-stepdad. Too emotionally exhausted now to care, I nodded and walked back up to my bed where I stayed all day as I listened to her on the phone. She didn't stop with him; she called everyone in our family and cried all over again with each conversation. I slept on and off that day. She never did get dressed or eat her eggs and neither did I. Over the weekend, various friends, neighbors, family members stopped by to console her.

I watched it all from the top of the stairs. My sister came

to sit with me a few times and hold my hand. She whispered to me that she was sorry and hugged me softly so I wouldn't pull away. My brother just looked confused and tried to console me though he didn't grasp why everyone was so upset. White hot rage replaced the hollow feeling in my gut. She'd spent the weekend telling everyone we knew about the secret I'd held for so long and now they came to console HER. I decided then not to show such a weakness again to anyone.

The following Monday, school friends approached me with pity shining in their eyes. Apparently their parents had told them. I had listened while Mom told everyone we knew but didn't expect people at school to approach me about it. When my counselor, Miss Nancy, asked to see me, I went into her office as my rage rose around me like a cloak. My fists clenched at my sides as I listened to her offer to talk to me about what had happened. I stayed icy calm on the outside as the rage burned like an imaginary flame. I'd been completely exposed, my private hell blown wide open. "I don't want to talk about this right now....at school...if ever. I didn't give her permission to tell you...or anyone." She kept me in her office for a few minutes trying to dig my feelings out, but I refused to discuss it any further, agreeing instead that she could attend the police interview as a witness.

A short week later, Miss Nancy arrived at my sixth period class to accompany me to our "meeting" with the officers. She excused me from the rest of my afternoon classes after a brief conversation with the school principal. I was embarrassed to walk out of school with the school counselor. My high school crush was loitering in the hallway and winked at me as I shut my locker, Miss Nancy on my heels. I blushed pink and stumbled before I could say hi back to him, but by then he'd already turned around to face his own locker. "Get to class, Ian!" Miss Nancy admonished over her shoulder.

We arrived at the police station and were immediately led down a long, jaundiced hallway made nauseously ugly by florescent lighting. The officer opened an institutional metal door and admitted us into a rectangular room painted boring beige. I stopped dead past the entry. It appeared I had an audience. There were already four adults in the room. With Miss Nancy and me there were now six people in attendance. There were two male officers in their black uniforms, a female plain-clothes officer and a woman with soft blue eyes and frizzy blonde hair who was introduced as the police psychologist.

The female officer to my left smiled warmly at me. She had light brown hair pulled tight into a curly ponytail. Her sparkly blue eye makeup was applied heavily and her mascara clumped her lashes into a few thick triangles. I regarded her with total ambivalence though I was seething inside. No one told me there would be this many people! I'd been unable to eat anything for breakfast and now my stomach churned nauseatingly. No one else made any noise of any sort for a minute. There was not a nervous shift in a chair or a single cleared throat. The officer indicated a chair next to her on her right and sweetly introduced herself as Officer Jenny.

"Okay, Alesa. We know this is going to be very tough. Just let us know if you need a break. We'll be happy to get you something to eat or drink. Feel free to take your time with this. It's been a long time and you may not remember much, but we'll stay as long as it takes."

I swallowed a sneer. She had no idea how much I remembered and she was right, we could be here a long time.

"Can we bring you water or anything?" The thought of food

or water made me woozy so I shook my head.

"Let's just start," I said impassively.

"Okay. We've placed a recorder here so that we can capture everything you say and reexamine it after we are done. We don't want to lose any detail. However, one of our officers will take notes, as well. I'm going to open the first cassette and start the recording...if you're ready."

I gripped the wooden bar under the table and nodded at the recorder. She pressed the red "record" button and the cassette started to spin. I focused on that small moving part inside the machine so I wouldn't have to look at anyone's faces. I let my bangs fall forward to cover my eyes. There was a box of Kleenex next to the machine. I didn't want to cry so I found the burning flame inside and drew strength from that place of hurt and anger.

Officer Jenny started speaking. "This is a child abuse case we're calling Teague versus Griffin." She listed the date and time.

"Alesa, you claim to be abused by Jim Griffin. Do you remember the first time it happened?"

"Yes, I was seven," I said with complete detachment.

From there I recounted each incident. The location. The time of year. My age. His clothes and anything that made them unique. I described his girlfriends, his belongings, the things he kept in his pockets. His moles and scar on his thigh. All of this I did with complete and utter detachment as if someone else read it from a script. I watched numbly as my second tape was replaced with a third. I shook my head at the proffered water and refreshment; in fact, no one else ate either. The tissue box in front of me was now half empty though I had yet to grab one. Everyone else clutched them in their fists or twisted them around fingers like Miss Nancy.

Toward the end of the interview, my expressionless accounting seemed to have taken a toll on everyone else in the room. Even the male officers had grabbed tissues. The only sign of discomfort I showed was trembling in my forearms from pressing so hard on my legs. My muscles had been tensed for hours. I felt uncomfortable with their tears, yet also guilty over causing this heavy sadness.

Finally, I described the last incident when he'd broken into our home and I hid from him in the cellar. One officer struggled with his composure as he put both hands over his face. I sat in silence after that, unsure of how to indicate I was finished, when Officer Jenny asked me if that was everything. I nodded. Everyone leaned in to talk about the next course of action. I tuned them out and missed most of what they were saying. It was nearly seven at night, I was exhausted and terribly hungry for fried chicken.

Officer Jenny knelt next to my chair. Her breath hit my arm. I flinched and closed my eyes with the effort not to wipe at my skin.

"I'm sorry, honey." She leaned back but stayed face level. I was too ashamed to look at her so I pretended a fascination with the pattern in the tabletop Formica. "Alesa, you should know that you did very well today. We have a lot more detail than we thought we would ever get today. Sweetie, we are going to ask that when or if this goes to trial, you won't have to be there. We are going to bring him in for questioning. Our officers have been tracking him and we know where he is currently living. Are you okay with that?"

"Sure," I whispered. "Can I go home now? I'm very tired."

"Yes, Miss Nancy is going to bring you home now. Thank you for doing this, honey."

We lived in Wyoming for two more years and I never heard a word about what was happening. I tried to forget and reminded myself they'd told me too much time had passed. During my junior year, we moved to Colorado. We'd been in our apartment for almost a week when Grandma called with some urgent news.

"LeLee, it's your grandma," Mom's voice sounded strained.

Afraid that Grandma was upset with me for something since she never asked to speak with me right away, I dragged my feet all the way to the phone.

"Grandma?" I squeaked in a little voice. I cleared my throat.

"LeLee, I have some very big news. First, I want to tell you that I'm so proud of you!" I became perplexed at that. She'd never said that to me before. I looked at my mom. She was wringing her hands with anticipation. It looked like Grandma had filled her in on whatever news she had. She continued, "The first thing that I want to tell you is that Jim has been convicted, honey. He received a nineteen-year sentence...." I gasped. My heart dropped. I'd almost forgotten about the trial. They'd told me they wouldn't be able to prove anything...been too long, they said.

"The other thing is...Oh, this makes me all choked up!... Honey, you did something pretty major for the whole state of Wyoming, not just the city of Lander. You single-handedly changed the circuit courts of Wyoming! Your testimony was so well done, you remembered so much....the police were able to track him and use the evidence you gave to verify everything! You have such a wonderful memory! You should be proud of yourself. This means that they now have to investigate every single rape case in Wyoming no matter how longs it's been! Before your case, they turned people away if it had been over a year. They believed no one could remember enough. Well, your most recent episode at the time of your testimony was more than two years with the first incident being nearly seven years prior... You recounted everything with such clarity and precision...you had so much detail about his truck, the inside, his bedroom..." By now huge tears ran silently down my cheeks. I held one hand out toward my mom to keep her from grabbing me. Grandma cleared her throat twice. "So, now they are looking at all cases no matter how long it's been." At last, the enormity of the whole thing made me gasp. My knees almost buckled as I said hoarsely, "Thanks, Grandma...It means a lot. I don't know what else to say."

The black, varnished beams above my head wavered in sinuous lines and became solid again as I tried now to focus on the beautiful room Francisco had given me. I sighed and rolled over. My thoughts so overwhelmed me that I didn't get up to brush my teeth before drifting to sleep again.

CHAPTER TEN

Morning light spilled softly through my window. The warmth in my little room tried to lull me back to sleep. There was no one scrambling to race out the door, no talking or loud-stage whispers. It was just me and my comfortable cocoon. No floorboards creaked with activity. Everyone was still sleeping. I thought if I hurried, I could beat Ignacio and his group, get a head-start. I sat up cross-legged to check my blisters. They had dried into a hard, yellow patch of skin. Only mild pain remained along the bottom of my left foot. I massaged those muscles a few minutes before I stood. There was virtually no pain! I stretched luxuriously with a huge smile on my face. Feeling strangely peaceful and ready for the day, I washed up quickly. I stopped by the snack station and grabbed a bottle of water, orange juice, chips, nuts and a cinnamon roll wrapped in cellophane. I left some coins in the tray as I slipped quietly down the hall in hopes of sneaking out without waking the loud-talking Italians.

I hadn't had coffee but only six kilometers stood between me and Santo Domingo. I was looking forward to reaching this historical city. It had been named for Saint Dominic of the road. He'd left the church due to his illiteracy and moved to the area of Santo Domingo in the eleventh century. His passion had been for us, the pilgrims, and he spent a lot of energy making sure our roads and bridges were maintained along the way. I expected to see a lot of pilgrims there. The grand fourteenth century luxury hotel, the Parador, had been converted from a pilgrim's hospital to hotel. Mostly, I wanted to see a pair of chickens kept in the main church on the square.

I was murky on the details but apparently a miracle had happened there with a dead chicken, a love-struck woman, her lover wrongfully accused of theft and a hangman's noose. This story is told as "The Miracle of the Cock." Makes me snicker every time! Now the church had a special viewing box of two chickens that they rotate out with fresh livestock each week. How could I pass up the miracle of the cock? I snorted with laughter again as I quietly shut the front door of Casa Victoria behind me. Heavy hearted for a moment, I regretted not saying goodbye to Francisco and Maria. I prayed they were blessed with many pilgrims over the years who appreciated their hospitality as much as I had.

Completely uncaffeinated but hopeful, I reached Santo Domingo before nine a.m. I wound through the stone streets and aimed toward a café, ducking past a pair of women whose cigarettes dangled from their lips as they bent over occupied baby strollers. Their fingers searched for latches to unhook their precious cargoes as long, ashen nubs fell from their cigarettes unheeded as blue smoke curled inside stroller canopies. I hid my shock as they both looked up and nodded at me. I smiled back sickly and pushed into the smokeless interior of the café. I'd just settled into a chair by the windows when a cyclist with long hair nearly crashed into my window.

His eyes met mine. We both smiled at his clumsiness. He was gorgeous. His long hair was caught in a ponytail at his nape. His dark brows lifted in wing shapes from his large blue eyes. I toasted my cup to him as he laughed and came inside, sporting a self-assured gait. His flirtatious eyes were zeroed in on me. He said something fast in Italian. I laughed.

"No comprende! Do you speak English?" He looked crestfallen and asked me something else. I just shook my head and laughed again. He came closer to my table and peered at me as though I jested with him. I looked him in his beautiful eyes and just shook my head. He leaned down and kissed me on the cheek. Then he waved at me and went back to his bicycle. He'd only come in to say hi! I was flattered and smiled at him through the window. He clumsily pedaled away and I giggled at his wobbly path. He really shouldn't have been on a bike.

Perked up and smiling from the excellent coffee and the wild Italian cyclist's antics, I weaved through a sudden wall of pilgrims toward the Santo Domingo church. I entered what felt more like a museum than a church and waited in line to talk to a guy behind a big gray desk who asked me to remove my backpack and put it in a locker. I was instructed not to use flash photography. I had only come in to see one thing and sure enough, overlooking the elaborate, two-story tomb of Saint Dominic, was a built-in chicken coop with two live chickens! People reverently took photos of the fowl so I did the same, feeling somewhat silly for having taken the tour.

Leisure time over, I hit the trails with renewed energy but fought with Mother Nature once again. High-speed winds threatened to push me into traffic so that I walked at an angle into the wind. I walked now next to major roads, buffeted by big trucks and speeding cars, and taking rests on the wind-breaking side of trees and any low outcropping I could hunker against for a few minutes. My ears rang with constant wind and burned with cold, though I wore a hood. I crept down the trail to see a man rolled up inside his sleeping bag to escape the wind. After a few hours, I became a bit disoriented and wandered toward the middle of the road. Cars honked and whipped around me. There were no hostels along the way, so I had to keep going. Each step became a struggle to move forward rather than sideways. I cursed at the wind as it caught at my backpack. I felt like taking it off and chucking it into the bushes.

With only 1.5 kilometers to go, panic set in. My legs felt about to give out. I desperately prayed to not get killed by a car and for some extra strength. Just then, a rather wide, tall woman strode around and directly in front of me. She broke my head wind and I made a split decision—I stayed directly, unusually close behind her. A glance at her calves showed them to be larger than man-sized and very muscular. I was impressed by the size and strength of her. Her hair whipped close to my face but I didn't mind. I thankfully let her guide me and gave no thought to how she might be annoyed by my space invasion. I doubt she noticed. My huge, brawny savior led me right to the steps of an albergue. I veered off, never even thanking her as I threw myself into a chair at the check-in desk. It was only then that I wondered where she had even come from. For at least three kilometers, I had not noticed anyone behind me at all and she'd appeared when I needed her most. I thanked my guardian angels, just in case.

My forehead thumped hard on the desk as I clasped my hands over my ringing ears. My voice seemed to come from far away as I heard myself ask the woman if there was a private room. There was not, but plenty of beds. I chose one far away from the restrooms to cut down on the noise of people slamming the doors all night. Dinner would be pilgrim style and it would be vegetarian. I was delighted at that. I was so tired of spaghetti, chicken and pork. I nodded stiffly and glanced at a clock. There were three hours before dinner and my stomach already felt ready to attack my spine.

After sluggishly showering in lukewarm water and attending my aches, I tried to nap to make dinnertime arrive sooner. I slept for a few minutes from pure exhaustion but the ache of food deprivation drove me out of bed like a vampire seeking blood. I rummaged through my pack for any last crumb or scrap of food to stuff down my throat. I found a few crackers and the last handful of nuts. In one swallow it was devoured. My hunger was so vicious that it did little to calm it down. It shook me. I felt dizzy, so I got up and searched the whole building for any kind of vending machine but didn't find one. With resignation, I threw on my jacket, grabbed my purse and headed out to find a cafe.

Three minutes later, I was gorging on two slices of a mediocre-looking torta and sloshing it down with a glass of wine. Someone giggled as I raised the last bite to my mouth—I paused. Two pairs of eyes laughed at me, a man and woman staring at my carnal display. He leaned forward in a friendly manner. His wavy, dishwater blond hair was windblown. He had long eyelashes rimming bluer-than-blue eyes. She was a short, squat woman with laugh lines fanning her crinkled green eyes and round cheeks dimpled with her smile. I shoved the last bite in my mouth before engaging them in conversation.

"Sorry. That fucking wind today! Oh my God, I was so hungry...I think I still am."

Brita and Harri were Finnish. They told me in very formal English they had also been starving and stumbled here to find anything to eat. Between the two of them they'd had omelets, croissants, mochas, orange juice, olives, calamari and a cheese plate. They were still looking forward to dinner. I laughed at that. I was too!

Despite their laughs, sadness lingered in the lines of their faces. I took a deep breath, not feeling enough energy to find out their story just yet. I decided not to ask. When the wine and food kicked in, my fatigue decided to wallop me as well. I could sleep now! Having already showered and hung up my wet, clean socks to dry, I had an hour before dinner to collapse in my bed. We paid our tabs and walked back together, our heads bent down against the wind and shouting at each other above the brewing storm.

I lay in my bed, intending to check in with everyone on Facebook, but woke up with the alarm and the phone resting on my chest. The room was full now. People hustled around and gathered items to take last minute showers before dinner. My eyelids felt like lead. An older couple, clearly in love, held each other tightly in their little love-bunk. They nuzzled each other and kissed. My heart stirred with an intense, sharp longing. I sighed and tried not to stare at them as they held each other. It was too painful to watch them, so I rolled over to face the other direction.

During dinner, I chose a seat by Harri and Brita. An Irish man named David, with whom I'd sheltered behind a tree earlier, sat across from me. We laughed over our plight throughout the day and compared near-death stories as we dug into bread and wine. I asked him if he'd seen the large, muscular woman who'd saved me. He hadn't. As the scrumptious roasted vegetable paella was served, our conversation turned to the topics of our pilgrimages. Why were we walking?

David shared first. He was approaching forty and had never been married, though he desperately wanted children. In fact, he had been dumped in rather crazy fashion by his most recent girlfriend a few months previous. So, he needed to walk and gain some answers about himself on the journey. A shadow of sadness passed over his face. I took a long, fortifying swallow of my wine as the topic circled to me. I spoke of the changes that had barraged me all at one time. Their eyes grew wider and wider at each turn of events. I received a hug from Brita. Sympathetic tears shown in her eyes. She asked me if the cancer was gone. I didn't know but hoped it was. I'd lost my insurance with the divorce almost immediately after my last surgery.

When everyone's eyes rounded in concern, I deflected more questions and insisted my turn was over. Harri and Brita paused as they exchanged a soft, worried look between each other. They gathered themselves with deep breaths and launched into their story. Harri talked about the famous iron cross, Cruz de Ferro, along the Camino trail. All pilgrims bring a rock or two from home to lay at the base of the cross with any message, prayer or intention to leave at the base of the mound that has piled up over the last thousand years. I had opted for a shell from the beach in Miami and had collected small pieces of quartz or shiny stone along the way to add. Upon going to the cross, we would climb up the hill of rubble that pilgrims had been leaving there for a millennium.

He spoke of his son in the past tense. My eyes teared up before he could say it. He confirmed the worst when he said, "We carry pieces of… Emil's… our son's tombstone. We chipped pieces off at his funeral…" He pulled something out of his back pocket and showed us a piece of white marble. "…He was twenty-nine. He took his life." I now had my left arm around Brita's round shoulders. David held his filthy dinner napkin to his eyes as he shed tears for this couple. I was amazed at their strength and courage. To be there, so strongly together and loving each other, and having such a hard mission...I had thought at one time that things couldn't get worse. Again, I was grateful for my daughter and her health.

The rest of our dinner conversation was somber. There was no way to pull it out of the morose thoughts that plagued us. Losing a child would indeed be the hardest thing in the world to deal with. That night I sent Parker an email telling her how much she meant to me and how I couldn't wait to wrap my arms around her. I slept soundly in my bunk set against the far back wall.

CHAPTER ELEVEN

By eight a.m. the next morning, I'd already eaten breakfast and finished my third cup of coffee. My pack waited for me, leaned against the hallway wall outside the dining room. It felt like an old friend that waited for me to pick it up and shrug into its comforting embrace. I hurriedly said goodbye to everyone and stole extra fruit for my pack.

A few minutes later I sheltered in the doorway of the albergue, glaring at the heavens as rain fell in slanting sheets across my line of vision. To my right, under the awning, a couple of pilgrims fortified their lungs with cigarettes while they too grimaced at the skies. My humungous maroon poncho fell almost to my knees, though it happily covered my pack, too. My feet were going to get soaked. I wondered how long the bandages would stay stuck to my blisters. With a big sigh of resignation, I shoved myself out the doorway and launched out onto the trail. My backpack creaked as I moved, the sound my sole accompaniment in the downpour.

I walked with my head down against the onslaught of rain. Traffic nearly blew me sideways a few times. It was impossible to hear the cars approach; the drivers seemed to be going about eighty to ninety miles per hour and with no shoulder on the road. I became pissed off at whomever had let the trail run along that dangerous stretch of road and entertained thoughts of yelling at someone on the Compostela committee when I reached Santiago. My nerves were frayed with the intense concentration it took to not get killed by the time I reached Belorado, a midsized town of about 2,000 people. The place was half-wrecked, of course, but I was too pissed at the unsafe roads combined with unrelenting weather to take notice of architectural details. I needed a café badly, but this time I craved a couple shots of whiskey to go with my bad mood.

In due time I found myself at the bar with a shot of whiskey in one hand and espresso in the other, unsure which to down first. For a distraction from the hellish journey I had embarked on, I surfed the WiFi and found a touching and hilarious message from my daughter.

> Hi Momma! I sure miss you toooo! Holy Crap when are you coming home? I'm having fun with Aunt Renee, but Soren and Alec are driving me cray-cray. Mom, why are all my cousins boys? It pisses me off. Just kidding but not really.... It's not FAAaaair I'm the only girl. They don't play nice and they don't do what I want them to do. Well, sometimes they do. We have a cool babysitter when Auntie's at school. She takes us lots of places and is wayyy cool. You would like her. How is your hike thingy going? I hope you are getting some rest and having fun and not walking allll day. Crap, that would be boring. I'm so glad I'm not there...but keep sending pictures and are the boys cute over there? Gotta go now. Love ya. Bye. Xoxoxoxoxo!!!

She seemed like her nearly thirteen-year-old self. Apparently, she thought she was safe to curse since I was so far away. I giggled at her nerve. I would never have said those words to anybody in my family! We were going to survive this. I had promised to take her on a trip to California when I got back. I missed her huge, expressive eyes. They were an unusual color that could not be defined simply by "hazel" and included blue, gray, green, as well as the browns and golds. They could be more green or blue depending on the color she chose to wear. Her honey-colored hair hung to her waist in soft waves and she had the cutest little nose on the planet. Many girls would envy that nose someday, I always told her. She possesses an unconscious grace and towers over most of her friends. Her one bad habit is cursing like a sailor. She gets it from me and there is nothing I can do about my mouth. I've tried. I typed her a message back, sure to fill her in on the sights, sounds, and yes, the dark-haired boys.

The whiskey burned a path to my stomach as I cringed at the sting of alcohol. I ordered another as I chased the first with the espresso that had gone cold. Now I shivered in distaste. I truly was a coffee snob and espresso should never be drunk cold. An hour later, I was reenergized with caffeine, alcohol and my daughter's encouraging words.

As I'd sat feeding my self-pity shots of whiskey, the cafe filled with a pleasant crowd. French, Australian and Japanese accents mingled in the air. Despite the various nationalities in the room a common, unspoken language could be witnessed while watching pilgrims interact with each other. Though most of the time we could not speak to each other, we could share much with simple facial expressions and bodily gestures. This phenomenon made me wonder if words were really necessary. I smiled at a woman across from me who limped painfully to her table. I winced and pointed to my feet, too. She nodded in sympathy for me as I did her. That was the beauty of this pilgrimage.

My friendly overture brought her over. I smiled at her as she took the empty seat next to me. She introduced herself as Nicola. She was very cute with dimples that creased her cheeks. On the heavy side, she revealed she was only walking half the distance each day "as everyone else" because her ankles swelled badly after five to ten kilometers. She unwittingly pulled me out of my bad mood so that I stayed an extra hour while she ate and refreshed. I convinced her to have a shot of whiskey with me. After which, she ordered a beer. I liked her immediately.

Nicola had almost quit the Camino twice. Her eyes filled with tears as she described her tremendous physical pain. Along with that came a shattered heart. Her boyfriend had broken up with her because she couldn't lose the extra weight. He had threatened her over and over that he would, but she hadn't thought he would actually do it. She walked the Camino in hopes to win him back. I held my tongue and listened a while longer because there was so much I wanted to say. I decided we should be friends for at least a couple of hours before I set her straight about what a jerk he was!

Sadly, she continued as we made our way back outside, "I know I am fat. People tell me that. My father, he tells me this a lot. My mother, she is large but not SO big, you know. My boyfriend, he never told me I am pretty. 'Nicola, you WOULD be pretty if you lose weight,' he says." My heart felt sad for her. She needed to find a reason to walk this for herself or she would probably quit. I'd seen that happen many times already.

"Is that really why you are walking the Camino....for an ex-boyfriend, Nicola?"

"Yes. I would like for him to see that I am trying to do something very courageous and say, 'You are the woman for me always.'" She wiped her nose on the back of her sleeve.

"Honey, you need to find out why you are walking this for yourself. No one can walk for someone else. You won't change him. You have to change yourself! I don't mean losing the weight, sweetie. Lose it if you want to, but it won't guarantee your happiness!" I always wondered where these nuggets of wisdom came from and how come I couldn't counsel myself in the same way.

"I think there is a reason I ran into you today. I needed to hear that very much. I don't like it so much, but I have heard you."

The highway we tread on passed through the middle of Villafranca. It was what we called an "eyeblink town" back home. Blink your eyes and you've passed through it. In fact, the tiny market we ventured into was really a bar that offered two shelves lightly stocked with a paltry selection of food items. I found some chocolate and fresh bananas, bought more tuna and crackers. I looked at the sad barkeep who listlessly ran a rag down the oiled wood bar. Not a soul sat in the bar. I knew it was early and hoped maybe people would come as the sun went down. I paid for my items and tried to smile at him but he only looked through me with a bleak expression. Nicola and I split off at the only junction in town. She wanted cheap and I needed something a bit nicer. We promised to find each other in the morning for coffee, if not for dinner.

A castle-like hotel waited majestically atop the hill for me as I approached like a lumbering yak. My purple rain poncho covered my whole body down to my knees, making my shadow look like an oddly morphed camel. Out of breath, I walked through an enchanting wooden arched doorway that opened into a wide courtyard. The lobby was handsomely decorated with creams and mauves. An overly friendly, short man stood waiting with wide eyes behind black-rimmed glasses and a huge, toothy smile. His name was Emilio and he immediately told me I was his soul mate and should move to Spain, before he winked to let me know he was kidding. When he found out I was from Colorado, he nearly swooned in delight! Apparently, he loved Americans a whole lot, as his lingering grip on my hands proved. He gushed, "I want to move back to the states! I lived there for one year in college. I love America! My family is training me to run their hotels and this one has been in our family a long time, but I don't want to stay here....Take me with you! There are only a hundred people in this whole town. Can you imagine trying to find your soul mate in this town?" He wiggled his eyebrows at me. He was so excited that, had I not been holding my money out and waving it in his face, he would have forgotten to ask for it. He shut his rambling mouth and led me back out through the courtyard and around the side of the building to a side entrance where we smelly pilgrims could befoul the air without offending the other patrons, I gathered.

He opened double doors to a room that held twelve twin beds, rather than bunks, and they were semi-private with waist-high walls dividing them into pairs, three to each side. A nightstand was set between each pair of beds with an electrical outlet above it. I chose a middle cubicle on the right side of the room, not wanting to be near the door nor the tall windows at the end of the room, which could either be chilly or let in too much morning light.

Suddenly claustrophobic, I dumped my rain poncho and pack into a careless heap and crawled onto my bed. I pushed my legs up over the half wall, letting the blood drain, not caring that my feet stuck up in plain view. I put my headphones in and tried to relax my tense shoulder muscles. My feet moved to the beat of *Sometime Around Midnight* as I closed my eyes. I opened them a few songs later to find a pair of inquisitive, smiling eyes regarding me and my suspended feet.

That was how I met Nacho. The single most beautiful and amazing man I had met so far on the Camino, I was convinced. His whole face looked happy to be alive and he was good-looking, too. His wide mouth stretched in a smile as he pointed at my feet and said something. I had been staring so hard I forgot to take my headphones out!

"What!? Sorry, what did you say?"

He laughed. "What you do? With feet?"

"Oh! Well, my feet were hurting from all of the walking and so I am letting the blood drain downward and soothe the muscles."

He looked as if he didn't understand. He chose the bed on the opposite side of the room but directly across from me. I sat up fully aware that I had not showered and my hair was probably...definitely a greasy, tangled mess. I nervously smoothed my hair with my hands. He sat down and looked at me.

"My feet...they are broken!" he laughed. "Thirty kilometers!"

"Wow, that is a lot!"

He turned and began to unpack in that bed across from me though the room was empty and he could have slept anywhere.

"I am Alesa. What's your name?"

He grinned at me, showing his nice white rows of teeth. "I am Nacho."

My whole face tried to betray me and I fought to keep it smooth and expressionless. *Who knows*, I told myself sternly, *your name could mean salami in his language.* I wrestled but a small snicker escaped before I could control myself. I covered it with a fake sneeze and chastised myself for being an ignorant fool.

"You ...uh...have...not eat?" he asked hopefully as he leaned toward me.

"No! Nothing yet, how about you?"

"I...shower." He grimaced as he pulled at the shirt glued to his sleek muscles. He looked fine to me. "Then maybe eat a dog! You come!" His English was adorably horrible.

I shot up to my feet. "Okay! Okay, lemme grab my things and get ready and meet you back here? Or there? Meet here or there?"

"Here or there?" He sounded confused. He took out his iPhone and fiddled with an app. I was slightly annoyed until he spoke into it and asked, "Here or there?" I promptly heard an Italian response. He nodded and pointed "here."

Twenty minutes later I sat on my bed and brushed my hair while I waited for him. He limped toward me with a huge smile. I fought valiantly to remain unaffected by his physical beauty. His body was sculpted out of pure muscle. He wore a tight blue shirt that showed that he didn't have an ounce of fat anywhere. His shoulders were nicely rounded and I could see his carved biceps through his long sleeves. His waist narrowed to a nice V shape. I envisioned following him all the way to Santiago even if I had to walk thirty kilometers a day.

He inhaled and gasped as he limped, yet he never lost the humor in his eyes. I told myself the least I could do was hold his arm and offer some support to the restaurant. He grabbed a huge and expensive camera from his backpack, slung the strap over his neck. I grabbed my valuables as well, and offered my arm out of total sympathy—at least that's what I told myself. It took us a while to get there as he gasped. I wondered if his feet were truly broken.

Nacho was the quintessential Italian romantic. He offered me the first bite off all of his dishes and refused to eat unless I did so. He was extremely caring and sweet, without being a smarmy charmer of a guy. After the first course, I couldn't help it, I asked him where he got his name. After finding the right translation to explain it to me on his iPhone he told me it was a "very prestigious" name, handed down in high honor! I couldn't help giggling. "Why is funny?"

"Because in my country you are a delicious snack!" His gorgeous eyebrows winged upward in mock horror. I laughed so hard I wheezed while he looked confused and spoke very clearly "Dee-lish-us snack" into his iPhone. When the translation came I was nearly under the table from laughing so hard. He joined me. We slumped in our chairs with muscle-numbing mirth. I tried to explain that nachos were chips and cheese sauce. This made me laugh harder. Just when I thought I had my tears of laughter under control, he leaned forward and said, "Chips and cheese sauce." The translation came back, "Chips con salsa di formaggio." His shoulders shook with laughter.

Dessert came and he laid his fork in my hand. "Try please," he ordered in a polite tone. So our night went. We laughed and translated more than half of our conversation. I told him how I almost brought my favorite item with me but I had decided not to and now I regretted it.

"What did you leave at home?" the translator asked me.

It waited now for my English to translate for him. "My hammock."

His eyebrows shot up again and he put his hand on my arm as he spoke into his phone.

"I brought mine. I use it all the time."

"What?!"

Turns out he had the same yellow slashed with blue nylon camping hammock as me.

"You're going to have to show me when we get back," I spoke a bit more slowly.

"I will show it." This was said looking into my eyes, his were crinkled at the corners. His mouth quirked upward a bit.

The beds were full so we quietly said goodnight. He hugged me in a very nice full-length squeeze that turned me into jelly and then kissed both of my cheeks warmly. His breath lingered on my face and it didn't feel bad at all. My smooth cheek rubbed his stubble as I turned away to find my bed. As we climbed into our separate bunks, we had to face each other. He caught me staring then held his bag open! I was so very tempted but I shyly shook my head. His white teeth flashed in a grin as he whipped his shirt off. I sat there shocked at his rippling, smooth muscles. I swallowed hard and stared as he wiggled out of his pants, too. Then he blew me a kiss and winked at me. I could not sleep that night.

CHAPTER TWELVE

THE NEXT MORNING I WOKE up to find that my delicious snack had already packed his bag. He sat on his bed waiting for me to open my lazy eyeballs. He came over silently and knelt in front of me.

"It was a great day when I meet you. I go another …. thirty-five kilometers today, so I go now. I hope I see you again on Camino, Alesa!" He kissed my cheeks and held my right hand in both of his large, warm hands for a minute. Then he left. I felt sad! I watched him go. At the door, he turned and waved before disappearing down the hall. I had grown used to saying goodbye to new friends on this journey, expected it, but I hadn't been ready to say goodbye to Nacho! I had secretly called him "Chip" in my journal. It was then I remembered I had not seen his hammock. For some reason, this made me want to cry the most. I had at least hoped to have coffee with him.

Wistfully thinking of Nacho, I enjoyed a breakfast of sunny-side-up eggs, yogurt and lots of toast accompanied with marmalade, and washed it all down with three cups of coffee. Nicola found me just as I paid my tab. I stood and greeted her with a smile and hug.

"Are you ready to go?" she asked.

"You bet. Just going to brush my teeth and use the facilities before we go. I hear it's a tough climb today!"

She cringed and made a face. "I hear that, too. There are three peaks indicated on the map and they look steep on the down side!"

I was secretly thrilled. Though the terrain was gorgeous at every turn in the road, the trail was mostly flat. I missed the mountains back home.

We caught the trail right at the courtyard exit and began the uphill climb almost immediately. My breathing was even and steady, my legs worked in synchronized fashion with my breathing. It wasn't long before Nicola was falling behind. Her face bloomed red as she began to sweat. I showed her a technique to walk in zig-zags from side to side up the hill to cut down on the angle of the ascent. She tried that and gave me a weak thumbs up. I told her I would wait at the top of the rise for her. I continued my climb and smoothly outpaced many people. Once I crested the top, I waited a few minutes for Nicola's head to pop up. When her grumpy face came toward me, I patted the log I sat on. She staggered over to me and promptly drained half her water bottle.

"Look. Why don't you go on ahead? I am going to really slow you down today."

"Are you sure? Do you want some of my water?" I asked.

"Absolutely, I will be fine, just very slow! I'm going to take long breaks, too."

She patted her camelback in the side pocket of her pack and said, "I've got extra inside, too."

"I'll meet you in the next town for a coffee, then!"

She nodded and continued to sit while I took off again.

Surrounded now by forest trees, I listened to the wind sighing and softly rustling the leaves like chimes.

An arrow was laid directly in the middle of the path with

loose, palm-sized stones. I wondered how fresh it was and if someone was lost. Sometimes pilgrims left signs or writings for people who they missed, directing them to where to find their party. This was just an arrow about two feet long. I walked carefully around it in case it meant something important to someone. Another fifty yards there was another arrow right in the middle of the trail. I wound carefully around that one as well. Another short distance and another arrow appeared but this one turned sideways to the right. Curiously I looked just to the right of the trail and saw my name spelled out in small pebbles on a flat rock next to the trail.

A wall of trees stood to the right and before my eyes scanned their depths, I knew what I would see. Not far inside the forest wall a bright banner of blue and yellow stretched above a span of forest floor. In the middle sat Nacho. His feet were planted on the ground as he steadied himself. He lifted his camera from his lap. He snapped a photo of my silly, smiling face as I approached. Once inside those sheltering trees, the world seemed to recede and grow quieter. His eyes simply watched me. Their depths were hidden in this half-light in the trees but his soft smile encouraged me silently. I nodded. His smile stretched in a grin.

His boots were untied and loose so he lifted his feet clear of them and stretched out inside his hammock. I knew it was a two-person hammock, same as mine. My pack dropped heedlessly to the ground. He waited with his left hand holding the side open for me. I sat very carefully on his left side and tried not to topple onto him as I rolled in. I wasn't very successful. There was a bit of confused grabbing and pushing as I straightened onto my right side with my head resting on his left pectoral muscle. His whole body was very hard and unyielding but when he wrapped his left arm over me, it all felt right. The sides of the hammock rose above our faces. This meant our only view was either each other or the tree tops towering over us.

At that moment, I admit I forgot that I was on the Camino somewhere in Spain and that I'd been metaphorically flogging myself the whole way. There was no room for self-pity or any ill thoughts. I was content to listen to the sound of his steady heartbeat with my right ear and the sound of the wind in the left ear. I didn't know him, but I knew his character. I could see it plain as day on his open, handsome face. I looked up at Nacho and impulsively kissed his cheek for this surprise. I'd never been given such a romantic, impulsive gesture in my life. My muscles relaxed. In fact, Nacho's breathing had evened out so that I knew he was dozing. I decided to do the same. Within a few minutes the rhythmic sounds of his heart and the wind in the trees cast their spell. I slept soundly.

I awoke to Nacho holding his right hand over the chilled left side of my face. My right arm ached from lying on it but I didn't mind. The rest of my body was toasty and warm, if slightly uncomfortable. He stretched his long, muscular legs and brought his right thigh over both of mine. I looked at his gorgeous, chiseled lips. His face lowered to mine. He gave me the softest, sweetest kiss I'd ever experienced. He brushed my lips twice more with his before I reached up with my left hand and pulled him closer. This time he kissed me properly. It was strong and vital. I clung to him with my left arm, my head whirling from the power of his embrace. Before I was ready, he stopped the kiss.

We snuggled and kissed some more, but we both sensed this was not the place or time and we sadly parted our lips the final time. I forced myself to get off of that beautiful man and clumsily dumped myself out of the hammock, trying not to hurt him on the exit. Nacho swung his long legs over and to the ground and easily stood up. I helped him unhook the hammock and pack it back up. Before I could put my pack on, though, he snagged my arm and pulled me into another embrace before we stepped out of the trees together with passion-bruised lips.

We walked in companionable silence for a time with frequent smiles. We paused by a Camino de Santiago sign that showed a map of the region. Nacho took a photo of me looking out over the valley below us. We were now in the Burgos region. I had done some calculating of the kilometers that remained to walk to Santiago and the number of days I had left. I would need to take a bus, pass the meseta section of the Camino, and jump ahead to León. Sadly, I knew that only if Nacho continued to walk thirty-five kilometers or more per day, he could potentially catch up to me. Most likely, it would not happen and my heart was a little glad. I didn't want to fall in love with someone a world away from me! Or did I? I told myself I didn't.

Along the way to meet Nicola, I made a mental note of the things I liked about him. He felt light and joyful to be around, as if he were truly happy. This is what I wanted in my future, a man who was happy to be alive, who genuinely gave of himself. Someone who loved people and shared what he had with them. Nacho had a zest for life, anyone could see it on his face. I would never fall for a wounded, sad man again. No, I needed a whole person, a man who was content with where he was in life. A man who knew himself and was happy with that. I was grateful that he had spent a bit of time with me to show me how a good man behaved. I didn't tell him any of that, but I wished I had.

We came to St. Juan de Ortega and there was Nicola at a table. I wish I had captured the sheer surprise on her face when she saw us. She must've thought I'd gone on ahead and left her far behind. I blushed furiously. Nacho almost glided beside me. The man was very graceful even with a backpack and "broken" feet. He went inside to order us coffees while I laughed at Nicola's sputters.

"Wha....? WHO is that? I thought you went on ahead! You found a man in the woods? Tell me, are there more of them? Ripe for picking?" I doubled over with laughter as I quickly tried to fill her in.

"Ohhh...my God......Really? Oh my God. That is the most romantic and beautiful story I've ever heard. If you're not gonna keep him, may I? I mean, look at him. He is perfection."

Just then he reappeared with three coffees balanced in his large and capable hands. He set them down in front of us and went back inside for sandwiches that he'd ordered. He'd stuck a long loaf of bread into a side pocket of his pack. He set a sandwich down in front of me and Nicola. She started to protest, but I waved my hand at her. I explained his limited English and that he'd just done it because he is generous and it would have been too much effort to ask us what we'd like without his translator working. There was no WiFi in this tiny village, for certain. I tried to pay him for at least my share but he wouldn't let me. We enjoyed our food while Nicola made baby doe eyes at him.

When we finished, I turned to Nacho. He'd told me he needed to catch up to some friends who were meeting him. He still had a long walk ahead of him today.

He clasped my hands, his eyes a bit sad.

"Your hammock...was good thing?"

"So good, Nacho! Very good! Thank you! I can't imagine a more romantic gesture. It was a beautiful morning... I.... know you have to go now and you move so much faster than I do.

You still need to go twenty-five kilometers today and you need to catch up to your friends..." I hoped he understood most of what I said.

"Yes, I must go. Alesa, I enjoyed...with you...in hammock.... and eating foods. We laugh....a lot... I am glad you are here on Camino. I leave you one kiss." With that he pulled me toward him and gave me one of those soft kisses. It was perfect. Nicola and I wistfully watched him leave. We sighed in unison when his pack disappeared from view. She turned to me with one eyebrow raised in mock accusation.

"They say everyone is offered a romance on the Camino!" Her eyebrows waggled at me. "I don't believe you... Did you really not....make love?"

"No!" I squeaked. "I couldn't...I mean. In the trees? No, I hardly know him....I don't know if I could have stopped him if he tried. He was so powerfully sexy..." I trailed off remembering his kisses.

We continued down the trail obsessed with Nacho, devising schemes to see him again, though we knew they were futile. It was only then that I realized I hadn't asked for his contact information. I almost threw my backpack on the ground. I couldn't believe how idiotic I'd been in this digital age! We could have been Facebook friends. I was lost in the joy of being with him for a little extra time and hadn't stopped to even ask his last name. I gasped at the thought. Now I was horrified that I'd kissed and snuggled a guy whose last name I didn't know! My grandmother's disapproving face popped into my mind. I pushed it away and dreamily let Nacho's visage float into its place.

That afternoon, I walked as far as I could, which was about twenty-five kilometers, before I had to find a place to stay the night. As four p.m. approached, my feet became bloated and sore. In desperation, I changed my tennis shoes for the walking sandals since they were softer. As I sat massaging my feet, I noticed the city of Burgos in the distance. Even with the change in shoes, after a few kilometers I was limping again. Nicola had suffered such pain in her knees from the previous hills that she'd decided to forget the last climb of the day. She'd stayed in Atapuerca, where there is a collection of prehistoric caves that claim to hold the oldest remains of homo sapiens in Europe. Historians claim our ancestors here were cannibalistic. Nicola loved archeology and was happy to stay and investigate these sites for a couple of days. We hugged goodbye and, for some reason, we didn't exchange personal information either. I began to think, "This is just the way. There are no expectations here. No pressure at all except to dig deeply inside oneself and be open to the miracles along the journey."

Just outside of Cardeñuela, I happened upon an old stone home that had been turned into an albergue. It was charming in its medieval way with rugs and blankets thrown over couches and chairs, but also cold as stone. The afternoon had become gray and drizzly again. I shivered as I stood at the desk and requested a semi-private room, the pilgrim's dinner and laundry service. I hardly noticed that I did it all in Spanish. The sullen man stamped my credentials with his blue Camino stamp and then he walked around the side bar, grabbed my pack and carried it up the stairs to the top of the house where a few rooms were located. I noticed a backpack lying on the other bed in the room. At least there were only two beds. I hoped it was a woman! Whoever it was had exited the room.

Once he left, I showered and gathered my laundry to leave it in the pink plastic tub outside my room. I then gathered a couple of blankets and wrapped them around me so that I could sit outside to look over the rolling green landscape surrounding me on three sides. To my right was a very small stone church, half in ruins. The walls surrounding the graveyard still stood. A couple of beer-drinking Asians came up the stairs then, laden with beverages in each hand and their packs being carried by the hospitalero. They bustled by me, noisily arguing in high-pitched tones, and continued to argue as they got settled into the room across from me. Another woman came up the stairs then. Her dishwater blonde tresses waved around her face in a pretty way. Her light green eyes lit up her face and drew the gaze away from her large, pointy nose. Her lips were full and lush. If it hadn't been for her unfortunate nose, she would have been fairly pretty.

"Hello...?" she said tentatively.

"Hi! I'm sorry, I was only staring because I didn't know you spoke English."

She laughed ruefully. "That is ALL I can speak. I just can't seem to speak Spanish, though I can understand it when I listen. I'm Celeste. Are you my roomie?"

"If you are in this room behind me," I tapped on the window behind my chair, "then I am!"

We chatted for a while about her holistic practice that she ran. I was familiar with it all since I'm a big advocate of the healing arts. We discussed the modalities that we liked the best. Her personality seemed a bit dry, but she told me she had been wanting to find a friend on this journey.

A bit surprised, I said "Really? But there are friends everywhere. You are never truly by yourself here unless you wish to be!"

Her eyes watered. "It's just that this is so hard and I can't stand all of the snoring. It's more expensive to stay in a better hotel without bunk beds or roommates but I can't afford that. I don't want to be absorbing people's energies and it seems there is too much suffering along the way."

"Why did you choose to come?" I asked a bit surprised at her experience of the Camino.

"My ancestors, my grandmothers told me to come walk the Camino during a women's chanting circle. After being here, I don't know why on earth they would give me that message. I don't know why I am here and why I have to be here." Her tone had turned rather whiny.

"Oh." I diplomatically decided not to question that one. "So, how are you liking the food?"

We chatted on the balcony until it was too chilly to do so. Still wrapped in my two blankets, I carefully descended the stairs that led to the dining area. Celeste followed me down and sat next to me in the middle of the long farm table. The beer-swigging Asian couple sat on my right, four older bookish-looking French people sat on the other side of Celeste, and three young college kids from Bolivia sat across from us. No one else admitted to speaking English so I was forced to converse with Celeste.

During dessert, the owner of the hostel came out holding a pair of my underwear. He pointed at them and then at me. I was appalled. He hadn't even grabbed the prettiest ones. These were not exactly granny panties, but they were a bit older. "Yup. Those are my underwear! Could you put them down?" He lifted his chin in arrogance as he held them higher, waving my pink Victoria's Secret size mediums in his fist. His other hand shot up with another green pair that were not mine. I narrowed my eyes at him, suspecting he knew more English than he let on. I shook my head. One of the young Bolivian women stood up with me.

He led us through a narrow hall past the bar/check-in desk to a tiny laundry area. Our clothing lay in a mingled heap in a large basket. He lingered there as we separated our laundry. I found it very strange that he stood and watched us and wondered why, until he reached past me and snagged a pair of men's boxers from the heap of clothes. I turned and gaped at his audacity! He'd thrown in his dirties! He merely shrugged at my outrage. I exchanged shocked glances with the young woman beside me. Feeling strange, I carried my warm clothes upstairs and laid them inside my sleeping bag to warm it up before I turned in for the night. Then I rejoined the group for dessert and wrapped my chilled body in the blankets I'd thrown off in my haste to collect my clothing.

"That was very odd! I can't believe that happened just now." Celeste was laughing though her eyes were wide with shock.

The owner was back in the room observing us and checking his watch. I got the feeling he wanted us to hurry up and finish so he could lock up the bar. Just to spite him and make him wait, I held my wine glass aloft and tapped it hard with my fingernail, indicating I wanted another glass. He regarded me coolly but got up to retrieve more wine. When he came back seconds later, I said very loudly and slowly, "Yes, he is a VERY strange man. I don't think he likes us much. Certainly doesn't seem happy with his job! Poor man must be MISERABLE." His eyes met mine steadily. I held his eyes. He knew what I'd just said. Yet he remained silent. My heart beat in my throat. It was so out of character for me to stand up for myself. Where had that come from?

Everyone at the table wanted more wine as well, so we ended up keeping the owner later than he probably wished us to. Oddly, I felt a bit sorry for him. There'd been something in his eyes that indicated a soul-deep pain. Celeste was speaking to me but I'd tuned her out. I'd noticed a negativity to her conversations that did little to interest me. I just couldn't bring myself to whisper with her about how rude the French were or how drunk the Asians. I finally turned to her, "You know, you surprise me. You're in the healing arts. Do you not see that all of these people are on their own journey? Why must you judge anyone? Think about why you are here and let's hope no one is judging you!" I stood then and left to go to sleep. I nodded to the young Bolivian woman. Her kind blue eyes met mine, twinkled with humor at our laundry experience. I waved at the whole table in general. "Buen Camino, peregrinos!" To the chorus of many well wishes, I exited the room.

Despite the biting cold, I stood atop the balcony viewing the darkened landscape with appreciation. Stars twinkled sharply in the cold night sky. My breath misted out in front of me as I wondered for the hundredth time how my daughter was doing. I closed my eyes and breathed in deeply as I imagined sending my energy out through the darkness, across continents and oceans to send her comfort. I envisioned wrapping my arms around her body and hugging her tightly to me as I kissed her soft cheek. No matter that she was turning thirteen soon, she was still my little buddy in so many ways. She holds my arm when we walk down the sidewalk, interrupts me when I talk with friends to say something funny. Always pulls my attention back to her. I don't mind usually. I thought I heard her voice softly whisper as if born on the wind, "It's okay, Momma. I'm fine. I love you." Content with that, I went inside.

Now as I settled into the middle of the bed massaging my feet and legs, Celeste entered the room. We made polite chit chat about the aches and pains we'd acquired along the way.

They were almost like badges of honor to me now. Almost insignificant compared to what was happening on a cellular, emotional and spiritual level. Celeste argued that we shouldn't have to suffer like the monks of old who wore no shoes and endured so much along the way. I listened to her and explained slowly as it dawned on me that there may not be true growth without some pain as we shed the past and all its regrets. We looked at each other. I felt the gap between our ideas dividing us as clearly as if a wall of stone were being built before me. Her eyes teared up a bit as if she felt it, too. She took out a little book of meditations and tuned me out while she read. Once I took some ibuprofen, I was ready to sleep but had just started my period. This was something I dreaded on the hike. I mentioned it to Celeste as a way of communicating something lighter than our previous discussion. She shrugged. "I won't get mine for a couple more weeks. I enjoy my menses. It's a cleansing time for me."

You would, I thought. I turned away so she wouldn't see me roll my eyes in reaction. This was oftentimes something I couldn't control whenever someone said something so ridiculously superior. I turned my back to her and let her read, pulling my eye cover on and shoving earplugs in my ears. I settled into my warmed sleeping bag. My clothes were now badly wrinkled again, but I shoved them in my pack in a wadded ball anyway.

Sleep claimed me swiftly that night. I fell through the veil between the sleeping and waking world as if only a thin membrane divided the two. My father waited on the other side for me. We stood on the balcony of the albergue I slept in. His back was turned to me, his golden hair was longer and wavier than it had been in life, flowing just to his shoulders. He turned and glanced at me over his left shoulder, his eyes shifted from green to blue to green. I never could remember the exact shade of his eyes. He'd died more than twenty-five years ago. His smile twitched as if he found it humorous that I tried to remember so much about him. He turned and held his arm out to me. I walked into the shelter of his left shoulder. We looked at the stars together. He pointed with his right forefinger at a cluster of stars. I'd expected to see a unicorn shape but I clearly saw the sign of a Cancer crab. Then a vague impression of my daughter's face took shape with a few star clusters. My dad looked at me and kissed my forehead.

"I see her, you know. I visit you often, too. Remember, this is important, we are all okay in the end. Everything will be okay." With humor crinkling the corners of his eyes, he left. He walked down the stairs as any man would. I watched his blond head disappear and turned my gaze again to the stars. I could no longer see my daughter's face, but the stars now moved and shifted as if they were alive. They danced. Shooting stars burst across the sky and planets swirled.

CHAPTER THIRTEEN

The next morning I woke with my arms and legs flung as wide as my sleeping bag would allow. Both of my earplugs had popped out. Oddly enough, I never found them though I searched everywhere around and under my bed. My roommate was up and making loud noises in the bathroom. Feeling disgusted, I was in the middle of inserting a new earplug deep in my ear canal when she burst out of the bathroom and glared at me! I paused in the act of shoving the plug in my ear and stared back. I felt guilty and didn't know why. Her hair was tousled and she had been crying.

I sat up and asked "Everything okay?"

"I need to talk to you."

"Okay....?"

"My period came this morning." She paused for emphasis. Lost and fuzzy in the morning, I shrugged, waiting for the important facts. "I am NEVER late. I take pride in being regular each and every month."

"Mmmhmmm?" I was starting to see where this was going and took a deep breath. It looked to me like craziness was setting in and having experience all of my life with such events, I could only breathe and wait. Crazy is as crazy does and there ain't no arguing with it. Just smile and nod, I thought.

"Don't interrupt. I am talking. Wait your turn." I nodded

politely and stood up to face her. I'd be damned if I was going to be verbally attacked while lying in bed. Seeing that I stood four inches taller made me instantly relax. I rolled my hand in a gesture that indicated she should continue.

"You are just not conscious!" My eyebrows lifted at this but I kept my temper in check. "Your energy is very strong....and your energy particles are mingling too much with mine. You need to be AWARE of your presence and keep it to yourself. You are sharing space with me here and I did not appreciate that you took the bed by the window. It's rather smelly by the bathroom." Again, I said nothing for her pack had been lying on the bed where she slept when I arrived. I simply glanced at the bed and back at her. *She must obviously be a pampered princess in her home*, I thought. I felt sorry for her life partner. Though she wore no ring, she had talked about a woman she cared very much for.

"Is that all?" I asked as tears leaped into her eyes. She nodded her head and folded her arms.

"Okay, then." I turned to pack my belongings into my pack.

"Aren't you going to say something?"

I looked at her a good long minute. "There is nothing a person can say to someone like you when lambasted with such bullshit first thing in the morning. Excuse me, please." I said gently and with no agitation in my voice. I pushed past her to brush my teeth and rinse my face, keeping watch in the mirror for any kind of attack. She simply sat at the end of her bed, her golden hair falling over her face, with her hands folded as if in prayer, and stayed that way until I gathered my things and left. I closed the door gently only because of the others who may be sleeping. I really hated being woken with a fight.

The breakfast table was almost full. I moved a chair to

the end of the table, effectively squeezing between two of the French. "Bonjour!" I nodded to them and grinned. They smiled, surprised, and tried to converse. I laughed and shook my head. Breakfast was simply the bread from last night toasted and served with marmalade. The coffee was the worst I'd had on the whole trip—it was instant and lukewarm. I gagged and almost spit it out. Today I was taking a bus from Burgos to León and skipping the meseta. It was a flat section that was mostly industrial. I'd figured this was the only way I could finish the Camino in time to catch my flight home!

Celeste came in looking like a haggard mess, with circles under her eyes. She sat heavy in her chair with her hands still folded in front of her. *Oh, little Drama Queen, it'll be good to see the last of you. I pray that you find what you need on this journey,* I thought at her. She reached for some toast and jelly just as I stood. My red backpack felt solid and now fit me like a glove. Feeling absurdly awesome and ready for the day, I parted the beaded curtain that kept bugs out and swept out without looking back at her.

The entry into Burgos was a depressing landscape of concrete and grimy industrial buildings. The streets were pocked with holes big enough to swallow tires. After passing one dingy, nearly empty bar after another, the depressing sights and sounds of the city played havoc on the peaceful feeling the Camino had instilled in me. Cars honked and people bustled around with gazes locked on the ground. A woman on a bicycle rushed through morning traffic with a box of donuts balanced on her handlebars. She wore a dress and was the only one who smiled at me and wished me Buen Camino. I needed to find an ATM to draw out some cash, but everywhere I looked there were hard-eyed men standing around the machines. I had been warned that the pickpockets here were terrible.

Dingy, faded fliers littered the ground and windows in these grimy businesses. Bar owners stood listlessly watching me pass by their stores. I had walked in one bar intending to use the restroom, only to immediately turn around and leave again. The whole bathroom looked as if it had been dipped in urine and filth. I felt dirty though I hadn't touched a thing. My hands itched with a need to wash them. I continued on though I saw no signs for the Camino, no arrows or emblems in the sidewalks.

Eventually, the rougher industrial area gave way to a few apartments and office buildings. I found an ATM without any mean-looking characters lurking about and quickly pulled out three-hundred euros, took my receipt and stuffed the card and everything into my purse, and that whole thing went deep into my pack. I swung the pack on my back and was walking as I buckled it on with quick movements, all the while keeping my eyes moving to make sure no one moved in my direction.

My senses reeled as the dingy roads and grimy windows gave way to a more upscale side of town. Sidewalks and streets were suddenly spotless. Windows and metal siding gleamed as if a giant squeegee had descended from the sky and scraped this section clean. I crossed through a park and came to a walkway by a wide river. It was here I finally saw yellow arrows. Looking back along the tree-lined path, it was now obvious that this was the trail. I had gotten off the main track somehow. People walked thoroughbred dogs or leisurely rode bicycles as they meandered along the path. The river led to the Burgos square, where stately, handsome townhomes squatted along the riverfront. This was a much different place than the filth riddled, hard-eyed city I'd just walked miles through.

From afar, the square and cathedral looked impressive. I promised myself to check it out if I had time. I needed bus tickets to León so I could skip the meseta and get back on schedule. Once free of the square, I walked up and down the area where I was told the bus station sat. It didn't appear to be anywhere close by. Finally, in exasperation, I asked a passerby and of course he pointed to a glass door right behind me. He smiled tolerantly as the doors opened for me suddenly. Remaining a bit doubtful, I went through the doors and saw that it opened up to the back and housed many waiting buses.

Since there were a few hours to kill before my bus to León left, I walked the few blocks back to the main square to tour the historically impressive, stunning Cathedral. With an English translating headset and hand controls, I was joined by several English-speaking pilgrims for the tour. Halfway through, I became bored with the different chapels inside. This one was for that saint and each more opulent than the last. I split off from my group and became lost as I tried to find an exit. By the time I found it, I caught up with my group. Wearing a sheepish smile, I handed in my tour gear and collected my belongings to go sit outside by the river.

Since the sun actually made an appearance, there was an excellent opportunity to relax by the river. With my pack against a tree, my legs stretched out long in front, I closed my eyes listening to the river. My mind wandered to the beginning of my journey and back. I missed Andrew. Nacho. Nicola. I wrote about them in my journal, wanting to capture as much of them as possible. I sighed and laid my head back, enjoyed the sun on my face and wished for a man in a hammock.

CHAPTER FOURTEEN

Once on the bus, it was disorienting to be seated on a moving vehicle. The landscape raced by too fast. The sky was lit bright blue with big puffy clouds that formed shapes I tried to decipher. An odd feeling took hold as I sped by the meseta. My whole being wanted to be out there with the pilgrims walking. My soul nearly cried for it. I had spent the last couple of weeks traveling approximately 220 miles by foot, now I was going to skip over about a hundred miles in just under two hours. My blisters still hurt, though I paid them little attention now. My shoulders ached from the constant weight of my pack. I was exhausted at the end of every day. Yet, I felt I was cheating myself out of something important. People had told me the meseta tried a person's patience in the beginning for the sheer monotony, but this was the only way to go deep inside oneself. It became meditative. I almost asked the driver to stop.

Two hours later I forgot about the meseta as I stepped off the bus into "the land of the castles," or Castile y León. This is the region that the most pure version of the Spanish language, or Castilian, came from. The castles here were built by Christians who fought the Moorish invasions from the eighth and ninth centuries. More medieval castles can be found in this region than anywhere else in Europe, a true testament to the strength of will the Christian-led kingdoms had when they united to reconquer

Spain from the Muslim rulers. Aside from the medieval section of town that houses the cathedrals, museums of the Knights of Templar and other monuments, there is one of the best-preserved aqueducts built in Roman times that has lasted more than 2,000 years. Oh, yes, I planned to spend a couple of days resting and relaxing in this fascinating city.

Once inside the grand city of León, I found the San Marcos plaza where the Hotel Regia was located. I'd heard it was a good location, good enough to stay and recuperate for a couple of days. The room was a dark sanctuary, painted a rich emerald green finished with dark wooden accents and furniture. Nearly black beams crossed the ceiling. A giant corner tub finished with brass knobs made me squeal in delight.

For two whole days, I ate and slept late, took naps and walked minimally. I left my pack in its lonely corner and ignored the gray straps that reached for me like a friend's warm embrace. I wore my sandals without socks and didn't worry about the weather. I visited the cathedrals and the places that had hosted legions of armies in León, giving it its namesake. León is derived from the word "legion." The Gothic style Casa Botines impressed me most with its pointy spires on top and its sculpture of Saint George slaying a dragon above the front entrance. This building was one of the first of its kind to be resurrected without load-bearing walls, using cast-iron pillars and open framework instead. The building, though it was constructed in 1892, has never had foundation issues. The cathedral here sported regal flying buttresses and sculptures engraved in every crevasse.

The second day, I leisurely made my way to the river and practiced yoga and meditation along the banks. Ignoring the persistent chill in the air, I tried to focus instead on the warmth that filtered intermittently from the peeking sun. I shivered as

I let the sunlight cascade and penetrate shallowly into my skin. After ten minutes, my yoga/meditation instructor's smiling face came into my mind and I gave up on pretending to meditate. I mentally stuck my tongue out at his laughing blue eyes as the chill invaded my senses and I could not stand another minute of sitting still.

Following a route off the Camino this time, I tried to be just a tourist and not a pilgrim. However, I felt a little bereft without my backpack. At one point, a pair of pilgrims across the busy street turned one way and then another seeking the yellow arrows. They were a few blocks off and still heading in the wrong direction. I ran over, feeling light without my pack, and halted in front of them. They stopped yelling at each other and turned to me with slightly wild-looking eyes. They were lost. I wondered if they'd just arrived. This was a point in the Camino where new pilgrims often would start, as most couldn't get the whole time off of work or other commitments to complete the entire trek from St. Jean.

"Hola, peregrinos," I grinned at them. "Camino....?"

"Da!" Aha, Dutch. I led them back around the other way from which we were headed and pointed to the small brass shells embedded in the sidewalks, as well as the yellow arrows on the posts. Using my hands in choppy motions like an air plane traffic controller, I motioned them to continue ahead and wished them Buen Camino. They smiled in gratitude. I watched them as they started to figure it out, remembering my first day in Pamplona when I'd been grabbed from behind and forced in the opposite direction. Watching them go, I felt a profound urge to collect my backpack and take off. I wavered in the direction of the meandering pilgrims before turning to retrace my steps. I'd been on my way to another museum. I would leave tomorrow. I felt comforted knowing I would rejoin it all soon.

Content to eat dinner in my room, I sat squarely in the middle of my bed and watched a little television though I could hardly understand any words. Content to eat alone? I realized I was fine and not one bit lonely. Before coming to Spain, I'd felt a deep desire to meet a man and settle into a relationship. This was a profound need that sometimes saddened me, weakened me. Of course, I tried not to let it show in front of my daughter, but it was hard some days to get out of bed. That need had given birth to some ugly dating choices, I reflected. I laughed a bit as I recalled some horrible dates that I would have given my left arm to get out of quickly. I supposed the need to find someone had arisen out of a need to compete with my ex-husband since he'd found a girlfriend the moment I made him break up with his mistress, my youngest friend.

My psychic friend Laura had told me before leaving on this journey, "Alesa, don't be in a rush to meet 'him.' He is out there waiting for you to heal yourself and arrive at his level. When you are there, he will be there. I see you going to Spain and noticing all of the men there but you are the one who is picking and choosing what you like. You like this, not that, like this, not that. Write a lot on your journey and see if I'm right when you come back. You will find the bits and pieces in a few men that make up one perfect soul mate for you." I'd been frustrated with her at the time, but now could see that she was right. I was so glad to be single and free to choose on this trip!

Of course, Parker and I had long, emotionally exhausting conversations about this subject. At first, she'd wanted me to not date anyone. We enjoyed our girl time very much. When she was eleven, that had been fine. Now that she is becoming a bit more independent with her friends and enjoying more activities away from home, she is worrying more about me and my dating life. Her views have changed and she wants me to find someone before she goes to college and "leaves me all alone." In the beginning, I dated more than I do now. Maybe I didn't want to be hurt anymore, I thought, couldn't open up anymore.

These thoughts brought the worst of the dates to the forefront of my memory. There'd been the desperate New Zealander, Ted. He smelled like an odd combination of Old Spice and engine oil. He wasn't my type at all. I found him depressing and groaned in agony when I saw his long, hang-me-now face coming in the store day after day. We talked about his woman issues and he always looked at me kind of sideways, like he was scared to face me straight on. He wore me down after he found out I was separated. He'd been coming in to my coffee shop nearly every day. When I said, "Okay....I'll go to lunch with you," he didn't seem to mind that I wasn't thrilled. He droned on about stories I already knew. He had never married, never had kids, suffered depression and worked the same boring job every day for the last fifteen years. He finally revealed a story about how he liked to ride dirt bikes through lightning storms and scream at the sky. He leaned toward me with a maniacal gleam in his eye then and said, "You ever do that? You know what I mean! Just scream at the sky! It's great!" I hid my alarm. Later, I mentally kicked myself as he skipped to his car and waved at me.

After two more strange yet mostly repetitive lunch dates with him, I finally told him I wasn't feeling anything for him. He yelled at me and said it took time to develop feelings. I just needed to give him a chance. I said "Nooooo....but thanks..?" After Ted, there was the landscaper. We lasted about a week before I could see that his marijuana and alcohol problems were out of control. He needed a sugar mama to finance his lackadaisical lifestyle. I told him so and he still texted and called me for six months before I threatened him with the police. There was the chef who cried about his wife's cheating throughout the terrible meal he'd prepared. The chef was followed by the super wealthy egomaniac. He promised me some lavish gifts if I slept with him before I abruptly told him to take me home. I banged my head on his passenger door trying to escape the kiss, to no avail as it landed on my lips regardless.

Though my girlfriends hungered for my dating-disaster details as they provided them with comic relief, I suddenly put a hold on dating. I'd had enough. Something was seriously wrong with me for attracting these odd men! I felt closed off and out of sync with myself. I wasn't sure how I was going to move forward in my life after the Camino, but a mental break was definitely called for. I was tired of shutting good people out and wanted to receive all of the goodness that life had to offer but I wasn't yet sure how to do that. I'd spent so much time pushing people away except for my husband and my daughter, how did I learn to embrace this world instead of fighting it and keeping it all at arm's length, a safe distance away?

Overwhelmed by my thoughts, I prepared for bed and pulled the covers up to my chin as my head sank into my plush pillow. Momentarily suspended between the world of sleep and waking, my mother's face came into my mind. This was the calm and loving mother I yearned for growing up. She leaned toward me with a lightness in her eyes instead of the heaviness she usually wore. She kissed my forehead lightly and softly whispered, "Let it go, baby. You carried all of this long enough. Come out of solitary confinement. Open your heart to yourself, your soul path, your insights, thereby opening yourself to the truth, to real love. Don't be afraid to simply be." Her face changed into

Laura's as I sank further into the dreaming world. "You need to get yourself out there and have some fun. Don't be so serious all the time. Be lighter....go dancing. Be free and happy, sweetie! You know we all love you."

CHAPTER FIFTEEN

On the way out of León, I was so excited to get going again that I nearly skipped coffee. Nearly. People smiled and nodded at me. I smiled back. I already had my music in my ears, letting the beat of the drums decide the pace today. I hummed aloud and watched birds whirl and dive in the air above my head. A heart-shaped cloud emerged as I looked skyward. *Yes,* I thought, *I will open my heart today and let go.* Strength surged through my legs as new energy flooded my veins. The trail beyond town enticed me into that familiar wakeful/dreaming state I needed in order to tune out the tedium of the journey. This was the state that allowed me to just "be" as my dream-Mother had asked me to be and open myself up. In order to let go, I needed to remember.

Owning my own business had started out being about proving I could be a business owner like my grandmother. I'd felt it was important to be as motivated and strong as I viewed her at that time. When the opportunity came, I'd thrown myself into it with the steam of my ambition to prove something. When my life began to fall apart—first with that cancer scare, then a failing marriage and other disasters, finally with the real-deal cancer—I'd blindly done something I tried never to do. I reached out to people and asked for help. It had taken me being at the lowest place in my life with the only other option being to just end it all, for me to realize I needed someone to help me. I could not continue to do it all myself any longer.

The mayor came over to the shop in her robe and slippers one day, per her usual habit, and asked to help me with dishes. I'd been slammed that morning and she could see that I was still a bit underwater. She helped bail me out. We chatted and cleaned. I gave her free coffee for helping. Since she lived just a few doors down from Cannon Mine on Cannon Street, she came often and late in the morning. Any time she helped me out, I gave her a coffee credit on her tab.

Then there were the "townies" or the regular local customers. Most of them loved our little town and sought to improve it and support it. They gave me the news on the street and tried to talk politics, though I am not sold any which way in that arena, so my conversations tended to either humor them or just bore them. They were the ones who ate more than one meal a day at my shop if they felt business had been slower than normal. Caring and hard-working people, those townies. They started fixing little things for me, such as the swamp cooler and shelves that tilted occasionally. They just knew I needed help and didn't ask for anything in return.

As if from afar, I watched myself growing invisible roots with these people. Their lives intertwined with mine. I cared about them. I trusted them. I couldn't leave now. Panic would set in from time to time, for my wandering side is very strong, and to feel beholden to a community was foreign to me. City council members had meetings in my store and listened to my opinion as if I mattered. I felt like I did matter for the first time in my life! How could I pick up and leave?

When things were going wrong with Derek, I started to pull at those roots. I clammed up. I thought no one would notice I wasn't happy. I tried to just handle it all without expressing any of my pain about what was happening. One day shortly after my first anxiety attack, I cried a bit before opening the store. I made lattes as fast as ever that day but then my friend, the mayor, came in and looked at me point blank and said, "What's wrong?" My face crumpled then and there. I cried on her shoulder. It was she who told me that reaching out takes more strength than keeping things in. Shortly after leaving Derek, I lived with her for my transition period. It made sense since she was just steps from the store. We drank wine together and cried every night for a week. After that experience, I began to reach out to a few more people.

Thankful for my little community that had pulled me out my personal hell, I focused once again on the landscape of greens and reds. I met many pilgrims that day. We smiled and took photos of each other. We shared short humorous anecdotes in passing and promised to dance the Camino Shuffle in Santiago. I noticed the small ways in which we all helped each other. This was a community as well. Our commonality was being here. After ten kilometers or so, I noticed a pilgrim giving out bottles of water close to a small town. He passed them out as we entered the town. His eyes smiled with an inner light. His backpack, with the scallop shell, sat leaning against a hip-high wall. A short time later he came in to the bar while everyone cheered and someone bought him lunch. These small things made me so glad to be a part of the human race.

Later that afternoon as I walked around a bend in the road, I came upon a tug of war with a hairy, bearded pilgrim and his donkey. The donkey's head was lowered obstinately as his owner tried to coax him to turn around. One ear stuck straight up into the air while the other pointed left. His back was laden with camping gear, balanced with pots, pans and other odds and ends. Though his rope was being pulled rather strongly, he'd set his forelegs in a stubborn stance against the pulling man. They hogged the road and so I backed up a few paces to enjoy the show.

The man finally let the rope go and rummaged for a treat. He produced a carrot from the bowels of his rucksack. This he tried to entice the mean animal with. When both of the donkey's ears went down, I figured it was safer to walk by but made a wide berth around the two as I cut around to rejoin the path. I loved not knowing what I was going to run into from one day to the next. Wild cows and bulls ran in pastures right next to busy roads. The other day I'd come across a man with a stick he'd stripped. He was standing in the middle of the road observing his loose cattle. I had tried to make him laugh by yelling, "Toro! Toro!" but all I got in return was the Marlon Brando smolder, complete with square jaw and deadly eyes. Well, I had thought it was funny.

I made my way into a small town that was so friendly that a group of townsfolk stood by the trail and waved at us, yelling "Buen Camino" and clapping as we entered their town. It was amazing how that small act of welcoming encouragement made my feet lighter. They still tended to ache at the end of the day's walk. Again, I headed to the first albergue I came across. This time it was Albergue San Antonio de Padua. As I settled onto a lower bunk near the back of the room, I heard yelling coming from the bathroom. A man wrapped in a towel ran out holding his groin as he bee-lined for the correct bathroom. Amidst a handful of claps and cheering, he slid and slipped, wet from his hasty shower, and almost lost his towel before he made it inside the men's room.

Dinner that night was made by a very old and rickety gentleman who could barely stand straight. His long gray hair was pulled back into a thin ponytail at his nape. The long weathered strands straggled across his back. He had a large electrical element made for the paella pan. He smiled kindly at me as I passed the open door leading to the kitchen. Another younger male cook put the finishing touches on salads and bread baskets. The aromas of spices and roasted vegetables wafted over me. I sat next to a younger woman from Florida and we giggled over how hungry we were. Bottles of wine were already opened and set out, one bottle for every two chairs. We poured wine as the room filled quickly. The elderly cook, Pepe, came out with our meal, also a vegetarian paella, and served us all with his big silver spoon. He winked at each woman as he dished her up. He served us the best salad I had on the entire Camino. There were field greens and sunflower seeds, vine-ripe tomatoes with a nice vinaigrette.

That night I wrote another note to my daughter. She had not responded yet to the other that I'd sent, but I knew she was busy with summer fun stuff. I missed my friends. Suddenly lonely in the dark, I wished I had someone to hold. Sighing in frustration, I wondered when I would find a man I'd actually want to keep. Was I still capable of loving a man properly? I wasn't sure. I had days where I craved a mate and others where I thought that idea was utter bullshit. How could I put my heart on the line again? I tossed and turned all night with these conflicting emotions in my head. I didn't sleep well that night.

CHAPTER SIXTEEN

NEXT MORNING, THE CUTE ELDERLY chef from the night before poked fun at me when I poured a fourth cup of coffee to go. With a twinkle in his dark blue eyes, he pointed at me, "Americanos! Muy gránde café! Eh? Gránde, gránde!" I laughed delightedly. I quirked my eyebrow at him and dryly asked, "Si! Dónde está el Starbucks?! Eh?!" He snapped his white towel at my ass as I turned and ran up the stairs to grab my pack and brush my teeth on the way out.

Just before I left, I had an urge to read my Facebook messages for some reason. I found that Mom had sent me an urgent note informing me that Grandma was deathly ill. I sat down in a plastic chair in the entry and reread the message over and over with my head in my hands. After some time, I decided there was nothing I could do for her here besides pray! I sent a quick message to my mother asking her to tell Grandma I would pray for her all day and night until she was better, that I had to keep going, but to give me updates. Large tears dripped onto my hands as I typed the messages to my mother. Grandma had been steadily watching my progress through Facebook. I hoped I hadn't caused her extra stress.

Since I had not updated my phone before I left for Spain, there was no way I could call home. My phone simply wouldn't work and I wasn't familiar with how to dial in an emergency.

Plus, I didn't know where she'd been taken. Tearfully, I stumbled onto the trail with my hands clasped in prayer for her.

My grandmother has always been a real force to be reckoned with in my life. If someone told me that Grandmother was disappointed in me, I quaked. She expected a lot out of us and she demanded respect. We behaved very well at her house. Our days were filled with cleaning and chores first, before play. At night, Grandma would relax with us after the kitchen was cleaned and dishes were all done. We would then curl up and watch movies and hope that dessert was already made. Otherwise we'd be back in the kitchen making a homemade dessert and washing those dishes again. Discipline first—then we could have fun. All of us respected her tightly controlled household. She ran it like she ran her business.

Other times, Grandmother joined the groups that my sister and I were in. She was a Girl Scout volunteer so she could go camping with our troops. She became a Camp Fire Girl leader so she could follow us around. She introduced the troops to her horses so we could ride them in our outings. She taught Renee and me to build dams in the creek by her house to make a large swimming hole. Grandpa and Grandma loved to snowmobile and camp. They never had a dull time. Though it was often more about getting things done than having fun, they were a steady and hard influence on us. We feared them, but also respected them and when Grandma decided to have fun, she could be entertaining.

I loved being with Grandma most when she told long, inventive stories. During my younger years, I could snuggle in her soft arms. She was the only other person besides my dad who I trusted to hold me that close. She smelled amazingly like apple pie and flowered lotions. Her hands had the softest skin I could imagine. I loved to hold them while she talked and talked. She would sometimes ask me why I was so quiet and she would wait for me to say something. She never pushed but I could tell that it bothered her a bit at times like those. I would just shrug and whisper for her to "go on and keep talking." Her voice was soothing while her laugh was shocking. I laughed the hardest when I heard her laugh. It was exactly like a witch's cackle and I couldn't understand how such a strange, loud sound came out of such a beautiful woman. To me, she looked like a glamorous actress from the fifties. Her vibrancy could be felt from across the room. I'd hoped to grow up one day and be just like her. Once in a while, I slipped and called her Mom. She never corrected me, just hugged me tighter.

A couple of years ago, I'd gone to their beautiful California-style custom ranch home in Wyoming. Their house was built on eighty acres and was set on top of a hill like a jewel. Every facet of the home had been handpicked by Grandma and she had impeccable taste. Even from afar, as soon as I saw the house I felt as if a warm embrace enveloped me. I thought, I'm home now. Grandma's voice would ring out from somewhere in the spacious rambler "LeLee! I'm so glad you made it! What do you want for dinner?" She always wanted to make us our favorite comfort foods. I usually worked side by side with her while we caught up on events.

This time, I had arrived a little earlier, so we reclined on her plush sofa in her formal living room while we talked. The conversation was more serious this time about the divorce and her worries for me. She was more emotional and she told me she was feeling things more with her old age. She had some regrets, she said, and she wanted to tell me about them. "I am so sorry, LeLee, that we worked so much back then and could not help you kids out more. We should have done more. I see that now. We just let you guys suffer. I wish I could have been there more for you." I had stared at my full cup of wine not knowing how to take this. It was the first time she'd ever mentioned anything of this magnitude.

"Can you tell me what he did to you?" I swallowed and shook my head. I touched her amazingly soft hands.

"Grandma, it's okay now. I've never told anyone at all. I don't talk about that. Let's not think about it, okay? It's over and he got nineteen years for it."

"Oh! I just think he should have gotten life for it!" Her eyes were surprisingly full of tears. Not knowing how to handle this, I let her pull me into her warm embrace and cry for me. It was not something I thought she would ever want to discuss, so her need to do so now was a bit shocking. Worriedly, I asked, "Grandma...you're okay, right? You're....healthy? This doesn't seem like you." She hugged me tighter and assured me she was. It was a while before we got up to make dinner together.

Tears were leaking from my eyes onto my t-shirt as I walked, finally stopping at Puente de Orbigo. This bridge, according to my guidebook, was "one of the longest and best preserved medieval bridges in Spain." It was truly impressive. I paused to take in the arches underneath that ran the length of the bridge and the turret-like structures that gave extra support. I walked over its long expanse into town and noticed a festival of sorts being set up. It looked as though they were celebrating the jousting and renaissance events that actually happened on this medieval bridge. Jousting poles rested with their tips pointing up against a fence. Colored banners flew from the staffs. There were tournament arenas and multi-colored banners where the spectators would sit in bleachers along the far side.

While sitting in the plaza eating what felt like my eightieth ham sandwich, I prayed again for Grandma to recover. She didn't understand my driving need to take this trip. Gossip had arrived in the form of my aunt who called me the day before I left, "Your grandmother is very worried about you. We all are. You've been through a lot. You just sold the shop and now you're heading off to Europe. Do you have any money? Where are you going to work? We'd just like to not worry." These kinds of things made me crazy with anxiety. I didn't feel like justifying anything I did at the ripe age of forty. I sarcastically replied to my aunt, "I have somehow managed to make it this far. Don't worry. I'll do what I've always done and take care of myself….cuz God knows no one else will." I felt bad about being so sarcastic. My Aunt had really made a big difference in my life and been loving, a soft place to land when I really needed someone. I wished I could take the words back.

The rest of the day, I tried to figure out how to open the dam inside my chest and how to tear down the walls I'd spent a lifetime building. I felt naked at the thought. How could I leave my pride, ego, rage, and other manifestations of anger on the altar of the Camino and become whole again when I felt incomplete and scared without these precautions? How did I start over again? My heart lurched at the thought. What would a real, grown-up relationship with myself feel like? I almost fell down on the trail at that thought. Trust and love myself completely? That meant letting go of everything! Who I thought I was! Who was I? I had to forgive myself and mean it this time.

I craved an existence where I thrived rather than just survived. Surviving was a weakened state of mind, I felt. *Might as well call myself a victim*, I thought. I felt like screaming just then. It was hard to let go. There was so much! I wondered how

I could possibly begin. The only thing I knew for certain was that I wanted to lead my life from now on and stop following, stop trying to measure up to what others expected, to grow up finally. Yes, I wanted to feel like a grown up.

Coming into Astorga had been odd. Without warning, the pain in my feet became terrible again so that I limped the last two kilometers. There was a stretch of trail by this absurdly long industrial building that seemed to go on forever. At the edge of town, there were railroad tracks that were fenced off so we couldn't cross at the ground level. We had to climb up a man-made metal bridge that switched back and forth, climbing higher and higher, up and over, before going back down. I wondered if the suicide rate was especially high right there. My dream in Pamplona came rushing back and I flinched at the thought of being hit by a train.

Once in Astorga I paid five euros to stay in the biggest albergue yet! It was the common one and right on the plaza, so it sat in a good spot. The showers were shockingly cold and I had to share water with the person next to me. We each received a cold blast of water, but if the other person hit their water button, the other shut off! We had to call to each other when we needed water for rinsing off soap. I was laughing and shivering by the time I was done. Once back in my room, I saw that it was filling up with pilgrims and there were English-speaking people! A woman from New Zealand introduced herself to me. Her name was Zen and she was rather short with a pretty, friendly face. I liked her immediately. She asked me to join her and her companions for dinner on the plaza after nap time.

As I dug through my pack, I came across the six fruity flavored condoms that my roommate had insisted I bring. I'd have to find a place to toss them when no one was looking, I told myself. I wasn't that kind of girl anyway. I shoved them farther down into the bottom of my pack self-consciously. I crawled into my sleeping bag to warm up after the cold shower and slept immediately with wet, tangled hair. I woke sometime later shivering to the sounds of snoring and rustling. A man was standing next to my bed in his boxers and he seemed to be indecisive about whether he should lie down or stand up. He seemed a bit odd. He sat down and stood up, sat down and stood up again. Feeling perturbed, I quickly stood up and grabbed my toiletries to brush my tangled, still-wet hair and find the group I'd promised to meet for dinner.

The restaurant teemed with laughing people and loud conversations. It was well-lit from the floor-to-ceiling-paned windows that let in the evening sun. Since it didn't get dark in this region until 10:30 at night, there was still plenty of daylight to enjoy. The bar was square shaped and centered in the middle of the restaurant. Tables surrounding the bar were all full. I saw my party at a long table set against the far wall. I had to squeeze through crowded chairs to reach everyone. Voices mingled with laughter, creating a pleasing harmony that rose and fell to the ceiling and bounced off the walls.

Zen had saved a seat for me at a large table of pilgrims. When I entered, she raised a glass of wine toward me and flagged me over. I sat between a heavy-set man with hard eyes and a young good-looking man. The heavy man's name was Glenn, from Tennessee. He ate fast and hardly seemed to chew his food. A greasy film circled his mouth. I ignored him and turned to Zen and Taylor, the young man from Minneapolis. I liked Taylor. He was very skinny and had ordered the largest meal on the menu. We laughed as his greasy platter of meat and potatoes was set in front of him. The meat alone must have weighed three pounds.

It made my hamburger look like the healthy option.

Zen asked me if I'd met anyone intriguing along the trail. I hesitated a moment before Nacho's name escaped my lips. She whipped out her video camera and asked me to talk more about this mysterious Nacho. I told them a few details and, of course, I blushed to the roots of my hair just mentioning him a little. Steph, a young woman about Taylor's age, from Florida, spoke up then and told me that Zen had been collecting bits of video for weeks. I asked her if she was going to make a documentary. She shrugged and said, "I just want to remember everything and have records." We drank wine and visited more. I then learned that the next day was Steph's birthday, she was turning 21!

"You are walking the Camino on your birthday by yourself?" I was intrigued by her.

Steph leaned toward me so I could hear her over Taylor, who was talking to Glenn on my other side. "Yes, I did the Camino with my parents at the age of fifteen, but I hated it! As I got older, I realized that I needed to do it again because I felt badly that I'd hated it. I am so glad I came because I love it now." I was impressed. I would never have thought to do this at her age.

Later that night, I donated my fruity condoms and chocolate bars I'd accumulated to the surprise birthday party everyone was throwing for Steph. We got up at six a.m. and filled condoms with air, then tied them to her bed and backpack. Zen set out Champagne and the dozen chocolate bars she'd collected. Several pilgrims were mad at us for waking them early, though we'd tried to keep it a bit quieter. Steph had learned that I was a certified yoga teacher and so she asked me to lead everyone in a morning yoga routine for her birthday. I nodded enthusiastically.

A couple of guys helped us move tables aside in the breakfast room, clearing a space that would fit about ten people. I started slowly with some sun salutations. As other pilgrims noticed what was going on, a few of them joined in on our spontaneous and rather hilariously uncoordinated yoga class. I called out the subtle changes in positions of feet and spines to lead us through some of my own well-rehearsed poses. Fifteen of us crammed into the small area, making it impossible for me to move around to assist anyone in their yoga postures. I wasn't sure how many people spoke English, but there was a crazy feeling of unity for a few moments before Steph complained about the fruity smells emanating from the condoms she'd tied in her hair. My class dissolved into laughter as pilgrims in the doorway applauded.

Coffees and croissants disappeared quickly amidst laughing conversations. Steph was still trying to perfect the dancer pose. We stood outside in the plaza and messed around with goofy yoga poses. We set a croissant on Taylor's head while he stood in tree pose, his arms flung out in opposite directions and the toes of his right foot secured in his groin area. He tried to slide the croissant down his face while standing. Steph ran up behind him and tickled him. The croissant plopped to the ground where pigeons immediately converged and squabbled over it. We wobbled through triangles and sloppy warriors as the sun climbed higher.

Before long, we disbanded to reunite in Rabanal that evening. The guys walked really fast and so we let them go. Zen asked me why I didn't teach yoga. Despite the morning's mayhem, she thought I had potential there. I told her it was too complicated, but I hadn't really become a teacher to actually teach.

CHAPTER SEVENTEEN

"Well, then why go through all of the expense and time to teach? Why didn't you just go on a retreat where you could be pampered instead of an intensive teaching program?"

"Someone pampers themselves when they feel they deserve it, right? I wanted to immerse myself in the culture and heal... you know? I was trying to do what this trip is finishing for me. It just wasn't time for all of it to come together yet." She nodded sympathetically, talking about how quickly life can blindside a person's peace and comfort. We talked and when I tired of talking of myself, I asked, "Why are you here, Zen?"

"I just thought it would be lovely to get away," she said breathlessly and looked away a moment. "I saw the movie *The Way*. It struck me, you know?" I nodded and listened, hearing the pain of the silent words behind her evasive response. I respected that. It was hard to open up, and who knew that better than me?

This part of the Camino seemed to call for deeper reflections as we passed through abandoned villages that at one time serviced the pilgrims along the Camino. Now they were just relics and nearly crumbling to the ground. My spirits fell as we walked the empty streets of El Ganso. Old thatched roof homes with collapsed roofs and walls stood empty of all life. I passed by one that had been used as a toilet recently. White clumps of paper littered the floor with weeds growing three feet high.

Just around the corner of this long-lost town sprung a bright cafe called The Cowboy Bar. Zen and I paused here to grab a coffee from the owner. He was a nice guy, but had many other customers besides us as this had been the only place to stop in quite some time. We sat outside in the weak sunlight. I watched as a young female pilgrim from Belgium placed her sweaty, blistered foot next to her lunch plate on top of the table. She extracted a needle from her bag to tend to her blisters right next to her lunch. She also had a cigarette in her pretty little mouth. The whole picture was gruesome. Glad I'd already eaten, I couldn't look away.

There were only seven kilometers left to reach Rabanal, our stopping point for the day. However, all of it was uphill and tiring. Zen put her earphones in so I took that as a cue and did the same. Soon the beats of my favorite songs took over and my feet settled into their own rhythm without thought. Purple wildflowers grew abundantly in the sage and small yellow flowers sprung up from under bushes, vying for attention. My feet were tired but my heart was lighter with each day. I was close to understanding something very deep but didn't know what yet.

We reached Rabanal to the cheers of the many who'd arrived much earlier. They were seated outside in the cobbled streets. The last hill into the town was brutal. My calves had tightened after climbing uphill nearly four miles. However, it was different from the sharp pain of blisters, so I didn't mind it at all. I would just take some vitamin I (ibuprofen) and be fine in the morning. We drew nearer to our cheering friends as Steph yelled, "Hurry up! They're almost full!" I glanced behind me and saw a few pilgrims so I shuffled a little bit faster to reach the front door of the albergue. They laughed at my awkward gait. I grabbed the handle and yanked the door open to startle a short woman behind the front desk. I apologized in Spanish and threw my pack off, searching for my documents.

Zen and I claimed two of the last three beds just as a group came in behind us. We hurriedly threw our packs on bunks, not caring who we slept next to. This was the way of the Camino— you just had to be happy with a bed! Zen went out to join Steph's continued, impromptu birthday party in the courtyard as I sat on my bed.

Suddenly, in my spirit I felt an uncommonly strong urge to let go of a few things. I sat with my heart pounding its urgent beat into my head as I wrote letters to those who needed my forgiveness. My ego wrestled with my heart as I started with a note to Derek. I thanked him for the eighteen years we'd had together. I realized if we'd never been together, I would not have the person in my life who had made me a better woman— my daughter. She'd changed me in ways I didn't know could happen. She was the first person to come into my life who I would have died for unquestioningly. She had opened my eyes to the true meaning of love. Being a mother had turned out to be the best gift in life. I visualized her beautiful eyes and her long arms wrapped around me in a characteristically tight hug. I was grateful for her. As I wrote this letter, a wave of warmth radiated up from my toes to my heart. This was the beginning of friendship that I'd unknowingly longed for with Derek. A common ground that could bridge the gap that had torn us irrevocably apart. Intense, hot tears leaked onto the pages as I wrote, each one searing my promise to myself and him to let it all go and be a better friend. I visualized his handsome smile and his hug. To feel that again in friendship would be an immeasurable relief. I reread the note several times as I felt this warmth for him that I hadn't felt in so long.

We had an uncommonly happy relationship for the first decade. I thought back to the passion we had shared so unashamedly. He'd been a friend to me in those early years when I'd shared my past, he'd listened. When I needed a shoulder, he'd been there. It was over time that things had degenerated and I could no longer point to any particular thing that had started the divide. It no longer mattered. I was tired of pointing out his wrongs and looking for answers. In that moment, I accepted the change and with it came a sense of peace. I really was a single mom. There it was. The truth sat in my mind and I was okay with it.

I moved on to a long letter to my mom, grateful for the friendship we enjoyed now. She followed me on my journey, through Facebook, along the Camino and we both hoped for this healing of our own rift. Again, I felt the warmth of peace. Next, I gave up being angry at my father. With this letter came a sense of humor. He knew I forgave him for taking his life. He was here with me, after all. Lastly, I wrote to Jim Griffin, The Creep. This one was the hardest, but it had to be done. I no longer identified with that victim and could no longer give him the power over me that he'd had. Though I'd vindicated myself through his prosecution, that act had instilled a sense of righteous anger that had never left me. Now I needed to release it. Rather than feeling weak like I thought I would feel, I felt stronger in peace and surrender.

I rose from my bed, tucked the letters that I never intended to mail into my pack, and rejoined the group outside with a sense of peace enveloping my heart. Steph and Zen immediately offered me glasses of wine, one from each of them. I took them. We ate and drank to Steph's health. We were all a bit inebriated by the time we decided to go to the local church. We didn't want to miss the chanting Gregorian monks at seven p.m.! They resided in this town and had a pilgrims' mass every night. We traipsed drunkenly up the cobbled streets to the humble church.

It was practically in shambles! There were no ostentatious gold wrapped sculptures. Beams poked through holes in the masonry. Two-by-fours propped up stones inside the walls. We shuffled into the shabby church to sit through the mass sung in Latin by the chanting monks. There we waited in drunken stupors for the solemnly draped holy men to file in. It was the first service that I'd been to that actually filled the church. By seven o'clock there was standing room only, so we squeezed together tighter to make room for more people. We must have been obnoxiously drunk because there were many pointed glares in our direction to quiet down. When the service started, everyone hushed. We listened as the monks chanted and sang the service. I'd missed their approach, but could now see them in their black cowls lining the walls of this plain and nearly ruined church. Their voices rose and filled the space above our heads with their melodic tones so that I wondered that no stones fell from the torn ceiling.

At the end of the service, many voices in the church were still singing so we stayed and enjoyed the happiness of the crowd. The monks waited for us as we filed out. They smiled and offered hugs as they thanked us for making this time-honored pilgrimage. I felt a bit bad for being intoxicated and hid it as best I could as I engaged a monk in conversation. I don't remember what I said to him, but he laughed. I took that as a good sign.

That night, we carried on with partying until eleven, the latest I'd been up on the whole journey! Zen had purchased sparklers somewhere so she handed them out to everyone in the courtyard. Just as they opened the last bottle of wine, Taylor decided the dinner table was the perfect dance floor. His sparklers nearly caught his hair on fire with his sloppy dance moves. I had to get a boost into my top bunk, but thankfully most everyone occupying that room was in the same drunken condition. I didn't even bother with my ear plugs or eye cover, just passed out.

"Get up, lazy! They'll kick you out any minute anyway!" I peeked blearily at Taylor's laughing eyes. Oh, to be younger and able to drink like that with no ill effects! He very sweetly handed me two ibuprofens and a bottle of water. I thanked him and swallowed the pills dry before washing them down with water. My head pounded harder once I moved but there was no choice. I jumped down and nearly yelled when my feet and calf muscles seized. As I moved, the tension eased somewhat so I could limp around. I threw my sunglasses on though the day was gloomy again; the weak light still stabbed my eyes. This time as I walked past the little church we'd visited last night, I stumbled for different reasons. I felt woozy and vowed never to party with twenty-one-year-olds again. I looked left at the small church in time to see one of the monks waving at us from the side courtyard. I thought about asking him to pray for my hangover.

CHAPTER EIGHTEEN

The journey from Rabanal continued steeply uphill until we were truly in the mountains. We would climb to the highest point on our journey at 1,500 meters. I paused several times to spin in all directions, thoughtfully taking in the mountain peaks surrounding us. There were snow caps in the distance. Those purple flowers rioted over the hills, cloaking the shoulders of the hills in lavender splendor. Here and there, yellow streaks of wildflowers ran in veins along the purple fields. I breathed in the beauty around me, completely at peace as my headache faded, replaced with an infinite sense of pleasure that welled from somewhere inside me. As we crested that first mountain top, we came to the famous iron cross, Cruz de Ferro.

Was this plain-looking iron cross the one we carried stones for? Its simple silhouette stood atop a tall wooden mast rising from the center of a large mound of rubble. Traditionally, since the eleventh century, pilgrims have laid a stone at the base of the cross to symbolize their journey. It's usually a stone from their home country. I'd forgotten to pack my rock the morning I left Colorado. With the layover in Miami, I'd gone to the beach and picked a shell. I thought it was fitting since we'd first had marriage trouble while living in Florida. Along the Camino, I'd pick up four pieces of shiny rocks and crystals that had caught my eye. These five pieces were now gripped tightly in my fist as I waited my turn to walk up the millennium-old mound that countless pilgrims had traversed before us and across time.

My first step on that mound brought a strange pulse of energy up my legs. I gasped at the palpable, residual emotion that clung to this place where people had prayed fervently and left their offerings. Shiny blue and pink bits of plastic stood out amongst the stones. These were obviously baby pacifiers and toys left behind by bereaved parents. Creased and faded photos peeked out from under heavy rocks. My legs shook all the way to the base of the cross. I laid the shell down on a relatively flat area and thought of Derek as his face flashed through my mind. Cognizant of others who wanted turns, though a small crowd could have fit up there with me, I laid a piece of quartz north of the shell. Another dark piece of stone was laid to the east, and so forth. The mini cross symbolized my need to cleanse all areas in my life in all directions. I prayed for healing to be free of my past, the whole past. My palm touched the wooden base of the iron cross that rose high above my head. "Please, let me come back to myself now. I'm done being angry."

As I climbed another peak a bit later, the sun chose to peek out from behind its cloak of clouds. My insides warmed with the sun. Tears filled my eyes as I looked around at the landscape. I was immeasurably glad to be here and free from my responsibilities so I could do this walk. I cried in joy for a moment, feeling silly but not really caring when a few pilgrims passed me. They didn't stop but smiled at me as if they felt it, too. They understood. I let a big fat tear roll down my cheek. I breathed in a huge lung full of air, amazed at how infrequently I ever drew a full breath of air. It was marvelous!

My odd burst of joy was short-lived as my concentration focused on the downhill slope. It was so steep that my weary ankles buckled a few times on loose rocks that slid from underfoot. By the time I made it halfway down the mountain, my knees felt watery. They were swollen. I came upon the picturesque mountain village called El Acebo. It was nestled so perfectly in the middle of the mountain that I knew I'd stay there rather than continue on. I was slightly worried about that squishy feeling in my knee, anyway. A new looking hostel, called La Casa del Peregrino, sat on my right. With a wide smile of delight, I greeted Steph and Zen. They stood waiting for me in the pretty courtyard in the House of Pilgrims, surrounded cheerfully by round iron tables with large red umbrellas stuck in them. I hugged them both, glad to see them. They had been there long enough to eat and enjoy a glass of wine already!

As soon as I sat down, the handsome bar owner came over to charm me. He practiced a bit of English with me and told me I was very pretty. I laughed and asked if he had a room available. He did, just one left. I started to hand him my credentials, but he waved the paperwork away. With that, he picked up my hand and placed a kiss in my palm, never taking his eyes from mine. "After you rest and eat, then you pay me." I nodded dumbly. *What WAS it with the men in this country*? I thought. It was nice to be appreciated so often.

My friends chatted with me for a few minutes and urged me to continue on with them rather than stay behind. I sadly shook my head and rubbed my knee as I explained. They stood slowly and prepared to leave. Both women had strict schedules and people would be waiting for both of them in Santiago. I felt a twinge of jealousy at that, though it was selfish to wish someone would fly to Spain to see me finish the walk. This time, it was harder to part from my new friends. We promised to stay in touch. Zen kissed my cheek and I watched them walk a ways down the street. They would catch up to Taylor and Glenn in Molinaseca, just nine kilometers farther.

Before sadness truly set in, my food was set in front of me with a flourish. The handsome owner sat across from me. He asked me, "Why does such a pretty woman travel alone on this journey?" I laughed at his charm. I had seen his wife giving him the evil eye. I thought about his question. I didn't want to give him the whole story.

"When a person wants to change their story and become a better version of themselves....When they are searching for something beyond their mere existence and they've tried everything else they know how to do....there may be a stirring in the soul that won't be ignored to come and walk The Way. That is why we go and walk the Camino alone...to find out why our souls called us here. There is discord in our lives until we do it."

His eyes lit up. As he slapped the table, he said, "Good! Now tell me. What you do for a living. You are American. You do not take so much time off work!" His eyes teased as the corners lifted in humor.

I relaxed into coffee shop talk. I did miss it. I missed the people so much. I missed a few of my employees, but most of all I missed my friends there. I talked about making espresso drinks and the joy in singing publicly for the first time even though it scared me nearly to death. I'd been a wreck and my voice totally choked. I loved the musicians so much that I had actually done it again and this time sang three songs instead of only one. I didn't die either time but I had sure felt like I would! He laughed at that. His eyes lit up as I talked about owning a business. How it involved the whole family whether they wanted to be involved or not.

"That's why she's a mean one!" He laughed and pointed at his wife. Though she scowled at him, I could see she wasn't seriously upset. On that note, he saw a glint of sadness pass over my face. Mistaking the meaning, he said, "You miss the store! You should not have sold it!" I nodded and let him think that. I didn't feel like rehashing the same old story. He leaned in suddenly.

"Tomorrow is Sunday." I sat back a little confused. For one thing, I had thought it was going to be Tuesday. I hadn't consulted a calendar in days!

"Okay…?" I questioned.

"Do you get up early?" he asked.

"Yes…no, not really. I am one of the lazier ones…I don't have a set time but I would LIKE to be out of here by eight a.m."

"Well…if you could do a favor for me and make your own latte in the morning….I know you can use my machine…"

"Sure! Show it to me!" I'd finished my soup and salad, including the whole basket full of bread.

He led me inside a warmly appointed room. Dark wood finishes along the bar and floor were modern and sleek. Behind the bar an espresso machine much like the one I was used to sat waiting with shiny, clean chrome handles and milk frother. A formal dining area sat to my right.

"My staff will set breakfast out over here, but no one will be here to make the special coffees you might want." With that he walked behind the bar and led me to the machine. He showed me where to find the espresso beans and I was familiar with his Italian grinder as well. I nodded excitedly. He then told his barista what was happening and the man looked happy to be able to sleep in. He asked the owner something in Spanish.

"You might make more coffees for pilgrims?"

"Sure, I'm thrilled to try it!"

"Great! I will show you your room now."

He led me through a door and up a narrow staircase to my room. I had upgraded my stay for the night to a private room. The bed looked inviting with a new comforter and extra pillows! The bathroom had been recently updated with new earth tone tile work and a huge glassed-in shower with brass finishes. He handed me the key and told me to leave it under the bar when I left. For thirty euros, I felt it was a good deal. He kissed my cheeks in their customary way, then left me shutting the door quietly behind him. I sat on my bed, preparing to shower and wash a few clothes. There was heat in this room so I figured things would actually dry! I'd had to hang a few items off of my pack a few times as I walked, air drying my underclothes and t-shirts.

I woke the next morning cozily snuggled under sheets and layers of blankets I'd heaped on my bed, windows ajar to cool the room. I'd clutched an extra pillow to my chest, pretending my daughter snuggled with me. I hadn't moved a muscle and was in the same position as when I closed my eyes. Yawning and stretching a bit, I quickly pulled my legs back up when my calves seized in a cramp. I stood quickly before I could think about it, teetering a little back and forth. I took no time to process any of the familiar pain signals; this was now my routine. I limp/walked to the bathroom and drank two glasses from the sink.

Ten minutes later I rushed downstairs in my socks to make sure the espresso machine was turned on. If it was like the one at my shop, it had to heat the water for at least half an hour before it could steam the milk or brew the espresso. They'd left it on for me. I rummaged around for a steam pitcher and found one without too much trouble. I poured milk into the cool metal pitcher and tested the wand. Steam came out in nice, even pressure. I stopped steaming and ground some beans in the Italian grinder to the left. I giggled to myself about how familiar yet strange it was to be making my own latte in someone else's café in a foreign country. When the grinder stopped, I filled the portafilter until it brimmed a little and dusted off the excess and tamped it down before inserting the metal cup into the espresso machine. I placed a mug under the coffee, and by then I heard a couple of voices behind me. I turned to see a large blonde woman smiling at me. She pointed to herself and her partner. His dark brown hair stood up three inches all around his head. His brown eyes were large and round. He ogled me curiously, seemed confused about why I was there making my own coffee. Before long a line had formed.

After I'd made a dozen small cafés con leche, I made a fresh one for myself and joined everyone in the dining room. I enjoyed breakfast with my foreign customers. They all smiled and talked and I had no idea what any of them were saying. It was one of my favorite mornings on the Camino. They all either hugged me or shook my hand before they left. Many of them had insisted on paying me, so I divided the money and left half of it in a mug by the coffee machine. Before I went up to pack I rummaged around and found a larger coffee mug and made an American sized coffee.

CHAPTER NINETEEN

BEFORE I'D GONE MORE THAN half a block from the hotel, I heard a honk and turned as an old white car whizzed by, nearly hitting me. An elderly man with bright white hair drove the car but I focused on the other elderly gentleman next to him. This man's face was flushed bright pink and he wore blue eye shadow. To complete his Sunday best, he wore a long, curly blonde wig. They waved out their open windows to anyone who looked at them. I shook my head as this happy little car rounded the curve ahead and disappeared with more honking to announce their arrival. Who would have thought they'd see a drag queen in full regalia driving down a tiny mountain hamlet while walking this soul-searching journey? I passed a man standing in the middle of the road and giggled at his astonished expression.

A while later, to a chorus of "Buen Caminos," I walked into a lively scene once I entered the town of Molinaseca. There were numerous pilgrims dining on the square. Many had arrived by bicycle as they were all parked in semi-disarray along the square's perimeter. A group of Italian men lounged in their colorful nylon cyclist's clothing while they drank espresso and shouted at each other in good humor. When I arrived they gave a big cheer. I grinned and waved. It was so nice to be noticed by these good-looking charmers. They tried to wave me over to their table but I shook my head in search of my own coffee and sandwich.

This town had charming balconies overhanging the streets and round wooden doors with etched carvings around the moldings. Bustling shops and restaurants lined the streets in all directions. It seemed to be a lively place. Regrettably, I couldn't stay and make new friends as I still had over twenty kilometers to go. Still, the peace and harmony of the mountains once again entered my soul as I left the loud city streets behind and rejoined the trail.

Ponferrada bombarded my senses as soon as I entered the city. It boasted a population of 65,000 but to me it seemed as large as Denver after the eerily quiet, nearly abandoned villages I'd walked through. Cars whizzed by fast and threw my equilibrium off. I hesitated to cross at an intersection even though both lanes of traffic stopped for me. I delicately put my toe on the crosswalk and cautiously tiptoed across the street, making sure all cars were stopped. A man on the other side was laughing and pointed at me. Annoyed instantly, I watched him as I crossed and stepped next to him with my eyebrow arched questioningly.

"You are AMERICAN!" he laughed raucously.

"I am....what gave me away?" I asked dryly.

"From...hahaha!....from the way you cross the street!" He imitated me with both of my arms stuck straight out and tip-toeing across the street. "You were funny to watch. They have strict laws about hitting pedestrians, you know. Everyone will stop! They were stopped! But you looked like you were going to get run over any minute! You know, you should try it like the Europeans! They just go and don't look."

Embarrassed by the picture of me as he presented it, I turned on my heel as I said, "Pardon me for being cautious, I guess..."

I brushed by him on my way to see the Castle of the Templar Knights just behind him. As I passed him, he still laughed openly. I turned indignantly toward him again, "I'd look sillier dead, you know!" and walked up the bridge that spanned the moat to the entrance. Unfortunately, the castle was locked. I'd missed the two-hour window to go in and take a tour. Feeling a bit dejected at not seeing the Templar history inside, I sat on the moat bridge to make sure my antagonist was gone before going that direction again. The wall provided a backdrop to sit against while I ate my cold lunch of whatever happened to be packed amongst my underwear and spare shoes.

My hands pulled out a sandy apple that had been abused by my shoes, a few rice cakes, a can of tuna in oil, and a sealed bag of olives. I saved the apple for dessert. I sat there on the cold flagstones long enough for my ass to go numb with cold and my legs and feet to stiffen up. I switched shoes again, this time putting on my tennis shoes, though I had to loosen the ties because my feet were very swollen and red. When I stood, they felt like hot, liquid-filled balloons instead of feet. I ignored this feeling and prepared to go another few kilometers. Pain or no pain, I couldn't stay here in this loud, obnoxious city.

Passing through the city only heightened the need to get away from it. Outside the old, preserved section of town, it was obvious that people here were poverty stricken and full of angst. Once outside the main square, graffiti marked the walls over abandoned homes and businesses. Endowed with a macabre imagination especially when alone, I fully expected ghostly faces to press up against the grimy windows of these poor, lost places.

City sidewalks led through a town with more empty storefronts. They were barred or gated, outdated fliers flapped on their windows and doors. Here and there eviction notices were taped to a door or window. Eerily, no one else walked about. I hesitantly walked up to an ATM machine as papers and garbage blew down the empty street. I expected it be inoperable. I calmed myself by watching the reflections in the glass for movement. Surprisingly it spit out my cash and card and I stuffed it all deep into my pack and buckled it fast. I swung the pack back on before I had finished turning around. Had I known then that many pilgrims are mugged in Ponferrada, I wouldn't have gone to an ATM there.

When I limped down the dirt road out of this town, I wondered if I was crazy. Why couldn't I call a taxi and just drive to Santiago. What was stopping me? Who would know? I wouldn't say anything. Except, I would know. Damn my pride, I thought. All of this for a certificate of completion in Santiago. I must be crazy.

I walked until I thought my feet must have fallen off because my legs felt like bloody stumps. Below the knees everything was numb. The town of Cacabelos finally arrived. With tears in my eyes, I made my way to the very first place I saw, called the Montcloa Hostel. Vine-covered walls opened up to a lovely courtyard with more vines and greenery overhead. I walked through an open wooden door that led into this haven. Farther in, the courtyard revealed outdoor dining on the left with vine-covered trellis overhead, a restaurant entrance in front and a gift shop to the right.

A tree decorated merrily with colored yarn woven into intricate designs grew outside the retail shop and check-in counter. A warm and friendly young woman looked up. She saw my pack and quickly told me about the pilgrim discount at their establishment. Then she begged me to sit while she helped someone else, but first she fetched me a glass of wine.

"For energy," she said brightly! I wondered how she knew to speak English but was beyond trying to figure out that mystery anymore. I figured there must be something about the way I carried myself that announced, "I'M AMERICAN." I sipped my wine and looked around at the fun gift choices in the shop. I immediately saw a hundred things I wanted to buy for Parker.

The smiley girl came back, so I handed her my empty wine glass and got down to business. I dragged my feet slowly after her. She had to pause several times while I caught up to her. As we passed restaurants, food smells assaulted my starving stomach. I caught myself envying her for her feet. They must feel great, I thought wearily. She practically bounced where I scraped and dragged and grabbed at banisters to pull myself along after her. I gasped as we climbed stairs, wondering how I would recover to make it down to dinner. My stomach now warred with my feet. I almost laughed at the ludicrous predicament. Soak my feet or feed my belly?

She led me to my room and though it was gorgeous, the only thing I could think of was a bath. So that decided it. I thanked her as she cheerfully closed my door and then I nearly wept when I removed my shoes. My feet pulsed and pounded. Immediately I lay on my bed to put them up the wall. I needed to reduce the blood flow to the abused flesh without delay. Twenty minutes later, I rolled over gently to touch one toe to the floor and nearly yelped. A whimper escaped as I slithered out of bed to land on my knees instead. All I could do was crawl to the bathroom, where I ran a tub of warm water from my kneeling position on the floor, which is where I undressed too, and then pulled myself into the tub with my arms. At the same time, I shook from hunger. I had never experienced two such extreme and competing needs like this before. My stomach was now, I was sure, consuming my spine as I laid back into the soothing heat. I was so hungry the bar soap smelled delicious—I almost licked it just to see if it truly was.

Water filled the tub halfway before I shut it off. I quickly scrubbed and then lowered myself more so I could elevate my legs again. After about fifteen minutes, my stomach won. I needed food to reenergize and heal my body. I drained the water but was fearful of standing on my feet just yet. Pushing up into a sitting position, I gently set my feet on the bottom of the tub. *Not bad, not bad at all,* I thought. *Here goes.* Using my hands on the sides of the tub, I pushed up into a nearly standing position and almost bashed the back of my skull into the wall behind me when the pain rocked me back. Arms trembled as I lay back down in the tub and resigned myself to more elevating. I pulled the large towel I'd set on the toilet seat over my body to keep warm.

I woke up snoring in the bathtub. I shivered. I had no idea how long I'd slept! This time, it didn't matter how much pain I was in. After walking thirty-one kilometers that day, I needed to "eat a dog" like Nacho said. Breathing through flared nostrils to keep from making loud sounds, I took two seconds to acclimate to the pain before gingerly stepping out of the tub. I had to sit to put my pants on. I couldn't really walk, but I could shuffle really well. I slid my feet quickly over the wood floor and made my way clumsily to the dining room.

An older couple passed me and grimaced at my pain. "It's just the Camino..." I whined at them. Once free of the stairs, I shuffled through the dining area under the trellis and sat down waiting for a waiter. He was very handsome and tried flirting with me, but the dialect had changed so much we were incommunicable. I saw a man across from me eating lamb chops so I pointed to his dish and then to me and held up my wine glass. "Por favor!" I was quick to add. He laughed and nodded his head.

He served me a luscious regional red wine, a whole basket of crusty bread with butter, a big salad with greens grown locally, and finally, four lamb chops with French fries. I ate it all, every bite. The waiter seemed impressed with my appetite. Finally satiated, I paid my tab and shuffled toward the gift shop. Everywhere I went people pointed at my feet. They grimaced while they "oh'd" and "ah'd" over them. A white haired gentleman even hugged me, while somewhat comically imitating my shuffle in sympathy. Turning my attention to the shop's offerings, I chose a handmade orange suede wrap bracelet with hand-cut flower design all around it, for Parker. Orange was currently her favorite color. I knew she would love it. Plus, I could carry it without adding noticeable weight.

That night my feet hurt so terribly that the pressure of laying them on the mattress was too much. I devised a sloping hill of pillows to elevate my legs and dangled my throbbing feet off the edge of them. I drank a full glass of water and took four ibuprofen liquid gels before slipping into an exhausted sleep. By morning, my pillows had been kicked to the floor and my feet throbbed where they pressed into the mattress. I sat up to massage them vigorously until the pain receded again. I devoted fifteen minutes to each foot, diligently massaging each little muscle that connected everything and promising them I would be kinder and walk half the distance as the day before. As I stood, I found the pain had reduced to a dull ache. Feeling triumphant, I shuffled around as I packed my few precious things. I had pared down to only those essentials I actually used and I was acutely grateful to have each and every item.

CHAPTER TWENTY

Despite high hopes, my morning started rough with my feet throbbing at each step. Experience had taught me to crank my music up uncomfortably loud to ignore the pain. It was a wonder my ears didn't bleed. I was right; after a kilometer or so, I could turn the music down and focus on one foot in front of the other without the pain beating at me.

A woman running a small street-side market called to me so I replenished my food supplies before exiting Cacabelos. The hills continued to rise and fall under my feet as I passed the vineyards on either side. Pilgrims getting a late start that day rushed by me on foot and bicycle, wishing me a good journey as they passed. I tucked my hands in my pockets after eating my cherries and spitting seeds along the road. I knew I would catch up to a few of these faster moving people. In the beginning, I'd been reminded of the story of *The Tortoise and the Hare*. It struck me that pilgrims hurried to be the first to arrive wherever they headed that day, but they lingered over food as if they had all day, only to rush and pass me again at some point on the trails.

After a short fifteen kilometer walk, I knew I was done for the day. I checked into the first albergue that came along, and it was the first time I was extremely disappointed in a place I stayed and the people who ran the place. The woman behind the counter did not look up at me, though there were no other pilgrims presently waiting to be served. An older woman finally came in who walked behind the counter and reached underneath it to extract the pilgrim registration booklet and the stamper, which she set out for me to stamp my own credential. She never asked my name but held out her hand for the money. I asked about laundry. She nodded her head once, then signaled for me to follow her. I was led out of the reception area, up some nice orange and blue tiled stairs, down a long hall past other rooms, to a room with four bunk beds. She left without showing me where the other facilities were. I dumped my pack on the top bunk by the open window that had absolutely no view except for the roof of the first floor. At least I could sleep with the fresh air, I thought.

After suffering through the worst salad and worst service I'd ever had on the Camino, I vowed not to eat at that unwelcoming place for dinner. These people were not nice. The showers had been cold though the place wasn't full yet and it was early in the day. I walked into the dilapidated town and found a small, dark market. I halfway expected it to be closed but the door opened to the musty, dark interior. Thick layers of dust coated boxes of crackers and canned goods. I wondered how long they had been hoping to sell some of these items. I bought dried fruit and nuts, crackers, chocolate, cheese, and a plate of spaghetti bolognaise the woman assured me was "fresh" to warm up in the kitchenette near my room.

The owners of the hostel were still blatantly throwing me hostile looks. I swung my bag of groceries so they could see I wouldn't be eating at their fine establishment that evening. I remembered that the second floor had a balcony and ventured out to find tables and chairs. A couple of overweight French women chugged strong-smelling beer, spoke loudly and belched as if they were men. The horrid stench that burst from each belch was also due to the copious amounts of cigarettes they smoked. They smiled at me but I still moved a few tables farther away.

    A woman from Brazil named Nikki introduced herself to me. She was short and petite with very pretty warm, brown eyes that sat on either side of a long, thin nose. She traveled alone, though she wasn't opposed to traveling with friends for a day or two. We both preferred solitude. We shared a few commonalities in our stories as well. I asked her shyly if she'd had any miracles happen to her yet. She looked down at the tabletop and said, "Yes, I have! Have you?" I nodded. We talked until it was time for her to join everyone downstairs for dinner. I heated my spaghetti and ate it outside as the sun slid slowly to the horizon. It was then I realized I was eating alone and perfectly comfortable with it! I had been so afraid to be alone, and now here I was seeking it out. I squinted at the sun and thought of all the people in my life and my need to please them all. I couldn't do it anymore. I vowed to be my real self from now on. I would stand up for what I wanted and not care if it didn't align with everyone's ideals on where or what I should be doing instead.

    That night I'd fallen asleep in my top bunk near the open window as I journaled. The pages stuck to my cheek as I peeled the book out from under my face and laid it against the wall instead of dropping it to the floor and waking the room. Just then the fat French woman below me farted loudly and I nearly laughed with the shock of it. The funk that followed is indescribable but I can tell you that it made me want to cry. It was the sort of smell that had weight and lingered far longer than it should.

    Everyone, including myself, hurried to get packed and out of there next morning. I threw everything in my pack hastily, taking breaths in the open window every now and then. I ran down the stairs and past the owners who waited to take coffee orders. I had noticed a cute little pension offering fair trade coffee, El Puente Peregrino, the night before near the market so I hurried there.

Santago and his wife Elly greeted me with bright smiles. Their little pension was very sweetly remodeled with a mixture of modern and old-world charm. I made myself comfortable on a bar stool. Santago exuded charm as he leaned toward me on his elbows. We were making jokes right away. An Asian pilgrim came down the stairs, joining me at the bar. He'd had a wonderful night's sleep in a non-smelly room. I was extremely jealous and vowed that I would stay there should I do the Camino again. Elly laughed but refused to comment on her competitor. She merely winked at me and went into the tiny kitchen next to the bar.

Elly hummed while she made me a breakfast of scrambled eggs and toast, including free shots of fresh OJ and a finger-sized biscotti. Since we'd been talking about hiking in Colorado, Santago jokingly made me an Americano, which earned the distinction of my most perfect cup of coffee on the Camino to date. I gushed over the delicious brew. They engaged each pilgrim who walked through their doors with warmth and gratitude. I wished that I had stayed there instead! I hugged them both afterward. They had turned my stay in Trabadelo around. Their little café offered souvenirs for pilgrims, so I bought a few pins and key chains as gifts for people. Sometimes, I realized, it took a not-so-great experience to appreciate the kind and generous people who, in contrast, wanted to spread their joy to the world and specifically to us on our journey. Their warmth infused me for the rest of the day.

CHAPTER TWENTY-ONE

THE WAY TO O'CEBREIRO WAS gruelingly uphill all day and most of it on paved highways. There were options to take a trail through the mountains but I missed the turn-off somewhere. Trucks blared by, disrupting my thoughts. Though the sunlight was weak again today, I wore my sunglasses to protect my eyes from flying debris. At some points there were virtually no shoulders on the road and I found myself hugging bushes to keep out of the traffic's way. It was harrowing. For a couple of hours I feared I might get hit by a speeding car or truck. Several honked at me, but I had nowhere to jump to. I was already as far over as I could get. Out of sheer desperation, I prayed to my angel, Michael, to keep me safe. I was almost pissed. How could a pilgrimage that was so time-honored and traditional not have a proper path?

After approximately ten kilometers, the turn-off came. I was graciously thrust back into the forest and sheltering trees. It was amazing to feel the transformation from feeling pissed and angry on the road to feeling like I stepped into Sleeping Beauty's wooded glen once the forest trees and dirt trails enclosed me in their rustling embrace again.

A few farmhouses and cattle ranging around seemed to indicate some kind of town because suddenly there was a café with horses hitched outside. I'd forgotten the Camino could be done by horse! I stopped to pet the soft nose of a quarter horse that swished his tail over his hind quarters and stomped his back feet occasionally as he waited for his rider to saddle up and get moving. His large, liquid left eye lowered to mine and he stared solemnly into my eyes as I scratched his forehead. I held my fingertips still as he rubbed his head up and down, scratching his own itch. His ears went up suddenly and he took a step back as the door to the bar opened. I patted his strong, warm neck before leaving.

It was good advice to always have a healthy respect for someone else's horse. Don't treat it like your own. They had a tendency to show their true colors when their human wasn't around. On a crisp autumn morning, I learned that lesson the hard way. I'd suspected for years that my grandpa's beloved black stallion was evil incarnate. Turns out it was true.

Leading up to that day, I'd been nervous to learn I'd be horseback riding with Grandpa, just the two of us. I didn't know what to say to the man. He wore Stetsons and Wranglers and had a mean, hard streak that I'd witnessed unleashed on other people. Never me though. He stood awkwardly when I spontaneously told him I loved him, he took a step back, arched a brow and asked, "Ya do?! What fer?!" Then he would mockingly punch me in the arm. Though he'd longed for a son, he'd been given four daughters. He was disappointed at emotional "weaknesses" and only strong, back-breaking work seemed to please him. I worked hard around him and since I rarely spoke, he seemed okay with me. People told me I was his favorite. I wished he wouldn't show it with arm punches though.

This particular day, he told me I had to help him and I tried to act like I knew exactly what to do. I tried to walk tall and confidently around the horses, because Grandpa had told me they could sense fear. "If a horse knows you fear him, you will never be his master. He will be yours." He'd said this to me often. I had chosen the mildest horse, which ironically was their largest, named Wink. He was a giant of a quarter horse, standing seventeen hands tall. He only ever wanted bits of horse cake and apples. As soon as he saw the plaid coat of Grandpa's that I'd borrowed, he ambled over to me and delicately burrowed into the top coat pocket with his lips to dig out his treats. He was easy. I had his bridle and blanket on before Grandpa coaxed his evil stallion to him with a combination of whistles and calls.

Grandpa led the horse through thigh-high grasses to the fence and since he only had a lead rope on him, he handed it to me and sternly told me to "keep a tight hold. Show him you're boss," and then he disappeared in the barn. I stood nervously holding the rope to Grandpa's horse, Patch. He stood a full hand and a half shorter than my chosen horse. As soon as Grandpa disappeared from view, that damned horse tossed his black mane and turned his head to look me full in the eye. His dark, glossy stare showed the elongated view of my face in his pupil. I didn't dare blink. Patch snapped his teeth at my hand. Then, he kept his eye on mine as he lifted his left hoof and placed it on my right foot. Swiftly, he shifted his weight just enough so that my foot shoved down into the spongy earth below it, sinking at least two inches, pinned beneath the weight of his massive hoof. I leaned my weight into his neck but he refused to move a muscle. The more I pushed the more he seemed an impenetrable wall. I was grateful that Grandpa made me wear a pair of his cowboy boots for riding.

I struggled silently against that evil horse for a few seconds when out of nowhere Grandpa's fist smashed into Patch's jawbone. I thought he would rear up in pain or shock. Instead, he simply lifted his foot straight up and off my foot. He shook his mane in defiance but set his foot back down gently, safely on the ground. It struck me how very diabolically intelligent this horse was. He hadn't broken any bones. My grandpa chuckled under his breath. "Showed you, din't he?" His blue eyes winked at me in admiration. He was proud of me?! The rest of the day, we didn't talk about the incident but the quality of our conversation changed so that we showed a bit more respect toward each other. My horse did not give me any problems except for being extremely difficult to climb onto. I stayed well away from Patch after that. I was pretty sure he'd won the showdown.

I missed my grumpy grandpa suddenly, as I climbed higher up into the forest. He was a difficult man to have a conversation with but he and I seemed to understand each other now. Often, when women in our family would spend hours and hours talking about mundane things, he and I would share a glance over the papers or magazines we read, share a look and a "harrumph." It was his secret language and not everyone could understand it. However, he and I both led lives a bit more incongruous from the rest of the family. We were out of sync with the world around us. This made us silent allies though we never talked about it. I appreciated that, like me, he had trouble expressing his feelings but he'd always been there to support us in his silent, strong-man way.

A canopy of trees covered my head. The trail turned to black mud and sliding rocks; however, I moved more steadily going uphill than down. I started to pass more and more pilgrims. It had become stiflingly warm and humid, so I shed layers as I went, adept at unbuckling my pack and removing layers now without stopping. Every inch of that twenty kilometer walk to O'Cebreiro had been uphill. I climbed up the concrete slab that led to the village with my head down, putting one foot in front of the other. I was unprepared for the beauty of the Galician mountains that surrounded me at the top of the climb. O'Cebreiro was a very old village, with a cathedral that dated back to the ninth century. Every building was preserved in its original gray stone, which only enhanced the lush green landscapes of the mountains.

In the main square, the buildings were tightly knit together in a small space atop the mountains. I walked the perimeter of the town just taking in the views all around. I snapped photos of the mountains from each side. They mesmerized me with their layers upon layers of peaks overlapping and stretching so far back that they looked like gray cut-out shapes from afar. It was tranquil. I sat on the low stone wall that rimmed the city and breathed in the fresh beauty surrounding me. Half an hour later back in town, I was thrilled to see a great selection of tourist shops and cafés. There were several choices to stay in, but I chose the albergue, only five euros.

The new albergue had been built to accommodate over a hundred-fifty pilgrims. It perched on the precipice of the mountain town. Several pilgrims sat on the stone wall outside of it much like I had. The air smelled uncommonly good up here. I never tired of it. I went inside and was led to a very large sleeping room with approximately seventy beds. I chose a lower bed near a window this time and dumped my pack before collapsing for a nap. Though I'd sweated like a beast today, showers would have to wait.

During dinner, I found an English-speaking table and introduced myself all around. Everyone was, of course, exceptionally nice. I tried to ignore the prickly feeling between my shoulder blades that told me someone stared at me. I glanced behind to see a tall, blond man staring with brilliant green eyes. I smiled politely but turned quickly around to answer the woman next to me, though I hadn't heard her question. I noticed him before at a couple of other stopping points but had managed to avoid his intensity. It seemed we were destined to talk at some point. I sighed and sipped my highly recommended Galician stew. I savored the warmth and felt my bones melt with each sip off my spoon.

I felt uncharacteristically unsociable this evening and felt a sudden need for solitude. Upon reflection, I realized those feelings had been trying to surface for days. One glance at the handsome blond man showed he hadn't shifted one bit. I closed my eyes and savored my stew. As more bottles of wine were passed around, I stood to get some air. The noise of everyone talking abruptly became too intense. I paid my tab and slipped out without glancing at the man behind me though I felt his gaze all the way to the door. Since it was only nine p.m., it was still light out. The sun wouldn't go down until nearly 10:30. I went back over to the stone wall I'd sat on earlier and perched there again with my toes dangling over the side, pointing down the mountain. In fact, I saw that if I tipped over, I would fall nearly straight down to the valley below.

The quaint stone village sat neatly atop this lone peak. There was a strong Celtic feel to the Galician region, as evidenced in the shops in town. Tourists looking for more unusual keepsakes can now buy Celtic knots, comical witches and evil eye wards—blue glass tokens with black and white spots of color that resemble eyes and are believed to protect against evil. The region was heavily influenced by its former Celtic inhabitants so there is a carving of a witch in the gate leading into the church, which is the oldest one on the route, hailing from the ninth century and predating the Romans' influences on architecture. Inside the church is said to be a holy grail that offers miracles. History in this beautiful town is so well-preserved that there remains the oldest operational lodging house along the Camino from Roncesvalles, the San Giraldo de Aurillac, which also hails from the ninth century.

As far as I could see, peaks and valleys rose and fell. I wondered how many more of them I would climb. My legs were stronger and leaner, the muscles tighter, my pants looser. I gripped the wall strongly with my hands and leaned forward a bit. I felt alone, yet not lonely. My body hummed with an almost impatient, vibrant urge to make it all the way to Santiago, but I knew there were larger more vital changes happening in my body and mind.

A softness inside was taking hold. I no longer felt the need to hang on to anger. Some of the relationships I'd lost in the divorce would never be the same and I was beginning to see that there was no need to reestablish those connections. Forgiveness did not mean maintaining unhealthy relationships. Rather, it was a tool to use so I could let go. Forgiveness, when I had thought about it before, meant sacrificing too much of myself. My pride and ego hated the idea. Why should I be the one to apologize? I would have these thoughts and the red hot steel of my anger would rise again. I'd feel it coursing through my veins like my very own vigilante. I felt justified.

Looking back on that sad, lonely little girl I had been made me terribly sad. Tears rose and fell unheeded as I thought of my scared smaller self. I'd been so quiet and so "good." I wished I could go back in time as myself now and talk to her. I'd appear as my older self and tell her to yell and scream and throw a fit. "Speak your mind," I would say, "it'll all be okay."

Growing up hiding my pain, I'd learned to keep everyone at a safe distance. I let them in just enough but guarded my heart. The only emotion I seemed capable of feeling was anger, but only under extreme situations. Then, I took it out with a vicious vengeance on the person, almost with a sadistic delight. It felt amazing to feel, even if it was anger that infused me. Angry with those in my family who'd wanted me to "get over it," I felt they just wanted to push it all under the rug. No one wanted to hear about the things going on at home. So, as soon as I could I'd moved out at eighteen and in with an abusive boyfriend...until I became angry enough at him to leave and stole his hidden cache of money to move back in with my mother a couple of years later — one of many starting-over points with us.

I knew then what I needed to do. I'd forgiven as much as I could but needed to forgive myself. It sounded trite and sort of ridiculous. It made me want to scoff at the sky and throw a temper tantrum. What did I have to forgive myself for? I knew deep down. I forgave myself for hiding from everything, being afraid, for letting myself be abused. For the anger. For losing my baby at the age of twenty and not leaving the jerk right away. I felt myself melt as old anger deep inside slowly released. My pride wrestled to keep it from happening. Anger had made me persevere. It was my backbone and that familiar place I went to when I needed strength. As I sat there, I realized I was at war with myself on different planes — spiritual and human. As the sun faded and my body trembled with cold, I hardly noticed. I was lost in transition.

Much later, the cold seeped into my awareness so I pried myself off the icy stone wall. The magical twinkling lights of O'Cebreiro caught my eyes as I stood and felt a stirring inside. With certainty, a familiar pull at my self-conscious tugged at me as I walked back toward the stone buildings. I knew I'd been here before in another lifetime. I neared the restaurant and glanced inside to see most everyone had left. The intense blond man was outside on the patio leaning his elbows on the low wall. His green eyes tracked me like a predatory feline. I watched him, too, in case he had strange ideas. Even after a lengthy exercise in letting go of anger, it was still ready to surge to my protection if there was a sudden need to karate chop him in the throat or something. Of course, only under extreme duress would I resort to such measures, but I felt a little extra power course through my muscles as I passed him uneventfully.

The next morning I opened my eyes to see the shutters flung wide open and half the beds empty already. I stretched, not caring about the time and in no immediate hurry to get anywhere. It was almost as if I forgot briefly each morning that I had to do the same thing all over again. Extricate self from twisted sleeping bag, try not to pee my pants while adjusting to the pain in feet, shuffle to oddly co-mingled bathroom, shield eyes just in case, and take care of business...Oh yes, and get ready to hike another twenty-k or so.

Ten minutes later I was walking to the same little restaurant and found the last seat available with the group from last night before the place became a zoo. The same middle-aged woman who had served us dinner calmly handled the mad rush. She simply yelled orders to the fry cook behind the front counter and went to the next table. Her once-blonde hair was pulled back into a loose, curly pony tail. Just when she'd written our orders, a group of cyclists came in and added to the barely controlled chaos.

All around, men and women bickered about how far to go and where to stay. Some already had their phones out in order to make reservations ahead of the rest of us. A woman sat crying across from me and showed her friends bandages around her knees and ankles. I cringed at that. Today was going to be all downhill. I hoped she knew that and chose carefully. I chewed slowly and absorbed the buzzing activity all around me. As I slowly finished my breakfast, everyone seemed to decide at once to disperse. A few people threw me Buen Caminos as they ran for the door. I wanted to laugh, feeling again like the tortoise. Dirty plates, silverware and cups were abandoned where they sat. A couple of pilgrims besides myself lingered.

    I stood and busied myself, picking up dishes. My waitress came over to put her hand on my arm as if to say "no need," her cornflower blue eyes opened wide. She gestured at the open door as if I should join the others. I shook my head and picked up more dishes. She let me take them behind the counter to stack by the sink. Within minutes she stopped encouraging me to join the masses and handed me a rag. After we pushed chairs and tables back where they belonged, I turned to wave to her but she held my arm and led me to the kitchen. She cut enormous pieces from two types of cake, wrapped them in foil and shoved them in the top pouch of my backpack. I thought she was done, but she threw in a bottle of water, too. Then she grabbed my hands and said a little prayer for me. Though I had no idea what she said, she could have wished me to be blessed with seven children for all I knew! I hugged her. She kissed my cheeks. Her blue eyes looked a bit happier than when I'd arrived.

CHAPTER TWENTY-TWO

Tranquility had settled over my heart and in my bones during my stay in O'Cebreiro and hummed throughout my body. My mind felt lighter. It was as if a window had been opened in the attic of my mind and a clean wind had swept away the old pain. Thoughts toward my mother were full of love and compassion, rather than vengeful anger. I thought about the many times when I'd tried to force her to take ownership of her involvement. My yelling and cursing had only invited more of the same from her. I saw her for the first time as a woman who struggled with how to cope with life. I had an understanding, a glimpse into what it must be like, as if a shroud had been lifted so I may have a peek inside. I only wanted to hug her and accept her and be a daughter to her. No more histrionics.

Now, as I reviewed the events of the last couple of years I found them oddly...right. Everything seemed as it should be, for some reason. I felt at peace with it all. I giggled to myself as I remembered spending the last year and a half looking for the next Mr. Right as purely competition. Here on this mountain in Spain, I could see it all so clearly. I'd been desperate and seeking someone, anyone...without even knowing what I wanted in a man! I nearly choked at the thought of what I may have unintentionally taught Parker. I had always wanted her to be independent and strong—how could she grow into the confident woman I saw her as if her mother was needy like that? This newfound levity inside refused to feel guilty about the past anymore. I shrugged as I continued walking, thinking, *I'll meet him when I meet him...no big deal.*

I was certain my heart had been cleansed in that church just a few days ago...or was it weeks? Time blended together. Somewhere along this trek my mind and soul had been scrubbed clean. I felt the strength of my own spirit as surely as the hardening muscles of my legs and in my shoulders that more easily carried me now. In the beginning of the journey, I'd been afraid since I'd never traveled alone. My soul had led me here though I could never explain WHY I needed to go, just that I had to. Now there no longer seemed to be any shame or regret, no hatred or blame. This was why I laughed and smiled on the trail that day. I was on the cusp of comprehension, and with that knowledge came a lightness I could not remember ever experiencing before.

After twelve kilometers all downhill, my toenails began to ache. My ankles felt a bit strained and my knees were tightening up even though I'd been careful to bend them slightly as I descended. Just when I needed a rest, the small town of Fonfría popped up. I stopped at a small café to order a sandwich and take a rest. I ordered my *bocadillo* with ham, cheese, lettuce and tomato and took it with me to sit and ponder the mountain vistas. The mists that shrouded the peaks that morning had become leaden gray clouds, heavy with rain, so I sat against the base of a tree huddled in my poncho. My pack rested beside me as I ate. Steam rose from the neck hole of my plastic coat.

After lunch, I passed through a very tiny little village where I couldn't help gagging over the smell of animal excrement that smeared the walkways. The rain had made it slick so I watched my step as I slid in pig and cow shit. Just ahead a short little woman in a farm dress and head scarf herded her dozen pigs with a long stick. She looked at me briefly over her shoulder but kept a vigilant eye on her herd. She was in no hurry to get out of the road. Due to the poop-slicked road, I walked carefully around the fat, grunting rush-hour traffic. Chickens and geese chased each other across the streets in these little towns. Impoverished and rundown as they were, they retained a certain old-world charm in their ancient stone walls.

It seemed a cruel joke that the steepest hill came at the end of this day's walk to Triacastela. By this point I had slowed so that I could zigzag down the hill to cut down on the angle and relieve some tension in my ankles and knees. Though I was tired of the constant physical aches and pains of the journey, I was also aware of how sad I would be for this to all end. However, when the town appeared in its low-lying valley, I was relieved to be near a resting point! I decided I didn't care about finding a quaint place to stay and stopped into an albergue right on the main road. It looked like a laundromat from the outside. It was a non-descript concrete building with a long glass window that faced the main street. Inside, I saw several pilgrims sitting at small tables and a few vending machines.

As soon as I claimed my bed, I went quickly into the sole bathroom and found a shirtless old man brushing his teeth. I quickly closed the door and took three steps back before he pulled it open. He gestured that I could come in, but I politely declined and stood to the side until he left a few minutes later with a big grin as he held the door for me. I ran into a stall and locked myself in the shower while I undressed. Unthinkingly, I turned the shower taps on and gasped loudly as the freezing water hit me with icy needles. There was nowhere to go to escape the cold blast. I suffered for a few seconds until the water heated enough to take the sting of cold away. After my shower, I longed for a nice, hot bath. I'd thought ahead to make a reservation at the Parador my last night in Santiago, and I looked forward to the luxurious bath they would surely provide!

After my customary snack and nap, I got up to go rummage for a proper meal. I found the courtyard where everyone seemed to be gathered around a few restaurants. Most of the outdoor tables and chairs were full already, though it was only six o'clock. I didn't want to take a whole table for myself and looked inside the darkened interior of the restaurant. Its gloom was not inviting, so I remained outside and waited for an empty spot. My name was called. I glanced over to my left to see Nikki, from Brazil. Her long brown tresses were still wet from her shower. Her pretty face smiled openly as she gestured for me to take the chair across from her. I joined her just as a group of males moved to converge on her. She smiled gratefully at me. I winked at her.

She turned her attention to the male in front of the group. His young, ruddy face looked a bit crestfallen. Nikki spoke to him in another language for a few minutes. I ignored them as she gestured at me and pouted into his hopeful face. His shoulders slumped a bit for a moment, but he brightened and asked her something, again sounding bright and hopeful. She shook her head and again gestured at me.

"Are you telling him I'm your lesbian lover?" I asked half-jokingly.

Her eyes widened in surprise. "No! Should I? I am telling him we are old acquaintances. We met earlier and now we are catching up." I nodded and waited as she conversed with him for another minute.

"Okay, he asked me to walk with him tomorrow and I told him I would walk either alone or with you because I have missed you so much! I think he is thinking we are interested in each other now." She laughed behind her hand. I looked at the young men as they retreated.

He glanced back over his shoulder at us. Nikki grabbed my hand. I looked deeply into her eyes, leaning slightly forward.

"I think I'll need some wine for this charade," I said with humor coloring my voice. The waiter appeared and we both ordered *tint vino*, or red wine. I told him to just bring me the best dishes on the pilgrims' menu. He smirked. My choices were between pork or lamb chops. I chose lamb.

We visited and laughed for hours before I remembered the dire warning on the albergue doors that they locked up at nine-thirty. I explained to Nikki that I had to hurry back and she said hers had the same warning posted on all the doors. I thanked her for the lovely evening in my most sarcastic tone and promised to go on another date with her. She hugged me and we ran in opposite directions, hoping to catch the doors on time. I made it back with three minutes to spare. I quickly prepared for bed and crawled in, convinced I wouldn't sleep, but that was my last conscious thought of the day.

CHAPTER TWENTY-THREE

Someone snapped the lights on promptly at six a.m. I'd forgotten my eye cover again and glared at the woman who'd been so rude. She smiled apologetically but started talking to her friend who still reclined above me. The whole room started grumbling at her. People shifted in their sleeping bags and sighed loudly. I kicked off my coverings and stood; my ligaments and muscles groaned. I walked stiffly to the bathroom sink and stared at myself in the mirror. I'd lost some weight. My cheekbones stood out in sharper lines on either side of my face. My leg muscles wrapped tighter against my leg bones and my pants were loose everywhere. I cracked a wide yawn as I stared at myself. *Now that is not a pretty picture*, I thought, as my molars became visible. I splashed more water on my face and shuffled out to the bunk room to collect my belongings, pack up and head out.

I'd have to find another market and stock up on snack items, I thought wearily as I sat on the edge of my bed. The idea made me grumpy. Lethargy stole through every fiber of my being for a moment as I fought the urge to lie back down and stay there all day. My head spun with weariness. I stood a bit slowly and grunted as I hefted my pack. It felt heavy. I wanted to whine to somebody, or call a taxi, or hand my pack to my boyfriend to carry. Oh, yeah—didn't have one of those. Out of options, I shuffled to the front door and out into the dawn's light. Panicked after a few yards, I backtracked inside and made a beeline for the espresso vending machine. No bars would be open this early. "Silly girl," I told myself, "this is why you don't vacate early."

"Stop judging me..." I whined softly to myself. I hated arguing with myself. It was not a good way to start the day.

I choked down two vending machine lattes. They were phony, chemical-filled approximations of the real thing. Of some mild concern was the aftertaste that lingered for an hour afterward. I kept taking sips of water to get rid of the phony coffee taste. I hoped it had at least contained a small amount of caffeine. I took the main road south out of town and came to a split in the road. I could either walk a longer route over more highway than natural trails, or take the shorter, more scenic route. I would have loved to have seen the historic monastery in Samos but that route was by concrete and much longer, so I chose the nature trails. I split right at the fork and shortly climbed up a steep hill to the highest point of the whole walk for the day.

After a torturous, coffee-free ten kilometers, I found a café where I ordered a *real* coffee. I sat inside at the bar hunched over my hot elixir of life, warming my hands when Nikki arrived looking harassed. I looked past her annoyed visage to see a familiar tow-headed young man in hot pursuit. My omelet and croissant were set in front of me as I pulled her next to me to sit on the bar stool to my left, away from the door. She unbuckled her pack and set it next to mine. For one split second I was absurdly happy my backpack had a friend.

Nikki settled in and ordered a coffee while I watched the young man approach the door. I stood just as he entered, his eyes searching the room for my petite friend. He saw me and hesitated a moment. He came forward as I took one big meaningful step backward and put my arm around Nikki. I couldn't speak his language but I could convey a lot of meaning with just a look. I lifted my chin a bit in challenge as Nikki's right arm stole around my waist. She whispered, "Thanks!" in my ear. I looked at her and touched my fingers to her chin. I really didn't want to have to kiss her and I knew she didn't either. Thankfully, the man adjusted his trajectory so that he stepped right and up to the bar just a few feet away. He pretended nonchalance as he ordered. He finally took his coffee outside and I sat down and dug into my food while Nikki dissolved in laughter.

"Oh my God, Alesa, if I still smoked I would have one right now. I would have one for you, too!"

"I'd have my own, thank you very much! I like smoking now and then. Not often, though," I admitted.

We giggled and ate a ton of food together. Both of us had missed breakfast in Triacastela. I took out my slightly flattened package of cakes and shared them with Nikki. Though we both preferred to travel alone these days, we enjoyed each other's company and decided to walk a while together. It was a nice break to not be alone anymore.

We passed through very poor farming villages along the way with few places to find sustenance in the hamlets we walked through. More often than not the cattle, including cows, pigs, geese and chickens, outnumbered people. The streets in these villages were slick with animal waste and smelled horrid. We passed elderly people who sat on buckets and waved to us wearily. I wondered if their grandchildren would pick up where they left off or would they let these places fade away like the castle ruins in Triacastela?

As we moved carefully down one poop-smeared road through a gray, sad village, an itsy-bitsy Spanish lady smiled encouragingly at us as we passed. I was charmed instantly. She held her delicate, blue-veined hand out toward me so I stopped. She stood as high as my collar bone. Her fine white hair was pulled up into a loosely styled bun with a red flower stuck into the middle of it. Her floral printed blouse was in direct contrast to her mod-patterned skirts. She wore socks with fuzzy house slippers. It was the light in her eyes that captured me. They positively danced. She moved toward me and hugged me harder than I thought she could have. I hugged her back gently. "Buen Camino, peregrina," she said in her thin, high voice. I leaned way down so she could kiss my cheeks. I kissed hers in return, wishing that I could carry her in my backpack for a few kilometers. She was the cutest little woman I'd ever seen. She kissed Nikki's cheeks as well, before we again headed out in the direction of Santiago.

We traveled quickly together, talking and laughing at the day's events as we trekked ever downward and away from the mountains. We reached Sarria where Nikki said she needed to find some of her friends. They were planning to meet up once a week or so, if possible, to check in with each other. I promised to look for her at dinner. Sarria was a bit larger than the towns I was accustomed to at this point. Vehicles traveled on the roads instead of livestock! There were street lights at the corners and many types of businesses and homes.

I was the second to arrive at the Don Alvaro albergue. The owner was a woman and she filed me into the "women only" room. I hate to admit I was disappointed. There were so many interesting men on this trek! I laid everything out as usual and gathered my toiletries and other important items to bring with me to the bathroom. Once finished, I curled up in my bed to watch the foot traffic below and write in my journal. The room was chilly but I dreaded closing the window as traumatizing memories of smelly French women invaded my memory banks. I finished writing and set my journal under my pillow after pulling the wool blanket at the foot of my bed over me.

My growling stomach woke me with such hunger that I felt punched. I sat up panicked to find food immediately. I hopped down from the bed and rummaged through my bag for the last piece of cake. I tried to eat it slowly, knowing that this kind of hunger would take time to ease its painful ache. Crumbs trailed me out to the courtyard patio. Roses of every color burst from planter boxes and bushes. I followed the cement walkway to a room that looked older than the rest of the house. A fireplace and large mantle took up a good portion of the room. Benches formed a U around the fireplace. Instruments hung from the walls waiting for the lyrically inclined pilgrim to strum them.

With the edge of hunger abated, I had only to walk around the corner and was at the main plaza with a restaurant waiting there. I sat down at a waiter's nod and took the table he indicated. He promptly delivered a menu as he passed inside the restaurant. I opened it hungrily just as a man's voice broke in.

"Have you tried pulpo yet?" I looked over to the small table next to mine to see a man with the sharpest nose I'd ever seen looking at me. His glasses were perched at the end of his spiky proboscis, which thankfully happened to feature a bump large enough to hold the spectacles on his face. I imagined he must push them up all the time over that narrow ridge. His intelligent brown eyes regarded me with only a hint of humor.

Guardedly, I replied, "No...It hasn't been something I've been looking forward to. I imagine I will try it at some point. It just never sounds appetizing." My stomach protested. Even pulpo sounded appetizing right then. "Are you ordering it?"

"I did! It's delicious here. I have enjoyed it a few times already. Would you like to try a bite of mine? You can sit with me. No sense taking up two tables."

That was how I met Barry, an Englishman. It felt great to be able to speak at my normal speed without having to edit what I said for fear that I would be misinterpreted. We ordered wine. I was tempted to order my own pulpo, but decided against it. I ordered the Galician stew, with a bocadillo.

"Why are you walking the Camino, Alesa?" he asked with intensity. His intelligent eyes seemed to bore into me. I looked down at my glass of water and traced a finger down the line of condensation.

"To be at peace, inside and out. To heal." I smiled mysteriously. His gaze did not relent. "You won't get more than that before the appetizer, Barry."

He sat back and the intensity of his energy diminished. The pulpo arrived on a wooden platter. Purple and white octopus tentacles swam in butter and flakes of cayenne pepper. Barry immediately grabbed a hunk of bread and dunked it in the broth.

"Try one of the white, fleshier pieces first...one of the pieces without the suckers."

I imagined those tentacles sticking to the back of my throat as I swallowed. Sticking my fork into a fleshy white chunk, I plunked it into my mouth experimentally. The butter and red pepper melded quite nicely with it; in fact, it didn't have a fishy flavor at all. At Barry's encouragement, I tried a couple more before digging up the courage to try a tentacle. They were delicious and did not magically suction to the back of my throat or inside of my cheeks at all.

We talked about our strangest Camino experiences while enjoying the pulpo. Between us, we drank a whole bottle of wine and ordered a second bottle. We kept the conversation light throughout our meal. Barry's meal arrived just as a bagpipe's startling blares burst upon the square. As one, we all stopped eating to observe this display. The sounds rose sharply, astounding our ears on the first notes, but then mellowed. There was an ancient reverberation to them. These mystical sounds vibrated in my bones as the men played their melodies. We listened to a few songs, unable to speak over the volume of sound. After half an hour the men stopped, a few people wiped their eyes, overcome with the emotional music. A hat was passed around and we all tipped them, which encouraged more music.

Since Barry was also staying at the Don Alvaro, we corked our half-finished bottle of wine and brought it back with us. We walked through the courtyard to the fireplace room. A man stopped me just in the entrance when he saw my wine. "No vino! No, no!" he admonished with a wagging of his finger. I guessed this was the owner's husband. He then pointed to a table with liquor and shot glasses and from the tone of his voice, I knew he'd had a few shots already and wanted me to have some. The fire was roaring away behind him. I held up my wine bottle and shook my head. He frowned in disappointment but as Barry made his entrance, his attention was diverted to him. Barry also declined the shot. My attention was riveted on the fire that roared in front of us.

I'd become accustomed to being cold and slightly damp from the unseasonably wet weather patterns all across northern Spain and hadn't realized how deeply chilled I was. The effect was intoxicating in itself. My toes wanted to curl so I removed my shoes and extended my feet as close to the flames as I could. I almost wept at the warmth that spread through my body slowly. Next to me, Barry also stretched out with his toes reaching toward the flames. Neither of us spoke for a few minutes. I thought I never wanted to be cold again at that moment, and dreaded going back to my chilly room and less-than-adequate sleeping bag. I'd bought a light one thinking the weather here would be warmer. I was lucky I wasn't sick, I told myself. Plenty of other pilgrims had caught some serious flus along the way.

People began filtering in. We met Andreas from Denmark, "Erica from America," and several other non-English speakers. We all drank and warmed ourselves without feeling the need to converse too much. There was no need. Our common yet individual journeys bound us in companionship in an almost familial way. This feeling was as palpable as if it were a living thing. Several times, I choked back the urge to stand with tears in my eyes and proclaim my love for these fellow travelers. I barely refrained from making a drunken spectacle of myself!

That night I went to bed while my pant legs were still burning hot. I didn't even stop to brush my teeth. I didn't want to succumb to the chill again. I shucked my shoes and kicked them under the occupied bed below mine and hurriedly climbed into my sleeping bag with warmth still radiating around my calves. I was happy to see the window was still open a crack, prizing fresh air over smelly-pilgrim air. I doubled the wool blanket at the foot of my bed and pulled it over me, tucked it around my lower legs hoping to trap the waning heat. With a sigh of pleasure, I realized my feet felt absolutely normal for the first time in nearly a month.

CHAPTER TWENTY-FOUR

THE NEXT MORNING I STOOD at the sink brushing my teeth for at least three minutes. I could not believe I hadn't brushed them the night before. I brushed them thoroughly and then rinsed my mouth before brushing them again. Someone had left a box of Q-tips outside the bathroom on a table so I stole two of them and blissfully cleaned my ears. This was usually a daily habit at home, though I knew it was frowned upon by ear doctors everywhere. I could not stand earwax build-up. I applied sunscreen to my burnt ears and forehead, making sure to get every inch of visible skin, too. I was amazed at how much sun we were getting despite the overcast skies.

Erica from America met me at the restaurant for cafés con leche. Her blue-black sleek hair was pulled tightly into a ponytail. Her sleepy almond-shaped eyes blinked at me when I waved. We sat by a window as we sipped coffee and nibbled at croissants. We talked about her acupuncture business for a few minutes before she switched topics to her ailing father. She then leaned toward me.

"I have a sense that you have a huge story to share."

"Well, that's a creative way of asking the same old question," I was amused.

"I am intuitive...and there is something about you..." she mused with one eyebrow lifted.

I hesitated. She waited. I gathered myself with a deep breath before talking about my ex. I was tired of making him sound so terrible. I gave her an accounting of the trials we'd been through, my personal war with cancer and emotional distress, ending with my spiritual awareness and exploration. By the time I was done, she had tears in her eyes.

"You are so strong. You need to share this, you know. It's okay to reach out and open up."

I nodded. "I'm learning that. I couldn't have told you all that four weeks ago."

"Well, what about you? Have you met anyone since the divorce? Do you have a boyfriend? Please tell me you do after all of that."

I shook my head. "I thought I wanted that for so long, Erica. I'm only realizing now as I'm talking to you that what I really needed was myself! I didn't know that I was wrong in needing a man. I thought I would be fulfilled. Yes, ultimately I do want a relationship....but not with just anyone. He's going to be very special when I do find him. Yes, over the last year, I dated lots of men....I could not open my heart to a single one. I couldn't even get to the second date most times. I found silly things to break up with them over. My heart would pound with fear if I thought he liked me. My heart wasn't ready....I needed me more than I needed 'him.'" I gestured out the window at the pilgrims passing by on foot and bicycle. "I found myself here and that is what has been missing...pretty much my whole life. I never believed in myself until...just this moment. I am all I need." My thoughts were coming together as I spoke. My voice rose with emotion as the truth sank in.

I stared at her wide-eyed when I was done. Her right hand hovered over her coffee cup. A tear spilled down her cheek. I patted her hand.

"It's all okay, you know. Everything that happens during our lifetimes. It's fine. It's all okay in the end."

She laughed. "I know. Isn't that funny? I know that!" We talked for a few more minutes before preparing to leave. Since she had just joined the Camino yesterday, deciding to try it out for a few days. I advised her to stock up on a few items here in Sarria, since this region suffered from poverty more than others and most pilgrim rest areas were now closed.

We joined the pack of pilgrims marching out for the day. There were a lot more of them at this juncture now. Just like Erica, many people could not get five weeks off work and so they did the last one-hundred kilometers of the walk. This was the bare minimum that they could get credit for in Santiago. If they didn't walk a hundred k, they didn't receive their certificates of completion at Santiago.

We walked through dilapidated towns that had no signs of life other than a few farmers and the ever-present smell of dung in the streets. We were glad to pass through them quickly and get back on The Way. Thankfully most of the trail was through tree-lined streets or natural paths. Those small, depressing towns were becoming eerier with each one. We sat in a glade and ate our cake with orange juice to wash it down. As we topped the last rise of the day, I thought back to my conversation with Erica. I paused to let her pass me on the descent and took in the views from my vantage point.

My hair lifted with the breeze. I spun slowly to take in the views, my breath catching at the beauty all around me. Every cell in my body felt awake...alive! My heart thrummed at a steady pace. My left foot poised on the edge ready to start my descent, but I stayed frozen atop that hill for a moment. I looked up at the clouds just then and caught sight of another perfect heart-shaped cloud just in front of me. Everything came together then. A strange sensation slid through my body from the crown of my head to my toes. It felt as though my soul had come home, settled in and clicked into place. Without knowing what I'd come here for, I seemed to have found it. The answer was Me. With a silly grin and hot tears flowing freely, I followed Erica down the hill.

We joked with each other the whole way down the five-kilometer hillside, splashing through mud and carelessly slipping on loose rocks. The sky was a cerulean blue with white, puffy clouds that took on shapes of all manners of angels, pigs, sea creatures and babies. We passed pilgrims on the trail who took more heed than we did. My buoyant spirit must have been infectious, for Erica exhibited the same joy. We alternately hugged and kissed cheeks with nearly everyone we passed, leaving off with the more dour-faced pilgrims. To the grumpier ones, we waved or wished them Buen Camino. Many people we saw that day had just arrived in Sarria the day before. How well I remembered that wayward feeling from my first day in Pamplona!

Portomarin sat like the king's crown high above a beautiful valley with a wide river flowing before her banks. Beyond the modern bridge to the left was a cemetery, the crypts oddly cut into the hillside above the river. We crossed over and climbed steeply up some medieval stone steps into the heart of Portomarin, passing an albergue that promised a hundred and ten beds. That sounded awful. We marched through stone arched colonnades that led us to the castle-like church that sat quite literally squarely—for it was shaped in a perfect square—in the middle of the plaza. We decided to go inside and sit in the pews for a minute. My levity made me unable to concentrate on prayers at first, so I respectfully kept silent while Erica prayed. As I began to quiet myself, I just thanked Buddha, God, Jesus and the angels for the knowledge that no matter what happened in this silly little thing called life, all that mattered was the power of love, since that is all that transcends with us as we leave the human trappings of our bodies behind anyway. I was tempted to shuck my shoes and meditate cross-legged but before I could, Erica stood.

We checked into a nicer hostel with a private room, called Posada del Camino. A restaurant sat directly below us and the owner seemed very nice, though he had trouble with my limited Spanish vocabulary. We each paid twenty euros for the private room, though we still had to share a single bathroom with the whole floor. We threw our packs on our beds and I plugged my phone in to charge it and review the photos from the day while Erica showered first. Once refreshed, Erica weakly told me she was going to nap. She agreed to meet downstairs when she woke up. I took note of her pale face and asked if she was alright. She told me she just needed a nap and to have fun.

With that, I left and rounded the corner leading into the dining area which brought me face to face with Barry. We laughed and hugged each other warmly. He was eating a light meal with about ten other pilgrims. He introduced me to all of them, of course. They were from Hungary, Nova Scotia, Belgium, Germany, Saudi Arabia and the States. Cathy was a cute, short woman from California. Her sparkling blue eyes and dimpled cheeks charmed me right away. She wore bright red lipstick, the first real makeup I'd seen on this trip. Though I had brought a little makeup with me, I never even opened the bag. The young man at the end of the table stared at me with interest. When Cathy noticed, she bluntly asked me if I was single. I nodded, choking on my beer as I did so.

With that, the handsome, dark skinned young man from Saudi Arabia leaned forward. "Me too!" he said in a silky voice. Then he rose and dragged his chair over next to mine.

Cathy leaned toward me and stage whispered, "Don't take Ash seriously, he has done this to every woman on the Camino." I winked at her to let her know I knew his game. Ash put his arm around my shoulder and said, "Hi. Don't listen to her. I am a very nice man. Maybe we will go on a date tonight. Let us see if this is love. We could be married by the time we reach Santiago!" I would have been alarmed if not for the twinkle of humor in his eyes. "How old are you?" he asked.

"Forty." It was my turn to laugh as his eyes widened in shock.

"Well....I am thirty....Hmmm. It does not matter. You are very pretty."

"Thank, Ash. You can sit next to me and compliment me all you like, but I'd like to enjoy my meal without you touching me." I smiled widely at him as he removed his arm. Laughter erupted around the table. Barry sat on my right and Ash on my left. There was twenty years' difference between the two men. It felt nice to have male attention from generations that bracketed my own. I didn't order any food as Ash and Barry competed for my affections by ordering beer or sharing their appetizers.

I sensed the watchful, hopeful gazes of everyone else at the table. Since they had all traveled together for the most part since the beginning, it was natural they would want to find matches for their friends. It was true that everyone was offered a romance on the Camino. I had seen it in action with Nacho and other couples who had hooked up just for the Camino. Some of them would break up in Santiago, go home to their single lives or, in other cases, their married lives. Still others would cling to the hopes of a long-distance love affair. I was simply enjoying the male attention with no intention of taking either of these men as my Camino boyfriend.

We ate while we compared our strangest Camino stories. There were tales of being chased off the trail by unruly oxen by Cathy. She'd narrowly missed being trampled! Barry laughed about a young couple so enamored they couldn't hide their sexual acts in their bunk until someone yelled at them to stop. Then the terribly awkward moments that followed as everything went silent. There was the barefoot guru who practiced meditations along the side of the trail, would hold spontaneous yoga classes, and spent much of his time luring young women into his bed. Apparently he made his living on the Camino. Finally, I told my story about Nacho while Ash narrowed his eyes in mock jealousy and everyone yearned to know the intimate details. Nothing had happened beyond kissing, but they refused to believe me because I blushed just thinking about him.

When everyone finished eating, we decided to take our party across the plaza where most of the pilgrims milled around. Since Erica hadn't joined us, I decided I should check on her. Both Barry and Ash grabbed my arms to keep me from leaving until I promised to come back. They planted kisses on my hands and cheeks until I broke away and ran to my room.

Her pale face blinked at me when I cracked the door to look in. "Oh, sweetie! Do you need anything?" She shook her head and gestured at the water bottle on her nightstand. "Can I bring you some soup?" She nodded gratefully. Fifteen minutes later, the soup sat cooling on her nightstand.

The mother in me kicked in. "You should eat that while it's hot." I felt her head. I thought she may recover by morning.

"You're an angel," she whispered.

"Nah. Just get better. I'm going back out until ten or so." I hated to leave when she felt crummy but I didn't want to catch her cold either. She nodded and I retreated quickly and silently. I stopped in the restroom to scrub my hands thoroughly before rejoining my new friends.

Loud music was blaring from a portable speaker system and a dance party had formed. I grabbed Ash, to Barry's disappointment, and made him dance with me. It was hilarious—he could not move well at all. When our song was over, he asked if he could be my Camino boyfriend. Feeling silly, I said, "Sure, why not." He beamed at me. I laughed with the pleasure of feeling attractive again. Barry cut in a few times and I was just as happy to dance with him, though Ash reminded me I was HIS Camino girlfriend. I thought he was kidding.

Ash walked me to my hotel. "Wow, this place looks nice. You are traveling in luxury, Alesa."

I laughed at that. "Right, Ash, I've seen my share of bunk beds, don't worry."

He leaned in for a kiss. Faster than thought, I covered his mouth with my hand.

"I just met you!" I warned. I withdrew my hand.

"Meet us here at seven a.m. so we can walk together tomorrow."

"No way. I don't get up that early."

"Get up early for me tomorrow!" I shook my head. Stubbornly, he said, "I'll be here waiting and if you don't come out I will yell your name very loud and you will be...."

"Goodnight, Ash." He was still talking as I turned and left.

CHAPTER TWENTY-FIVE

THE NEXT MORNING I WOKE feeling energetic and happy. The same could not be said of Erica. She coughed as she laid with her back toward me. I stretched luxuriously on my bed, having completely forgotten about Ash. A huge smile stretched from one side of my face to the other as I sat up. In fact, I felt annoyingly happy this morning. It bubbled up inside and threatened to burst out of me. It was going to be a great day! I could feel it coming. Something wonderful was about to happen. I stood and stretched again, taking notice of all the small bones of my feet and stretching each muscle. No cramps shot up my legs, there was some mild pain along the bottom of my feet, and I was pretty sure I was going to lose my middle left toenail. I laughed to myself as I wondered if I'd get a ten-percent discount for a pedicure.

Erica turned toward me. One look at her crusty eyes peeping at me from her little cocoon had me checking her temperature. She seemed to be running a slight fever.

"Whatcha gonna do there, girlie? Stay here and rest today?" She nodded miserably. "Want me to let the owner know....or do you think you can come down and ask him to stay?"

"I'll come down in a few," she croaked pathetically.

"Okay. Gonna head down there for breakfast. Get yourself some orange juice soon as you can!" I couldn't help nagging her a bit. She smiled as we said our goodbyes.

    I had ordered toast and an omelet so when my handsome waiter set a huge piece of chocolate cake in front of me, I stared at him a moment. He saw my look and gestured at the cake, pronouncing something that could have almost been the word for toast....*Maybe I had ordered cake*, I mused, as he set my chorizo omelet next to the head-sized dessert. I shoved the cake to the side and dug into the omelet. I'd eaten so many on this journey that they tasted flavorless now. The cake stared at me. I stared back. *Fuck it. If this is the kind of day I'm gonna have then bring it on!* I thought and devoured the succulent chocolate cake instead.

    Sugar and caffeine pumped hyper energy into my happy energy, which combined to make me feel like time was moving too slow. I hurried past confused and lost pilgrims who'd obviously just started their journeys. I rushed to the first ATM I saw and could not work the machine fast enough. I vibrated with the need to burn some energy. My hands shook as I extracted my cash and card and shoved them deep into some pocket of my pack and nearly ran down the market square to get out of town.

    The scenery that greeted me made me sigh with pleasure as I hurried to join the trails. Mist hung over the green hills like a blanket of white cotton, offset by the blue, flowing rivers and sky. Lush greenery burst forth from one mist-shrouded hill to another. I bounced on the balls of my feet down the steep sidewalks that wound over the river and up through the forest on the other side, breathing in the beauty of it all. I felt idiotically ecstatic to be alive. I vowed to eat more cake for breakfast.

    Music was my companion. The beats of Mumford and Sons' song *Below My Feet* thrummed in my veins. The lyrics defined everything in that moment. The damp earthy smell of the forests filled my lungs with each deep breath in. I felt like I could run up the hill. An elderly couple struggling slowly upward seemed confused about which way to go to get out of my fast approach. They shimmied left, then right, before settling on left. I took out my earphones for a second and slowed as I passed the woman and, with a hand on her shoulder, said, "I'm so sorry. I had cake and lots of coffee for breakfast."

She laughed. "Honey! Never apologize for being faster than old people!" I smiled and waved, once again inserted my headphones and took off.

At the top of the first rise, I spun around as a man passed me. Our eyes connected with a mutual expression of utter joy. His wide, amber eyes sparkled with humor as I yelled, "OH MY GAWD! YOU SCARED ME. IT'S SO PRETTY!" I gestured stupidly around us. His mouth quirked in a sexy half smile on the left side. He said something to me but I couldn't hear him. His long legs carried him away before I had the chance to ask him to repeat whatever he said!

Disappointed that he was gone so fast, I came to the first stop completely unprepared to see him again. My amber-eyed man sat finishing a small cup of espresso outside a cafe. When he saw me, his golden eyes opened wide and he paused with his cup halfway to his lips. We waved shyly to each other as I passed to go inside and stood in a long line to order a coffee and orange juice. I peeked to my left and saw his head bent to the side to look at me. My heart hammered with some kind of understanding. I pretended not to notice him peering in at me from time to time as the line moved sluggishly. I casually brought my drinks to his table and set them down. I held out my hand and he took it with a long, warm hand and a soft smile as he waited for me to introduce myself. He seemed a bit dumbfounded that I sat right down and started talking, but his intelligent eyes held curiosity and warmth, so I rambled for a bit before I paused for breath. I looked at the steaming brew I'd ordered out of habit, deciding I probably didn't need it since I hadn't let him say a word yet. I shut my mouth and waited.

He'd listened to my rambling with that sexy sideways smile dimpling his cheeks and now he leaned forward and introduced himself. "I'm Niklas. It's very nice to meet you." His rich, deep voice sounded bemused. We talked for a few minutes while we finished our beverages. We stood to go and as he helped me lift my pack, he asked if I'd walk with him.

Niklas, from Germany, was tall and thin with wide shoulders. I guessed that he must have been about six-foot-three. He immediately told me he felt stupid for not saying something wittier on the trail and had mentally smacked himself, thinking he'd missed the opportunity. He joked about the speed at which I'd been traveling. Even his long legs had a hard time catching up. I loved his accent immediately. He was able to converse naturally on most things but he became lost if I used sloppy American English. Our slang words tripped him up. As we walked side by side, I found myself speaking a bit slower and more succinctly, my phrasing changed.

He'd been traveling with a man named Matthew from Australia, though he was presently missing. Niklas told me how they'd met in Pamplona in a cafe and immediately became friends. Matthew had been struck almost immediately by a strange illness and nearly died. He refused to go home and had been to the hospital a few times. Niklas was not in a big rush and had told Matthew's girlfriend back home that he would stay and make sure Matthew survived the trip. After four weeks of fighting illness, Matthew was finally on the mend and Niklas was free to stretch his legs and walk his own pace a while. Apparently, Matthew was behind us somewhere.

It was a strange coincidence that Niklas and I had both started our journeys in Pamplona, an uncommon starting point. We even shared the same first stamp from Francesco at the German albergue, Casa Paderborn, to start our credentials. We laughed at that. Our lives had run in a lot of parallels. Niklas was newly divorced from his wife. They had no children and had grown apart after numerous attempts to have them. His wife was unhappy with him constantly. He'd come to the Camino to process his grief over their relationship ending.

We spoke of our exes with more respect than I would have thought possible just four weeks prior. He was interested in my life. I talked about Parker a bit hesitantly until I knew he truly wanted to hear about her. I softened more toward him as he listened and asked questions about her. There was a sadness inside him centered around children and I knew he had passionately wanted them, but for whatever reason he and his wife could not conceive and this despair had whittled away at their marriage until it crumbled.

We took turns telling our stories to each other the rest of the morning. With each conversation I felt closer and closer to him. When he laughed, he leaned forward a bit and his dimples creased his cheeks. I admired his wavy, dark hair as he ran his long fingers through it. During a rare moment when we were a bit quieter, he revealed that he was glad he had not met me earlier, as he'd been very sad the whole way until yesterday. I gasped in astonishment and asked him what had changed.

"Me! I changed, Alesa. I woke up feeling like no matter what, this fucking divorce could happen and I will be okay." He paused, gathering his words. "I am not explaining it right.

Before the Camino, I quit my job of many years. I had a 'freak out'...is that what you say? I did this Camino but I did not really know why I wanted to do this! My feet hurt! My legs hurt! Every morning, I was saying to Matthew, 'Fuck, fuck, fuck, this shitty hurting feeling!'"

I grabbed his arm to keep from toppling over as I wheezed with laughter.

"Then, you know, it didn't hurt so badly but my soul became sadder and sadder. I met a woman in Sarria who read my cards... you know these cards? I forget what they are called...emm."

"Tarot cards?" I guessed.

"Yes, these tarot cards. This girl, she told me to take just one. It was a card with a woman on it. She told me I would meet my Camino angel very soon." He paused and looked at me sideways, "I think that is you. You are my Camina." He smiled shyly and blushed a little.

"Very charming of you, Niklas. How do you know it is me?"

"I just feel it." He linked arms with me. "Don't you?"

There was definitely no urge to pull away from him. I wanted to walk the rest of the way with him—every minute of it that we had left. He intrigued me. "Yes, I feel it, too. Yesterday, I fell in love with myself for the first time ever...."

He nodded excitedly, said softly, "Me too!" Tears came to his eyes. "...And now maybe you and I are going to heal each other." He looked up at the sky and stopped for a moment before turning to me. His eyes shimmered gold with unshed tears. He pulled me with his long arms into his chest and hugged me tightly. I stepped closer and snuggled in, putting my right ear to his flannel shirt. I heard the steady rhythm of his heart and smelled his aftershave. I had met him a few hours ago and felt closer to him than anyone I'd met on the Camino already, even Nacho with his blue and yellow hammock and his warm brown eyes, soft kisses...this was something different. Our souls seemed to know this, too.

Niklas's long-legged stride naturally carried him faster than my shorter legs. He frequently steamed ahead, only to find a wall or stone to sit on and wait for me to catch up. We stopped frequently to order coffees in every bar along the way. He hoped for a glimpse of Matthew to be sure he was okay. I marveled at Niklas's patience; he could have been to the next stopping point with that gait of his by now.

During a late lunch break just a few kilometers shy of our destination, he spontaneously grabbed my left foot and stripped off my shoe. "Let's see what is the problem with your feet," he muttered. He removed my socks to inspect the blisters, but when he touched the bottom of my foot I nearly leaped out of my chair. "It hurts, yes?" His wide eyes looked at me as he touched my sole again. "Yup," he murmured to himself as he gently began to rub my feet with his large, warm hands. I sat stiff and straight, ready to yank my foot away, but he tenderly worked at the muscles until they relaxed. "Now let's see to the other one. Come on, put your foot up here." I melted in my chair this time.

That afternoon, in Palas De Rei, we were able to find two top bunks near each other. We eyed each other nervously as we laid out our sleeping bags and arranged our belongings. He was sloppier than me, I noticed, nothing was organized in his pack. He spent significant time searching for his charger, convinced he lost it, only to find it in a random spot, meanwhile murmuring self-deprecating things to himself in German. He made me giggle before he grabbed me spontaneously and kissed me fast. His carved lips brushed over mine once, twice before he released me. I grabbed his strong neck and pulled his face close to mine again. I'd just begun to taste his lips when his starving stomach voiced its complaints, interrupting our kisses. It was time to shower and join the pilgrim rush for dinner.

Refreshed, we walked arm in arm into the rainy night and around the corner to the nearest restaurant and nearly smacked into Ash. He hugged me immediately and ranted over how he was mad at me for standing him up that morning. I blushed but didn't know what to say. Quite honestly, I'd forgotten about him. He pulled me, while I pulled Niklas, over to his table and there were Barry, Cathy and the whole group from the night before. Ash had been sitting at the end of the table near the window. When he saw me take the bench by the wall with enough room for Niklas, he complained. I ignored him as best I could while I tried to figure out what I would say.

"Well, well, well!" Barry murmured to me. "This is interesting indeed! Pulpo?" he asked as he slid his appetizer over to me. He winked at me when I shook my head. "Don't let Ash bother you. He's been behaving this way since we started, the insufferable bastard," he complained.

Niklas and I bent our heads over the menu, deciding we would share pulpo, bread and torta (similar to a slice of pizza). Ash was loudly trying to get my attention now. Niklas grabbed my hand under the table as Ash yelled my name, "Alesa! Alesa!" No longer able to ignore him, my eyes rose to meet his.

"Who is that? Where did you find him? Under a bush? You brought a German boy?"

I calmly looked at Niklas as I gestured toward Ash. "Niklas, meet Ash. We met yesterday in Portomarin."

Ash leaned forward. "Yes! But who AM I?" he asked with rude intensity. I could not tell if he was joking or not.

"I didn't know you were serious about being my Camino boyfriend or I would have said no...we talked and danced...that's it."

Niklas teased me, whispering in my ear "I am too late, angel?" He kissed my ear.

"No," I said loudly for everyone. "You are not too late."

Ash became furious. His face turned red. "Really, Alesa? You break my heart already? Who is this German man? He is better for you than me?" He turned to Niklas. "Who are you? Why are you here?" I looked around the table at Ash's friends. None of them seemed to know what to say.

"Ash, we had a couple of hours to talk and dance last night. That doesn't mean I am yours to keep. I didn't know Niklas yesterday, and I'm sorry but as soon as I met him it was all over for you." Niklas squeezed my hand.

Ash glared at Niklas. He begged and pleaded and finally argued about being my true love. I shook my head as his friends did nothing to quiet him.

Niklas finally leaned forward. "She is with me. Please be a bit more respectful. You only met yesterday. She is not yours."

"It's true, Ash." With nothing further to say, I turned to Barry and changed the subject as the two men glared at each other over the table. Barry leaned toward me and in a stage whisper expressed that he'd hoped I would be *his* Camino girlfriend. I groaned and put my head in my hands while everyone at the table teased me about being their girlfriend, too. Face red, I looked up and demanded, "Stop it right now! All of you!"

Just then, Niklas's Aussie friend Matthew made his appearance. He was a tall, good-looking man with long blond hair that flowed to his shoulders. He removed his wide-brimmed hat as he approached our table. He reminded me of

Brad Pitt. He clasped Niklas's hand and sat next to him on the bench. He was very open and friendly and soon had us all rolling with Australian jokes in between bold stories of flesh-eating kangaroos that stood ten feet tall and killer koala bears. My stomach ached from laughing so hard.

Later that night, Niklas and I lay in our sleeping bags facing each other, staring across the open space between our beds. I glanced down to see the woman below him wink up at me before she turned to face the wall behind her. Niklas reached out with his long arm to clasp my hand. His amber eyes stared brilliantly even in the darkened room. I dropped his hand after a moment and flipped onto my back to sleep, shutting his face out of my mind. "What is happening here," I wondered. "Did I really want a Camino romance?" I didn't want to lose a part of myself here in Spain. I'd just reclaimed every particle back again. My mind turned as I drifted to sleep. I turned my head to look at him. His eyes were now closed, but as if sensing my gaze they opened to regard me intensely. I waved. He grinned and waved back. It was my turn to face the wall, or risk not sleeping at all.

CHAPTER TWENTY-SIX

I SAT UP IN THE cool morning air at the end of my bed in a lotus position, quietly trying to meditate with my roiling thoughts. People bustled around preparing for their day's walk and interrupted my attempts to clear my mind many times, but with sudden clarity I decided to just let it all happen naturally. I wasn't going to fight this. If there came a time or day when things would progress to an intimate decision, I trusted myself to make the right one for myself. I nodded to myself as if agreeing when I heard his chuckling behind me.

"Make your decision, my Camina?" he asked in his silky tones. I glanced over my shoulder to see him also sitting up. His tousled curls rioted this way and that. His sleep-warmed body and tired eyes pulled at me so I slid down from my bed and scaled his ladder. I threw myself at his chest as he caught me and lay back. I ran my hands through his tangled curls and admired the dark-red tones in his hair. His half-closed eyes watched me. He waited with his mouth quirked up on one side, dimpling his cheek irresistibly. I brushed his lips with mine before laying a kiss on his dimples, then laid my head on his chest. He relaxed and just held me for a few minutes before I felt myself falling asleep again. I jerked awake.

"Let's get going."

He mumbled, "No, stay here all day. Who cares?"

"They will force us out in thirty minutes anyway, silly."

He growled and rolled over, kissing me a bit harder before leaping out of his bed in one smooth motion while still inside his sleeping bag. He held his arms out to help me down and stole a kiss before setting my feet on the ground. He shimmied out of his sleeping bag and we began gathering our gear. It was tough to pack between all of the hugs and kisses. Not a single person remained in the room by the time we joined the rush for breakfast. With his pack slung over his left shoulder, he grabbed mine and slung it over his wide right shoulder and grabbed my hand to drag me out by his side. Once in the entry, he withdrew my rain jacket from my pack. I hadn't even noticed the rain yet.

He settled me and our belongings into a table and casually ordered our breakfast in perfect Spanish. I watched his lithe movements across the room. He seemed taller without his backpack, I thought. He caught me looking and smiled a bit self-consciously. He even blushed. This was how our whole day went. It didn't matter that it was raining. I felt warm and protected. He massaged my feet at rest stops whenever he could convince me to let him. We sheltered under trees, inside our ponchos, when the rain became heavy. He bought us drinks to warm us up and rubbed the chill out of my hands. He was a natural caretaker. If I shivered, he pulled out his large fleece jacket and wrapped me up but did not chastise me for not wearing enough layers. I never noticed if I limped that day, too happy for his companionship and the marvelous warmth that his nurturing was spreading.

A deep voice behind us startled me suddenly. "Oh! So, you've found your angel, have you. Well, isn't that lovely. Now where is my girl to keep me warm on this fucking dreary day?" Matthew sighed with faked annoyance. "I suppose you'll be tagging along now?" as he winked at me. I shrugged.

"Be nice, Matthew, or I'll kick your ass," Niklas warned seriously. I sensed he was weary of Matthew's constant teasing.

Matthew shrugged, "Sorry mate." He looked at me. "You've picked the saint on the Camino, you know. He stuck it out with me even as the Camino tried to kill me multiple times. My girlfriend's going to be eternally grateful to this fucking German. He stayed behind when I couldn't walk for a couple of days due to fever and whatever the fuck else. He truly is the nicest guy here."

"Thank you for that," Niklas acknowledged kindly. I held Niklas' long hand in mine, trying to warm it as he'd warmed mine. This earned a kiss on the cheek before he rose to buy some food to share with me.

"Hey! You gonna buy mine, too?" Matthew whined.

"No. Fuck you, Aussie," Niklas laughed as his wide shoulders disappeared inside.

We sat amidst a crowd of pilgrims outside despite the threat of rain. There were small, weak rays of sun now and then that broke through the pervading gloom. I munched slowly on my half of the sandwich while I listened to Matthew harass and tease Niklas about his German heritage, as he made one off-color joke after another. I marveled at Niklas's extreme patience. Occasionally, a warning flash darkened Niklas's amber eyes. At one point, Matthew needled him about a particular aspect of war, having made countless mean references about German invasions, to which Niklas only shrugged. I tried several times to redirect the conversation but Matthew was relentless in his questioning of certain aspects of war that Niklas clearly didn't want to discuss. At one point, I leaned over and snapped, "If you really want more details about something he is clearly not wishing to discuss, maybe you could take the hint, drop it, and save your questions for the internet.....G-T-S, dude!"

Matthew paused and looked at me curiously, "What's G-T-S?"

"Google That Shit."

Niklas laughed so hard I thought he would fall out of his chair.

He finally sputtered, "Aww, angel. Thank goodness you have come along when you did. Your American humor is very funny to me! I must write this down." He giggled as he removed his journal and wrote the definition down quickly and closed it with a snap.

Curiously, I asked, "But, don't you have comedians at home?"

He arched his brow at me. "Name one funny German comedian." I paused, thinking hard.

"Hmm… G-T-S if you can't. Bet you won't find one."

Impulsively, I whispered in Niklas's ear that I wanted to avoid Matthew the rest of the day. He nodded in agreement and squeezed my hands. With a trembling breath, I watched Niklas shrug his wide shoulders into his pack. He turned to breathe in the crisp air and look longingly toward the trees and the beckoning trail as I stood dumbfounded at the burgeoning awareness in my heart. I was frozen with one hand gripping a strap of my pack, which rested in Niklas's abandoned red plastic chair. He half turned to say something to me, his words freezing on his mouth when he caught the look on my face. His golden eyes widened. We stared for a moment. He moved fast and softly grabbed my left arm, pulling my hand from the backpack, and lifting my chin with his other hand. He kissed me softly, whispered, "I know. We'll talk later." I nodded blindly as he helped me with my pack.

He waved to Matthew, indicating we would not be walking with him that afternoon. Matthew's handsome, boyish face looked a bit disappointed but he waved dismissively. I wondered how they had managed to stay friendly on the journey. They were such different people.

Niklas and I both had our earphones in, walking along to our own thoughts but enjoying each other's companionship in a strangely intimate way though we'd know each other one full day. Niklas's words, "I know," echoed through my mind. I didn't think he really did. In that moment, as the leaves rustled overhead and his focus had been elsewhere, I'd felt a shift vibrate through my whole being. I'd had an astounding realization about myself and my own capacity to love at that moment. Clarity about the truth of our relationship had hit me as I looked at his handsome profile shrugging into his pack, unaware of me at that moment.

I knew that I could love him unconditionally for the next few days until we parted ways. There was not enough time to change each other, to fight, to grow irritated with each other. We could enjoy the hell out of each other for the next few days. It would be a truly transformational time. More importantly, the newfound love and respect that I felt for myself was allowing this relationship to enter my life at this time so that I could heal. I would say farewell to Niklas in a few days. I was certain there would be a few tears. I also knew that I would be more than okay. In fact, I would be able to go home and be whole by myself.

In that moment, I'd heard my own voice in my head say, "Let it all go and be open to whatever lies ahead with him. Enjoy him, love him!" Then the weights of my self-judgment dropped from my heart. A doorway had opened, allowing me to give this gift and receive it back. I had trembled at the trust in myself and the Universe in general as I looked at this man who had materialized at the most pivotal moments in both our individual journeys.

I loved that he took the time to smell the varying flowers on this part of the journey. We saw less poppies and more purple bells and small yellow wildflowers. Once, he wrinkled his nose at a bad smell and pulled me away as I bent to smell it myself. "You don't want that inside your nose, honey," he said as he blew the air out of his own and made a horrid face. We stopped in each bar along the way for Niklas had a huge need for caffeine that seemed unquenchable. His long legs frequently carried him ahead of me so I mocked him by matching his steps in ridiculously long strides until he slowed down. He frequently forgot what he was saying as he watched me, his sentences trailing off until I poked his shoulder to continue.

Though this day's walk was relatively easy, we'd long ago left the mountains behind and it seemed to take us forever to get to Arzua. It was nearly five o'clock and I knew it would be tough to find a bed at an albergue, so I suggested we stop in Ribadiso, which was two kilometers short of our destination. When I mentioned that to Niklas, he suggested getting a taxi to Arzua and resting in a hotel instead. I shook my head, not quite ready for that. His eyes looked a bit sad but he nodded and said, "Whatever you wish. I won't push you at all. I am okay if we never have a private room. I just want to spend every last fucking minute with you." I laughed over his awkward use of his favorite American curse word.

We joined our fellow pilgrims at the fire pit after dinner, though we only had eyes for each other. He again massaged my feet, effectively ignoring my protests by gently lifting one foot and then the other into his lap. Several people asked us if we were married, to which we shook our heads and explained we had just met. They exchanged knowing glances with us and congratulated us on finding each other with genuine warmth and something a little like longing in their eyes.

It was awkward to feel the sexual tension between us and yet share a room with six other people, most of whom were already snoring. I tossed and turned, alternating between glaring at his lumpy shadow that seemed to be sleeping soundly or at the wall behind me. By morning I was a wreck and had pulled my sleeping bag over my face to try and get a few minutes of rest, shutting out the bedroom light that someone had flicked on at six a.m.

CHAPTER TWENTY-SEVEN

Niklas chuckled when he pulled my covering off and kissed my lips. I glared at him while he calmly gathered his belongings. "This was your decision, honey," he whispered before winking at my outraged glare. His smiled quirked up on the left side of his handsome face while he calmly whistled and packed, before grabbing his pack and walking out, saying over his shoulder, "Let's get coffee, my angel!" I pulled the pillow over my face to drown out his whistling, mocking retreat. "Might be time for a hotel," I muttered to myself.

I was the last one to get out of bed and get ready so I had the whole bathroom to myself. I took my time. Niklas had already downed his latte before I joined him but refused to eat until I arrived. He was such a gentleman that I melted even more. As soon as I sat across from him, he raised his finger to the bar owner and my café con leche was delivered a minute later with croissants for each of us and orange juice for me. I got up and walked over to him to hug him for his thoughtfulness.

"No more grumpy angel this morning? Hmmm?" I shook my head against his neck and kissed it before sitting back down. He reached across the table to hold my hand while he scanned the Spanish papers and sipped his coffee. I imagined him in Colorado, sitting across from me at my table. The image wavered and faded. It was not meant to last. I squeezed his hand

and stroked his fingers, trying to memorize this moment. Tears threatened behind my eyes but I refused to let them drop. I finished my coffee and another immediately replaced my empty cup. I thanked the owner without removing my hand from Niklas's while he squeezed my fingers. "Oh look, zee mean Germans are bailing Europe out of their recession yet again with billions of Euros....and we are so mean, huh? I should tell Matthew. Will give him a heart attack to be nice to me today." He winked at me with that crooked little smile dimpling his cheek.

With Santiago so near, we were both anxious to get started today. I wanted to see the incense burner swing at mass, blessing all of us who had journeyed so far. I was excited to know that in a couple of days I would make the travel plans that would bring me home to my daughter. And I needed to either punch Niklas in the arm really hard or find a hotel where we could forget about the world for a little while. I shifted back and forth on my feet while he infuriatingly, maddeningly sipped his coffee almost delicately and continued to read. I fumed. His eyes flicked up at me, wide with innocence. "Something wrong?"

"Nope." I refused to tell him what was on my mind. He knew anyway. "I have to get moving though. Feeling antsy." I walked out the door knowing his long legs would catch me soon. I'd removed my headset when he caught me from behind with one long hand gripping my pack. He slowed me by degrees so as not to yank me to a halt. When he turned me around, his eyes were huge and a bit worried.

"Did you mean to say something about ants?" His eyes were huge.

Sputtering with laughter, I shook my head. "Just have too much energy and I don't want to waste time today. Let's get there fast."

"Okay...what kind of place do you want tonight to sleep?"

"I would like a hotel, Niklas, with you and...um...with thick walls....privacy."

He actually snorted with laughter at that. "Oh, my God, you are so cute. Okay. Thick walls it is." He lifted my chin so I stared at his eyes rather than the hollow of his throat. "Are you sure?"

I hesitated. He simply waited. He didn't try to kiss me or fondle me or sway me. After a full minute, I nodded. He brushed his lips across my forehead with a sigh.

"Okay. Wow. I am nervous, too!"

I believed him for I was staring right at the vein in his neck as it throbbed with adrenaline.

The sky was bright cerulean blue again, with only a couple of clouds here and there. We shucked layers as we walked and tucked them into each other's packs. We filled the day with stories about our amazing grandmothers, our siblings, and finally compared our spiritual experiences on the Camino. We talked about friendships we'd made on the Camino and I told him about Nacho. He was silent for a few minutes as he processed that one.

"I wish I had a hammock for you, sweetie. I am jealous." He shook his head and continued to walk but would not release my hand.

Then with silly grins, we linked arms to continue toward Arca O Pino.

The terrain was mild, with only a few pretty stone paths laid in rivers to cross over and mellow hills. Eucalyptus trees provided shade along most of the route. My feet felt better and better with Niklas's attentive hands. I fantasized about tossing my shoes over a cliff somewhere though. I knew they were wrecked after all the mileage. The cushioning had broken down so that they offered no support whatsoever. I complained loudly that it felt like having no shoes at all. I switched them for my sandals. Niklas joked about my socks. I told him this was the height of fashion in Colorado. He thought everything I said was a joke. I assured him I would send pictures of random people with sandals and Tevas.

We approached Arca O Pino and I released his hand. We looked at each other nervously. An arrow led us to the right. There sat a nice little hotel situated in the crossroads of two intersections called the Hotel O Pino. We walked through a three-sided, windowed patio area that allowed people to sit outside even while it was raining, and into the lobby. I gestured for Niklas to go in and make the arrangements. I was too embarrassed to go in with him. He held a cigarette out to me as a joke while he went inside but I shocked him by taking it. He didn't say a word as he located his lighter. He kissed my forehead again and disappeared inside.

I sat down on the outdoor patio furniture and smoked the whole thing, though it caused my lungs to burn. I hadn't smoked in a long time. The nicotine hit my bloodstream and made me jittery, but it was a bit soothing to sit and smoke with the other people hanging out around the patio. I struck up a conversation with a Dutch man named Stefan. He had only been on the Camino for a few days, since Sarria, and had luggage rather than a backpack with him. He was a businessman and had heard about the Camino and wanted to try it. I teased him about doing it again for real sometime, with a backpack like mine. He looked distastefully at my pack and shook his head.

"I've no interest in causing pain or injury to myself, Alesa." He winked at me. "Have you and your husband done the whole thing?"

I flushed bright red. "We....are not married." I rushed out.

"Ahh!" he winked at me. "Did you meet on the Camino?"

"Yes..." Right then Niklas came out and met Stefan. They both spoke Deutsch and so they quickly settled in to conversing. I knew how that felt and wistfully thought of Barry and his friends. I wondered if I would see anyone I knew on the plaza of the Santiago Cathedral tomorrow. I could tell that Niklas and Stefan were talking about us and our meeting, but didn't mind. I just didn't want to be the one explaining. I reached for the pack of cigarettes when he threw the room key down on the table instead. I stared at it nervously but didn't touch it, continuing past it to the pack of cigarettes. Niklas's eyebrows shot up at that, but I ignored him. I smoked two more before Niklas stood up and announced it was time to shower before dinner. Now horribly red in the face, I swiftly stood and grabbed the key.

"Do you mind if I go first, Nik?" I asked. It was clear that I wanted privacy.

"Not at all, honey." He walked over and hugged me, rubbing my arms to comfort me a bit. "Go upstairs, turn to your right and up another flight."

I took my time, though I knew he was probably starving. My stomach was in knots, but I was also feeling anxious for the night to start. I had no hair dryer and I desperately wanted to fix my hair, but contented myself with brushing it until it crackled before twisting it up and freeing pieces around my face. I always tucked these loose strands behind my ears out of habit so I don't know why I bothered to do that, but tried it anyway. I wore my cleanest clothes, which was not saying much. I stuffed my feet into my tennis shoes for what I hoped was the last time before descending the stairs. I sat next to Stefan rather than Nik, which he thought was super funny. I snapped at him to hurry up and get ready.

Stefan invited himself to our table, which was fine with me after all. He was very nice and intelligent. He was kind enough to include me in the conversations once in a while, but I was content to listen to the rhythm of their language, which at times sounded harsh and at others almost melodic. I found it fascinating that so many English words were interjected, too. I felt I could almost follow what they were saying. I sat across from Nik and, aside from hand-holding, he did not rub his toes on my leg or anything suggestive or pushy. Occasionally he looked at me with a knowing look in his eyes before turning back to Stefan.

Our food that night was the best I'd had on the Camino. The salads had varied options, rather than the same old tuna combo that I'd grown so tired of. There were inventive pastas and tortas, and a five-course meal option that Stefan and Nik each ordered. I enjoyed a huge salad, afraid that I couldn't eat much. I was right. I did enjoy several glasses of a nice red wine that Stefan picked out. He paid our tab at the end of the night. With a bow over my right hand and a kiss to the back of it, Stefan excused himself from our table and wished us a goodnight. Nik's eyes watched me as he stood and came over to my side of the table, holding out his hand. I grasped his hand gently as I stood a bit unsteadily. He didn't say a word but guided me out of the room. I wondered about his upbringing that he had such decorum.

There were no crude jokes on the way to our room. He didn't grab my butt or accost me in the hallway. He was calm and confident. Those were the qualities that made me attack him once we were safely inside our room. It had been over a year since I'd been intimate, since I'd chosen celibacy over sleeping around, so needless to say I was worried that things would not work out well. I was surprised with how easily it all came back. I'd been afraid something would go wrong or I'd be somehow unable to accommodate him, but in the end it was truly beautiful. We both shed a couple of tears, already sad about our impending goodbyes, but we also discussed the changes within us and the hope we had for our futures. We knew the ending of our relationship was inevitable. While it was saddening, it was also a beginning for both of us. We talked for an hour afterward before we fell asleep comfortably entwined.

The man did not even snore! He slept like the dead. I woke up early and watched his sleeping face and stroked his stubbled chin since he'd grown it out for me, ran my fingers over his dimpled cheek and long nose. I thought he was sleeping until he bit my finger suddenly. I kissed the crease of his mouth as he rolled over to kiss me with an emotion he couldn't voice. By the time we went down to breakfast, it was almost ten a.m. Again, we sat down and enjoyed one of the nicest meals to date on the whole trip.

I sat outside with him while he smoked his morning cigarette, with my legs draped sideways over his as I snuggled into his warmth against the chilly air. I felt completely alive now. I was warm inside and out. We'd been safe so I knew there was nothing to worry about, except that I would miss him incredibly when the time came. We avoided that subject as we prepared for the last leg of our trip. I thought I saw tears in his eyes as he lifted my pack onto my shoulders. He turned me around to buckle my straps; though I didn't like to be coddled, I knew he just needed to do something for me, anything. He needed the contact. I leaned my head into his chest for a minute before we took off.

CHAPTER TWENTY-EIGHT

I LOOKED BACK ONCE AT our little hotel before it disappeared from view, then Parker's face rose in my mind with her large, expressive eyes. Even more than being here with Niklas, I wanted to go home and hug her, kiss her face, take her out for ice cream or new clothes. Anything. Soon, I told myself, soon this journey will be complete....then on with the rest of it, I realized. This was only the beginning of the rest of my life... I felt ecstatic that I would see her in a few short days. I felt lighter and happier instantly, and with renewed energy rejoined Nik. He must have felt a similar elation, for he was nearly bounding ahead of me. He tried to pull pranks on me the whole way, succeeding in drenching me by pulling branches over my head, sprinkling me with rain drops, and jumping out of the bushes when I thought he was far ahead of me.

We passed a small landing strip inside a decorated chain-link fence. Pilgrims had filled the fence with handmade crosses made out of twigs and wildflowers. Nik pulled some green sticks off a tree so we could make our own. I watched as he fashioned a heart and tied it together with green grasses. We picked wildflowers to weave inside of the opening. Then we hung it on the fence amidst the other offerings. With tenderness, we viewed our woven heart amidst the multitude of crude crosses before leaving it behind.

It was a clear afternoon as we slowly climbed the last hill on our journey called Monte Del Gozo, or the Hill of Joy. This is where we stopped to take in our first glimpse of Santiago as so many other pilgrims have done before us. We held hands as we stood there with breathless anticipation. A host of emotions rose within me at the sight. We were only an hour away. We could barely make out the spires that rose above the Santiago Cathedral. To our left at the crest of the hill squatted a large four-sided modern sculpture with reliefs showing religious depictions of pilgrims and Saint James. We found Matthew sitting on a low wall awaiting our approach. With his hat in his hand, he simply watched us as we came toward him.

"Shall we do this together then?" His eyes trembled with unshed tears as Nik and I embraced him in a tight three-way hug.

"Of course, my friend!" Nik said.

"Yes! Can you believe we're almost there?" My voice became a little choked. I sat down on the wall next to Matthew and took my tennis shoes out of my pack. Without looking at either of them I marched to the top of the hill, uncomfortably close to a pilgrim that was peeing. He didn't seem to mind. I threw first one shoe and then the other as far as I could. I never wanted to see those hated shoes again. I turned to see my two friends observing me a bit oddly, both of their heads cocked in the same direction. Without a word, we filed back to the trail and walked on in silence that last hour down toward the city.

There were now masses of pilgrims on the road. At times it seemed like a foot race to reach the end. We passed and repassed some of the same people as we jockeyed for the front positions. I have no idea what we rushed for. There was nothing to gain. Mass was over for the day, and I was pretty sure we had hours to go before the cathedral locked its doors. The city of Santiago came upon us with all of the modern traffic and lights of a traditional city, but soon led us into the medieval section. At this point, both men grabbed my elbows as we followed the footsteps of so many to the heart of the plaza.

Tall, gorgeous stone buildings with rows of stone arches marched us along the cobbled path as balconies hung with laundry heralded our arrival. Backpacks of every color wove in and out of the common pedestrians. Their white scallop shells shone like beacons in the darkened walkways. The spires drew ever closer. Bagpipes and beggars serenaded our arrival, the sharp sounds of the pipes cut only by the cries of the begging. Pilgrims lounged along the open walkway that led past a side entrance to the cathedral and down some stairs through a tunnel, suddenly opening up to the Parador Hotel to our right and the expansive plaza in front.

The square was filled with pilgrims. Some laughed loudly while others comforted someone weeping. Most were full of joy. The sun lit up the west-facing cathedral, its brightness so welcome after all of the gloomy weather. The three of us ran to the center of the square and immediately threw our packs on the ground. Nik grabbed me and swung me around in a tight hug, while Matthew teased that he was next. I made the guys laugh when I ran over and kicked my poor backpack. Immediately, I felt sad for having kicked my faithful red companion. Not sure what to do next, I merely lay down where I was with my head resting on my abused pack. I looked up at the figure of Saint James in the center of his church, blessing all of us. I put my hands over my eyes and wept a bit, grateful to be done but mostly for the healing that had happened. The guys had moved away to figure out where to go to the pilgrims' office so we could turn in our credentials for the certificate of completion, or Compostela. While they argued, I glanced to my left at the Parador Hotel. Built in 1492 as a pilgrim hostel, it was now a prestigious hotel. On impulse, I got up, grabbed my pack, and with a glance at Nik's questioning eyes, raised my index finger and told him to wait. I took off for the hotel lobby. The dark-haired beauty behind the counter spoke perfect English.

Ten minutes later I rejoined them outside without my pack. I would have skipped but I was tired from the walk. I reached Nik's questioning face and silently handed him a key to our room. His eyes lit up mischievously.

"My gift to you tonight. You can leave your pack there now, too."

"Thank you, baby! That had to be expensive!" I shrugged.

"Doesn't matter!" I kissed his lips to stop his argument.

"Do I get to stay, too?"

I looked horrified at Matthew. "Of course not!"

"Thought I'd ask! Don't worry about poor Matthew. I have no girl to keep me warm, but you kids go ahead. Have your fun."

"Better start looking, bud!" I gestured around us. "See all these pilgrims? They're taking your bed as we speak."

Niklas ran to dump his pack at the Parador while we waited in the middle of the square, seated in the sunlight and too lazy to go with him. I startled suddenly to see a brown hand in front of my face when I looked up to see a familiar face—there was Ash! I jumped up and gave him a huge hug. He kissed my cheek and congratulated me on making it to the end. He told me everyone was going to party at the Parador if I wanted to join. We hugged again when Niklas cleared his throat. I laughingly pulled away from Ash while he pretended to be hurt. The two men glared at each other as we separated to seek out the pilgrims' office.

Finally, with our precious, rolled Compostelas in our hands, we found a handsome square filled with shops and nice restaurants to waste time in. As we sat at a restaurant, pigeons flew around us scavenging for crumbs. The waiter suggested that we just trust him to find us the "best treats" so we agreed. He brought us red wine and an appetizer of mariscos, shrimp with butter, and warm rolls of bread. This was followed with green roasted and salted peppers Padrones, a regional favorite. Next a huge sampling of pork cutlets and tortas were served before they brought us each a piece of Santiago cake. We watched other pilgrims limping into town, searching for the pilgrims' office. Some looked disappointed at their experience thus far. I felt sad for them and elated for the ones who clasped friends with passionate enthusiasm as congratulatory shouts resounded from all directions.

Suddenly I received a text; my phone vibrated in my purse. That hadn't happened at all on the trip so it took me by surprise. I glanced at it to see a message from Barry: *Please join us tonight if you are free.* ;)

That flirt! I thought. I ignored the message, only to receive another.

Are you still with the German?

Yes, I am. :) I'm glad you made it, Barry! Congratulations, I responded.

Let me know if your situation changes, he continued.

I shut off my phone with one glance at Nik's far too curious look. He shook his head.

"Tell the boys you are with a man." I laughed hard at that. He merely smirked at his cake and took a calm bite.

"I am indeed."

He gently grasped my hand and did not let go, even when Stefan found us. His merry smile seemed glad to see us, though we were ready to turn in for the evening. We were aware of how little time we had left now. Ever the gentleman, Nik invited Stefan to have a seat with us as I fought my irritation. Matthew made conversation with me as they started talking in Deutsch again. I can't recall what we talked about as I was hyper-aware of the gentle squeezing of Nik's hand. He, finally, delicately ended the conversation and released my hand as he stood and stretched a bit. He hugged Stefan and waved merrily to Matthew before again taking my bereft hand and gently leading me away.

"Let's fucking get out of here before anyone else recognizes us and steals our minutes away." We made a beeline for our room, encountering no one else who wished to intrude on our remaining time. He opened our door and let me go in ahead of him, quietly shutting it and leaning back against it. I stood a pace away a bit uncertainly as various emotions warred across his handsome visage. He took a huge, shuddering breath and simply opened his arms as I stepped into him. Our lips met with the salty tang of tears. I didn't know if they were mine or his.

The next morning, the sun filtered through the filmy drapes for we'd forgotten to pull the heavy velvet drapes closed over them. We silently regarded each other in the semi-dark. I could just barely see the line of his smile and the dimples it created in his cheek. I rubbed my face on his stubble until he gripped me in a fierce hug.

"How come you have to go to Colorado?" he whined. "Bring Parky to Germany. She would love it, truly." He kissed my nose and waited expectantly.

I chuckled at the innocence of someone without kids.

"I'm sorry. I can't do that to her...or her father! I wish I could."

He snorted. "Yes, you can."

I shook my head. "No, let's just remember each other this way." I said throatily. I was getting a little choked up now. "You helped to heal the last piece of me, you know." We had talked a lot last night about our pasts and he'd cried for my pain. I kissed his lips. "Thank you for being my Camino angel, Nik. I won't ever forget that."

Just then his stomach growled loudly, adding much-needed humor to the moment and providing an excuse to get up. "Come on, you're starving! Let's go eat this delicious breakfast they promised! There's going to be fresh fruit and any kind of bread you might be craving, plus tons of bacon! I'll bet the coffee is exceptional, too!" I ran into the bathroom before his grabbing hands could detain me and slammed the door closed when he leaped toward me. I shrieked in laughter as I locked him out and jumped in the shower. He shook the door softly, begging to be let in.

I started the water, tuning him out. Soft sobs shook me for a few minutes but thankfully didn't last too long. The wide shower head had several settings, so I switched it to pulse mode. I let it beat between my shoulders where the pack had sat for so long. Those muscles felt like steel. The glass door steamed as I shaved my legs for the first time in over a month. I'd been delighted to find razors and shaving cream kits in the bathroom, along with toothbrushes, combs and mini tubes of toothpaste on the sink. I took my time grooming once out of the shower. With a touch of mascara and some tinted lip gloss, I felt like a different woman. I left my hair down and wrapped myself in a towel, opening the door to let the steam out. Nik sat facing the bathroom and when

I came out, his amber eyes brushed over my face as he stood to appraise me. "Beautiful! Just beautiful, my Camina." He kissed me as he passed, a light brushing of his lips.

An hour and a half later, we sat in the pews of the grand Santiago Cathedral on one of the sides where the giant *botafumeiro*, or incense burner, would swing over our heads. Our packs had been left at the front desk, where we stored them until our departure. We'd toured the church first, to be sure we got the best seats we could. We'd walked up the steps behind the statue of the apostle and knelt at his shoulders. It seemed to me that Nik had prayed. Being raised Catholic, he was more in tune with what the protocols were. I went up the worn steps that hundreds of thousands had walked on before me and felt awe over that simple fact. I had knelt at the statue of the apostle, my mind blank, but a great feeling of peace and well-being crept over me and I figured that was good enough. I exited on the steps on the other side where Niklas waited to escort me to our bench. He knelt in prayer, his dark red-brown curls falling over his forehead. I sat in quiet contemplation, observing everyone who came in and sat around us.

A short, meek little nun came out and stood front and center. Since we were on the side section of the altar, her profile was to me. The lovely, operatic voice that escaped her throat was so unexpected that stunned tears rose to my eyes. Niklas immediately stopped praying, made the sign of the cross, and sat next to me to watch her as she sang. We scooted closer to allow more people to squeeze into the pews. I didn't mind that I was practically in Nik's lap. He put his arm around me to bring me even closer. Before long there was no more room except for standing, but people kept coming, filling the aisles and steps behind us.

A bishop and his procession came in. They filed behind the podium to stand in rows. The nun continued singing but now the men filled in. I wished I could understand what they were singing. Their chanting filled the air. I sat in rapt attention knowing something profound would happen soon. With one last motion of her arm, the nun was finished. She closed her book silently, made the sign of the cross and stepped back, now hidden amongst the men's red robes.

Then men came forward one at a time to recite in different languages the number of pilgrims from each part of the world who had checked in to the pilgrims' office and received Compostelas. When the numbers were finished, people lined up for communion. I decided to try it as I'd never had the opportunity before. But when I stepped up to the priest with his little wafer, I simply opened my mouth. He looked at me and asked, "You are Catholic?" I shook my head. "Not for you," he said and smiled at me before dismissing me!

I whispered to Nik what had happened and he nearly choked with the effort not to laugh. He knelt again to continue his prayers while communion went on and on. I was beginning to fidget when a half dozen men in burgundy robes came out and stood near the swinging platform that would set the silver incense burner to swinging. The ritualistic silver burner was pure silver and nearly as tall as a man.

The bishop blessed the incense before lighting the bowl inside. Smoke filtered out immediately and the six robed men set it swinging. It took a few passes before it really started swinging overhead. The nun's voice again filled the church. Nik's hand gripped mine tightly as we both watched the smoking incense swing across the arches and up into the highest recesses. Except for the nun's voice, a hush fell over us all. A powerful feeling of love descended on me. Tears fell freely from my eyes as I closed my eyes to receive the blessings. I leaned my head on Nik's shoulder and he cradled my head with his left hand while his right swiped at his own falling tears.

We sat and watched everyone file out of the church once the incense burner ceased to move. Leaving the cathedral meant it was time to go our separate ways. Nik's eyes searched mine. He tried to smile his lopsided grin but failed at it. I leaned in until our foreheads touched.

"I'll always love you," I whispered hoarsely.

"I love you, too, my Camina," he whispered back.

We couldn't say anything else. After a few minutes, we walked back to the Parador together. I watched him retrieve his pack from the front desk staff. He'd made arrangements when he'd dropped his pack off last evening to be taken to the airport today after the mass. I walked him sadly to the entry, out and down the steps to the square. His taxi already waited. The driver threw his pack into the trunk and slammed it shut. We both flinched. He hugged me quickly and brushed my lips for the last time before folding his body into the car. I couldn't watch him drive away, so I turned away and walked quickly to the Parador and through the entry to the courtyard in the middle where I sat and shed a few tears alone. However, after a few minutes I felt the same feeling as I had in the Cathedral of Santiago, the church in that quaint town so long ago, and other times along the way.

With strong resolve, I stood in the sun with a small smile on my face. I was ready to leave. I still had what I came for and that was myself. I walked purposefully to the front desk and announced that I was ready for my own taxi to the train station. I retrieved my pack and nearly ran out to my taxi. My driver seemed shocked by the grin on my face. On the way to the station, I prayed Niklas would be as happy as I. I hoped he would remember this time fondly forever. Once at the station, I breathed the air of freedom and promise of home. At the ticket window, the man asked in halting English if I minded sharing a private sleeper cab with three other women. I asked him if he was kidding and showed him my backpack with the pilgrim shell. He laughed when I said, "Tres es nada!"

My train arrived an hour later. I was shown to my gray-walled "private" room. There were four beds inside and already housed the three women, none of whom spoke English at all. With a soft apology, I squeezed past a woman to stuff my pack in an overhead compartment. Then I stepped on the occupied bed below so that I could boost myself up to my bed. I was lucky to get the top bunk near the window with a view of the train station. I sat with legs dangling as I watched people running to board. I calculated that it would be three days before I reached home, since my plane left in two days. I would stay a night in Madrid before the long plane ride to Florida and the connecting flight to Colorado.

Without warning, the train glided smoothly forward and picked up speed fast. I began to sway with the motion of the racing locomotive. I pulled my legs up and hugged my knees as I watched Santiago glide away. The city pulled at my heart as it slid away from view. Soon, I leaned far left to catch the last glimpse of the cathedral's spires. My last night with Niklas lingered in my mind. After our passionate embraces, we'd lounged in bed and searched for German comedians on his iPhone without luck and laughed over some hilarious skits from American comedians. We'd snuggled for hours and every once in a while one of us would notice the time and hold the other with an urgent need for time to slow down.

Though neither of us had slept, morning had arrived quickly. With my hand on my heart I remembered our last moments together. It had been emotional and so very beautiful. He'd given me the gift of his love and I hoped he had received mine and kept it in a sacred place in his heart, too. I would miss him.

We now raced at full speed. Parker's face popped into my mind and I smiled with a huge grin so infectious the women across from me both smiled in reaction. I laughed. Happiness welled up from deep inside as I let my back settle against the wall. The train swayed comfortably as it safely rocketed toward Madrid, toward home where Parker waited…and toward the rest of my life.

Made in the USA
Lexington, KY
21 March 2014